3/99
Dawsons
16.99

Fashioning the Frame

Dress, Body, Culture

Series Editor **Joanne B. Eicher,** *Regents' Professor, University of Minnesota*

Advisory Board:

Ruth Barnes, *Ashmolean Museum, University of Oxford*
Helen Callaway, *CCCRW, University of Oxford*
James Hall, *University of Illinois at Chicago*
Beatrice Medicine, *California State University, Northridge*
Ted Polhemus, *Curator, "Street Style" Exhibition, Victoria & Albert Museum*
Griselda Pollock, *University of Leeds*
Valerie Steele, *The Museum at the Fashion Institute of Technology*
Lou Taylor, *University of Brighton*
John Wright, *University of Minnesota*

Books in this provocative series seek to articulate the connections between culture and dress which is defined here in its broadest possible sense as any modification or supplement to the body. Interdisciplinary in approach, the series highlights the dialogue between identity and dress, cosmetics, coiffure, and body alternations as manifested in practices as varied as plastic surgery, tattooing, and ritual scarification. The series aims, in particular, to analyze the meaning of dress in relation to popular culture and gender issues and will include works grounded in anthropology, sociology, history, art history, literature, and folklore.

ISSN: 1360-466X

Previously published titles in the Series

Helen Bradley Foster, *"New Raiments of Self": African American Clothing in the Antebellum South*
Claudine Griggs, *"S/he: Changing Sex and Changing Clothes"*

DRESS, BODY, CULTURE

Fashioning the Frame
Boundaries, Dress and Body

Dani Cavallaro and Alexandra Warwick

Oxford • New York

First published in 1998 by
Berg
Editorial offices:
150 Cowley Road, Oxford, OX4 1JJ, UK
70 Washington Square South, New York, NY 10012, USA

Berg is an imprint of Oxford International Publishers Ltd.

Library of Congress Cataloging-in-Publication Data
A catalog record for this book is available from the Library of Congress.

British Library Cataloguing-in-Publication Data
A catalogue record for this book is available from the British Library.

ISBN   1 85973 981 4 (Cloth)
        1 85973 986 5 (Paper)

Typeset by JS Typesetting, Wellingborough, Northants.
Printed in the United Kingdom by Biddles Ltd, Guildford and King's Lynn.

For my parents, with love.

A.W.

For Barney, the Unclothed.

D.C.

Contents

Acknowledgements

In writing a book, in collaboration, on fashioning we realized how much those three processes; writing, collaborating and fashioning, depend upon one another, and how many people have been part of them in different ways. We would like to thank some them here for all the contributions they have made, and in the spirit of collaboration our separate thanks are combined in one list.

A debt of gratitude is owed to several friends, colleagues, relatives and, last but not least, texts without whose assistance many aspects of the research entailed in this study would not have been initiated or completed.

Mary Conde is more responsible than she can know for setting one of us on the path that led to this book and, we hope, beyond.

Friendship in academic life is inseparable from intellectual stimulation and professional support and Harriet Evans, Rosemary Auchmuty and Gabriele Griffin continue to be friends in every sense.

We are also grateful to all our colleagues in the English department of the University of Westminster, particularly Mark Willis, Philip Tew and Leigh Wilson, whose warmth, intellectual generosity and companionship made our work a pleasure, and to Louise Maaroufi, Paddy Bostock and Tim Havard for the constancy of their encouragement and unerring knack for spotting stimulating ideas.

Our gratitude is owed too to Hilary Footitt and Alan Morrison, whose efforts made possible the sabbatical in which part of this book was written.

Finally, our thanks to Margaret Bostock for her generosity and to Martin Pyle, Izzie Thomas and Lizzy Bacon for their unfailing friendship and sustaining provision of entertainments.

Notes on the Authors

Dani Cavallaro is Head of English Studies at the University of Westminster. Her main research interests are in theories of representation, aesthetics and debates on postmodernism.

Alexandra Warwick is a lecturer in English Studies at the University of Westminster. She has research interests in late-nineteenth-century fiction and the gothic, as well as in theories of representation and the body.

List of Illustrations

Preface

There is no obvious way of demarcating the body's boundaries. Hair, nails, corporeal waste and secretions, indeed the skin itself, could be seen both as integral to the body's identity and functionings, and as dispensable append-ages. Any attempt to establish unequivocally the limits of the physical apparatus is further complicated by multifarious practices of body decora-tion, such as tattooing, piercing, painting, make-up, scarification, and, of course, *clothing*.

Should dress be regarded as part of the body, or merely as an extension of, or supplement to it? Even confining dress to the apparently secondary status of a supplement hardly resolves the problems inherent in the assessment of the relationship between dress and the body, since, as indicated by Derrida's analysis of the logic of supplementarity, the supplement operates simultaneously as an optional appendix and as a completing and hence necessary element. The notion of *dress-as-supplement* only serves to compli-cate further the already baffling partnership of body and dress.

The body has been the focus of much recent critical attention. The aim of this project is to offer an overview of some of this scholarship as a means of examining the body in relation to dress. Central to the present investigation is the idea that the body is both a *boundary* and *not a boundary*, that it is ambiguous and that this ambiguity produces a complex relationship between self and non-self. In Lacanian terms, dress could be said to function as a kind of 'rim', as that which is both inside and outside and thus problematizes the very notion of *boundary*. In *Adorned in Dreams*, Elizabeth Wilson observes :

Clothing marks an unclear boundary ambiguously, and unclear boundaries disturb us. Symbolic systems and rituals have been created in many different cultures in order to strengthen and reinforce boundaries, since these safeguard purity. It is at the margins between one thing and another that pollution may leak out. Dress is the frontier between the self and the non-self.[1]

If it is the case that cultural identity relies on boundaries as ideological and psychological structures designed to individuate the self, dress would

1. Elizabeth Wilson (1989), *Adorned in Dreams*, London, pp.2–3.

seem to challenge boundaries. It *frames* the body and insulates private fantasies from the Other, yet it simultaneously connects the individual self to the collective Other and fashions those fantasies on the model of a public spectacle, thus questioning the myth of a self-contained identity. The integrity of the body as a personal possession is questioned and the vulnerability of all liminal states is accordingly exposed. This vulnerability may be envisaged either as *contamination* – as in the image of the body 'assaulted' by the external Other – or as *self-dissemination* – here, the body 'disperses' itself into the outside world. Dress, then both defines and de-individualizes us.

Whatever status it may ultimately be granted, dress acts as a daily reminder of our dependence on margins and boundaries for the purposes of self-construction. This role is played out on both the level of the Imaginary and on that of the Symbolic. In the Imaginary, dress represents a projection of the ideal egos which we seek to embody and with which we wish to identify. In the Symbolic, dress is symptomatic of our introjection of sartorial and vestimentary codes and conventions, as instances of a broader network of intersubjective values designed to guarantee the socialization and institutionalization of personal identity and thus secure the cultural grooming of vision.

The subject's entry into the Symbolic coincides with the erection of barriers meant to prevent defilement and hence separate the self from the non-self through a clear distinction between the *proper* and the *improper*. According to Kristeva, this process of self-definition is characterized by the phenomenon of *abjection*. This consists of a series of moves towards the expulsion and rejection of everything that threatens the subject's existence as an autonomous and differentiated entity. The primordial object to be expelled is the mother-figure, as the main signifier of the subjects physical and psychological dependency and of its lack of a self-contained identity. Abjection is therefore supposed to guarantee a bounded selfhood. In Victor Burgin's words, the abject is 'all that we must shed, and from which we must distance ourselves in order to be'.[2]

Yet the abject is never totally erased or suppressed. In fact, it survives well beyond infancy as a puzzling object of both revulsion and fascination. In particular, it resurfaces whenever we are confronted with marginal or threshold phenomena that elude unproblematic classification and remind us that the body is only precariously bounded. As John Lechte puts it: 'the abject is above all the ambiguous, the in-between, what defies boundaries, a composite resistant to unity. Hence, if the subject's identity derives from the

---

2. Victor Burgin (1990), 'Geometry and Abjection' in John Fletcher (ed.), *Abjection, Melancholia and Love*, London, p.117.

unity of its objects, the abject is the threat of unassimilable non-unity: that is, ambiguity. Abjection, therefore, is fundamentally what disturbs identity, system and order.'[3] If the body itself is only uncertainly defined, dress reinforces the fluidity of its frame by raising the somewhat uncomfortable question: *where does the body end and where does dress begin?*

In defining dress as instrumental to the forging of margins and boundaries, it should be stressed that 'margin' and 'boundary' are not interchangeable concepts. In fact, whilst the boundary divides and frames, the margin blurs distinctions and frontiers. It is one of the paradoxes of dress to be both a margin and a boundary at one and the same time. As boundary, it frames the body and separates from the rest of the social world, thus functioning as a kind of container or wrapper. Dress as boundary is meant to trace a neat line between self and other: the limitation of physical visibility via clothing, for example, parallels metaphorically an intended limitation of psychological accessibility. As margin, on the other hand, dress connects the individual to other bodies, it links the biological entity to the social ensemble and the private to the public. This cohesive action holds the advantage of releasing the individual subject to the possibility of collective interactivity and communication, yet it erases its very individuality.

It would be misleading, however, to associate univocally the boundary with the Symbolic and the margin with the Imaginary, or vice versa. Indeed, both the boundary and the margin apply equally to both the Imaginary and the Symbolic. If it is the case that the margin may be reminiscent of the state of undifferentiation peculiar to the imaginary and the boundary of Symbolic compartmentalization, it is nonetheless worth noticing that the margin also functions as a metaphor for the cohesive tissue required by the Symbolic and the boundary as a reminder of the desire for sealed wholeness typical of the Imaginary and of the subject's rejoicing in the phantasmatic plenitude of its own misrecognized mirror image.

Disparate discourses criss-cross over the territory of dress. Whether explicitly interrelated or, alternatively, conflicting with one another, all these discourses exhibit overlapping and reciprocally fertilizing attributes which preclude the viability of rigid compartmentalizations. It is mainly for this reason that throughout this project, emphasis is laid on concepts such as the boundary, the frame, the margin. Indeed, the coexistence of diverse, yet subtly interwoven, issues and perspectives within the domain of dress compels a reassessment of conventional definitions of the boundary as a border demarcating a precise division, of the frame as an unambiguously insulating structure, or of the margin as a definite limit and posits, instead, a configuration of all putatively

3. John Lechte (1990), *The Works of Julia Kristeva*, London, p.160.

dividing mechanisms predicated upon principles of movement, fluidity and porousness.

Undeniably, the language of clothes and bodily adornment generally experiments relentlessly with ways of defining and redefining the boundaries between self and other, subject and object, inside and outside. The boundary never survives these alchemical processes as an intact and inviolable barrier. As regions to be playfully traversed, rather than frontiers to be crossed only at the trespasser's own irreparable peril, the boundaries proposed by dress are eminently disrespectful of notions of either integrity or reparation. Ludic activity and aleatory curiosity may well be the only criteria which ultimately define and constitute them. Therefore, these boundaries are far more permeable structures than any of those beloved of classical logic. Each side of the border may at any point spill over into the other and thus spawn, by osmosis and contagion, a hybrid clan of unpredictable mutants. Each of the seemingly bounded parties on either side of the partition is continually in the process of becoming otherwise.

Given fashion's penchant for obfuscating the very distinction between deception and truthfulness, even the boundary between 'telling lies' and 'telling the truth' becomes precarious and uncertain: the language of dress ironically intimates that if all telling, by dint of its complicity with strategies of narrative elaboration, is, at least potentially, a form of lying, then: 'we always graze against the lie, as long as we are in narrative. Telling truths is already almost lying'.[4] At the same time, the simultaneously aesthetic and commercial status of fashion images and commodities also problematizes the nature of the boundary between contrasting concepts of value. As Baudrillard reminds us, in the process of acquisition of fashionable objects, money is exchanged not simply for commodities but also, often primarily, for prestige. The meaning of money is transformed through a type of expenditure which replaces economic value with the 'sign exchange value',[5] namely the wealth of symbolic meanings which the commodity itself stands for, which the money spent to purchase it stands for, and which the operations required to obtain that money in the first place also stand for.

In the realm of symbolic exchanges which hinge on the deployment of vestimentary codes and conventions, categories such as self, subject, inside, truth are not, consequently, ineluctably counterposed to those of the other, the object, the outside, the lie, since each of the terms in the first series is fundamentally a function or an effect of the transformability of a corresponding term in the second series.

4. Tzvetzan Todorov (1977), *The Poetics of Prose*, New York, p.60.
5. Jean Baudrillard (1981), *For a Critique of the Political Economy of the Sign*, trans. C.Levin, St.Louis, p.113.

Figure 1. Tono STANO, *Sense*. © Tono Stano 1992. Courtesy of the artist and Dansk Votruba, Prague.

Issues of identity and history, time and space, meaning and language are continually raised by a sustained investigation of the roles played by clothes and ornamentation in their multifold relations to the human body. Whether the power of dress be associated with epistemological, ontological or aesthetic potentialities, with utopian or dystopian projections, assessing the relationship between the language of dress and culturally shared encodings of reality remains problematic. Some invest dress with the authority of a structure of knowledge (about individuals, groups, cultures), i.e. a means of 'finding things out' about the world. Others prefer to envision it as indexical of ways of being and hence a means of formulating hypotheses about 'what things are like'. Others still approach it primarily on the basis of the sensory and sensuous responses it elicits, with varying degrees of emphasis on the ideological implications of this function, depending on the extent to which the aesthetic is seen as enmeshed in, or else detached from, the political sphere. There is no way of ascertaining, moreover, whether the principal function of dress lies in transcending, counteracting, or indeed fabricating reality, since its discourses ultimately accord no authority to absolute definitions of consensual truth, depth and epiphanic revelation, any more than they hold out the promise of an iconic correspondence between reality and its representations.

Understanding the language of dress and its relation to the body, therefore, involves a forever provisional and constantly re-negotiable grasp of the activities of seeing and making sense as social practices, based on a wide range of conventions, largely dictated by concepts of history, memory, permanence and impermanence, fluctuations in function and value, and always inscribed in institutional frames which ultimately decree whether and how meaning accrues to images. The permutational and hence indecisive character of these encoding and decoding practices activates a process of continuous interpretation, where analysis does not *follow* production as a post hoc subsidiary or adjunct, but rather *coincides* with it: interpretation does not merely explicate or categorize the image, it actively makes it. Concomitantly, interpretation does not regenerate a given and wholly autonomous representation, but actually generates form and meaning and, in so doing, simultaneously fabricates the parameters that will, retrospectively, elucidate the hermeneutic operation itself. It is, to this extent, not only generating in a transitive sense but also, reflexively, *self*-generating.

The ongoing nature of these interpretative operations is, arguably, a corollary of the pervasive incidence of desire as an indomitable and insatiable force which impels us to want to act on the objects of our perceptions, rather than be sated by simply registering them. As Starobinski argues: 'sight opens all space to desire, but desire is not satisfied with seeing'.[6] Desire, more specifically, shapes our experience of time, by both contracting it into the eternal present of productive interpretation, where past, present and future are merely variations on the dominant theme of sense making, and yet mocking and frustrating the hermeneutic effort through relentless reminders of the imaginary status of that present (as the here-and-now, as presence, as the gift of meaning): 'The irreducible and untranslatable significance of images . . . is finally rooted in the intersection and inevitable contradiction between the world's always being present to us and its seldom being present to us as we desire it to be. Desire for the absent constantly transforms the present'.[7]

Any exploration of dress in relation to social structures through which bodily functions and rhythms are regimented and appropriate forms of desire accordingly sanctioned will show that clothing cannot be seen as simply *disciplining* the body or as simply providing a means of *transgression*. The ambivalent and undecidable nature of dress contributes, in fact, to the production of an eminently hybrid social space. Like power in one of Foucault's formulations, the strategies of control intrinsic to the discourse of clothing are simultaneously restrictive and potentially subversive, as:

Power would be a fragile thing if its only function were to repress, if it worked only through the mode of censorship, exclusion, blockage and repression, in the manner of a superego, exercising itself in a negative way.[8]

If clothing represses by constructing the body and organizing desire, it also holds enabling potentialities centred on pleasure and affectivity in the production of meanings and interpretations.

The power of dress to threaten boundaries (between self and non-self, the individual and the collective, discipline and transgression) is emphasized by items of clothing such as masks and veils, which epitomize duplicity and the co-existence of concealment and revelation, presence and absence. Such aporetic garments invite an examination of the workings of the gaze, and, relatedly, of issues pertaining to truth and simulation. The ambiguously screening garment conceals and arrests the flow of the gaze whilst simultaneously stimulating it, by provoking and increasing the desire for discovery and possession, hence effecting a magnification of the erotic. The veil's fascination lies in the prospect of unveiling, just as the attraction of dress in general has to do with its greater or lesser ability to intimate the possibility

6. Jean Starobinski (1989), *The Living Eye*, trans. A.Goldhammer, Cambridge, Mass.

7. David Summers (1991), 'Real Metaphor: Towards a Redefinition of the "Conceptual" Image', in Norman Bryson, Ann Holly and Keith Moxey (eds.), *Visual Theory: Painting and Representation*, New York, p.241.

8. Michel Foucault (1988), 'Body/Power', in C.Gordon (ed.), *Power/Knowledge: Selected Interviews and Other Writings 1972-1977*, Brighton, p.59.

of removal. In Barthes's words: 'Is not the most erotic portion of a body where the garment gapes? . . . it is intermittence . . . which is erotic: the intermittence of skin flashing between two articles of clothing . . . between two edges . . . it is the flash itself which seduces, or rather: The staging of an appearance-as-disappearance.'[9]

Intermittence highlights the fact that there is no seamless or immediate connection between the subject and the object of the gaze. What is tantalizing is not instant reciprocity but a gap, the filling of which is only ever transient and imaginary. Stano's *Sense* (1992) effectively encapsulates Barthes' ideas by representing the body as a gap produced by the frame of clothing. A sinuous, almost serpentine portion of flesh flashes ambiguously against a backdrop of engulfing darkness. Defying both anatomy and logic, dress metamorphoses the physical form into a disorienting sliver of light. Although specific portions of the model's body can be recognized, the overall effect is surreal and made all the more eerie by the somewhat incongruous naturalism of the head and toes placed at each end of the fragment. The body is portrayed as a fluid boundary glimmering between two edges of apparent nothingness. Yet it is that nothingness that defines it: the body is an optical effect accomplished by clothing. Its erotic lure is the fascination of the fragment, the slice, the cut, the seam. What is titillating about this image is that it does put the body on display as a whole object, a neatly bundled package ready for consumption. In fact, the pleasure it promises proceeds from a hint, or partial anticipation of things to come. The glimpse of the model's body we are allowed to catch is meant to activate the desire to unveil the portions of the body screened by clothing. The absent body becomes immensely more enticing than its present counterpart. Stano's photograph depicts the relationship between the body and dress as an interplay of presence and absence. It vividly reminds us that in, the face of a clothed body, we respond to a presence based on absence. Both the body and dress, as symbolic and linguistic structures inconceivable outside the domain of representation, could be seen as forms of absence, with dress concealing not the body but rather the absence of the physical body as a pre-symbolic or extra-linguistic entity.

The unfixable character of dress as both a personal and a communal phenomenon is largely due to its ability to quiz conventional understandings of the relationship between surface and depth. The conventional reading of dress as a superficial form to be penetrated in order to gain access to a deep content, obviously based on the primacy of notions of depth and content over those of surface and form, is radically challenged by a reading whereby

9. Roland Barthes (1990), *The Pleasure of the Text*, trans. R. Miller, Oxford, pp.9–10.

the superficial forms of people and objects are seen to possess their own kind of depth. This challenge triggers a shift from the type of analysis based on attempts to grasp the 'true' body's hidden depth beneath the supposedly deceitful dress to an examination of the surface itself. In the latter style of analysis, surfaces are regarded as yielding no less crucial clues to the fashioning of subjectivity than the depths treasured by more traditional quests and methodologies. Indeed, it could be argued that it is only by analysing the superficial language of dress that one may arrive at certain, albeit provisional, conclusions regarding both singular and group identities. Ignoring the surface would leave us with no hints as to the cultural and psychological significance of a sign system which is by definition superficial and whose depth lies precisely on the surface. In a Lacanian frame of reference, truth itself is inevitably seen as superficial, for the reason that the repressed (the unconscious) is not hidden but exposed in the superficial rhetorical displacements which characterize language in its multifold applications. Dress, in this respect, is a manifestation of the unconscious at work, in that it is a superficial phenomenon, like symbolic language, which, also like language, speaks volumes about submerged dimensions of experience. Clothing, then, does not just operate as a disguising or concealing strategy. In fact, it could be regarded as a *deep surface*, a manifestation of the 'unconscious' as a facet of existence which cannot be relegated to the psyche's innermost hidden depths but actually expresses itself through apparently superficial activities.

Whilst as a hegemonic tool dress conditions us and makes us schizophrenic by idealizing uniqueness at the same time as demanding uniformity, its ambivalent status as both a framing boundary and a loose, fluid margin makes it unamenable to absolute compartmentalization. In this respect, dress may be treated as a deconstructive instrument for the interrogation of ideas of difference and differentiation, of their ideological fabrication and attendant demystification. by inviting a shift from an analysis of the signified to an analysis of the signifier, through its emphasis on the superficial, rather than deep, character of all processes of signification, the language of dress may help in the questioning of time-honoured metaphysical categories (origin, truth, presence) and hence in the subversion of all binary mythologies.

Introduction: The Body in Philosophy and Theories of Representation

... though it has been penetrated by X-rays, opened by generations of surgeons, and had its cellular structure scrutinized daily by a multitude of microscopes – on some level the body remains as opaque and mysterious to us as it always was. For, as Silenus pointed out to the Cyclops, the body has something more than a mere physical reality. It is more than just a collection of organs, cells and enzymes. For one thing, it has a unique relationship to language, existing as it does in the domains of narrative and myth – as well as being the repository of all sorts of metaphors for the human condition.[1]

... we have dreams of moving back and forward in time, though to use the words back and forward is to make a nonsense of the dream, for it implies that time is linear, and if that were so there could be no movement, only a forward progression. But we do not move through time, time moves through us. I say this because our physical bodies have a natural decay span, they are one-use-only units that crumble around us. To everyone, this is a surprise, although we see it in parents and our friends we are always amazed to see it in ourselves. The most prosaic of us betray a belief in the inward life every time we talk about 'my body' rather than 'I'. We feel it as absolutely part but not at all part of who we are. Language always betrays us, tells the truth when we want to lie, and dissolves into formlessness when we would most like to be precise.[2]

The body has only relatively recently become the object of serious theoretical investigation. What we witness today, however, is a culturescape wherein the body literally saturates the output of legions of artists, writers, advertisers and photographers, which may suggest that the body is simply *in fashion*, or, alternatively, that it has gained a new urgency. Multiple factors may

---

1. Cecil Helman (1992), *The Body of Frankenstein's Monster: Essays in Myth and Medicine*, London and New York, p.4.
2. Jeanette Winterson (1990), *Sexing the Cherry*, London, p.90.

have contributed to the rampant popularity of the corporeal. According to Ewing:

> The body is being rethought and reconsidered by artists and writers because it is being restructured and reconstituted by scientists and engineers. In an era when parts can be routinely detached from one body and plugged into another; when the U.S. National Institutes of Health offer to replace corpses in medical schools with 'industry-standard digital cadavers'; when certain machines can appropriate the functions of human organs, while others are invested with intelligence; when the life of the body can be prolonged when the mind has ceased to function; when genetic change can be engineered and human beings cloned; when a foetus can be nurtured in an artificial womb, or jobbed-out to a surrogate mother; when we entrust automatons to land our jets or perform operations on our bodies; when the *New York Times* informs us that, contrary to what most of us had believed, there are three, four or possibly five genders; when we capriciously rebuild faces, breasts or thighs to conform to the moment's ideal of beauty; and when we dream of 'Robocops', 'Terminators' and 'Replicants', and long to live in a virtual reality – then concepts and definitions, values and beliefs, rights and laws, must be radically overhauled.[3]

Turner corroborates this reading by associating contemporary preoccupations with the body, its functions and limits, with 'a broader cultural *fin de siècle* complex' that parallels and re-echoes certain central anxieties and fears of the late nineteenth century, particularly regarding sexuality and reproduction: 'The body has once more become apocalyptic given the threat of chemical warfare, the destruction of the natural habitat, the epidemic of HIV and AIDS, the greying/declining populations of northern Europe and the apparent inability of national governments to control medical technology or medical costs.'[4]

The pivotal elements, in this atmosphere of crisis, exhaustion, decadence or decay, are not only the obligation to confront *the sense of an ending* as far as a century or indeed a millennium is concerned, but also the necessity to come to terms with the possibility of traditional understandings of corporeality drawing towards a close. It may be inappropriate, however, to regard the feelings of unease, uncertainty or even trepidation that surround contemporary theories of the body as an exclusively late-twentieth-century phenomenon. Although the restructuring of materiality effected by science and technology, or the disembodying potentialities of computer culture, may have fuelled our concern with the physical side of experience, these forces

3. William A. Ewing (1994), *The Body: Photoworks of the Human Form*, London, pp.9–10
4. Bryan Turner (1991), 'Recent Developments in the Theory of the Body', in Featherstone, Hepworth and Turner (eds), *The Body: Social Process and Cultural Theory*, London, p.24.

have not engendered from scratch, but rather exacerbated, ongoing anxieties about the body's uncertain frame and perilous cultural standing.

This study explores the burgeoning of critical perspectives on the body with a focus on the discourse of dress. The principal reason for selecting this specific theme is that, in our society, not just the body in general but the *unclothed* body in particular have been traditionally regarded as lacking and unfinished entities, and it is dress that has time and again been assigned the responsibility of transforming the incomplete body into a complete cultural package. The body, in this respect, has often been conceived of as a hanger or peg for clothing.

The present survey of theoretical approaches to the body and of related attitudes to the language of dress aims at highlighting the ways in which analyses of the body repeatedly confront the issue of lack. Lack is not only one of the most salient features of the socialized body but also, where physicality is concerned, a recurring characteristic of Western philosophy, both in so far as the body is conspicuously absent from mainstream philosophical thought and in so far as the conclusions drawn by those who have in fact engaged in systematic research in this field are patently, and perhaps necessarily, incomplete and provisional. Discursive practices centred around dress both point to the ability of dress to fulfil, round out and thus redeem the incomplete physical ensemble and expose the body's ultimate resistance to completing strategies.

This *aporia* is arguably attributable to the fact that dress foregrounds the difficulty of establishing the body's boundaries. Though both literally and figuratively attached to the body, dress is simultaneously part of the material being and independent of it: it separates the individual body from other bodies, whilst also at the same time connecting it to them. Often thought of as one of the main isolating mechanisms designed to secure an autonomous identity, dress actually constitutes an uncertain frame. Its ambivalence is further emphasized by the coexistence, within its discourse, of disciplinary, regulatory strategies and subversive potentialities.

In framing the body, however precariously, dress contributes to the symbolic translation of materiality into cultural images or signifiers. As a mediator between the carnal dimension of existence and the abstract laws of the symbolic order of language and institutions, dress aids the construction of subjectivity as *representation*.

The central premises on which much recent theoretical work on the body is based, and that the present project endorses, are the ideas that, firstly, the symbolic, culturally groomed body is void outside representations and that, secondly, there are no semiotically innocent representations of the body. A thorough examination of how these representations are both produced and consumed could break up the illusion of naturalness so frequently adopted to *dress up* reality. Without claiming that the natural body, as a biological or physiological apparatus, somehow does not exist, these positions emphasize that neither being real nor being natural are apolitical and objective states, though part of their mythologies is to make themselves appear to be so.

No representation is natural, and representations of the body, whether clothed or unclothed, are no exception. However, exposing the artificial quality of the representation becomes especially problematic when it comes to dealing with the body, owing to a tendency to take corporeal existence somewhat for granted, as a natural attribute or possession. It could be argued that this difficulty is further exacerbated by the ambivalence of the subject's relation to its body, simply on account of the fact that it both *is* and *has* a body. When the body in question is clothed, and hence defined by a symbolic intersubjective casing, denaturalization turns into a harder task still, as it is arduous to determine to what extent dress contributes to, or indeed confirms, the body's status as a disembodied representation, and to what extent dress, as a material phenomenon in its own right, reinforces a view of the body as an irreducibly corporeal dimension.

If it is difficult for the subject to decide whether the body is something it *is* or *has*, it is even trickier for it to establish whether the clothes with which it is intimately connected are part of its *being* or rather an item in the parcel of its having. The subject is a body and has a body; but it also is and has, at one and the same time, the clothes that it wears.

Recent trends in critical theory and philosophy, as well as scientific and technological developments, have underscored the incidence of processes of construction and mediation on all forms of representation. Dress, as a pervasive vehicle for the fabrication of culturally viable subjects, is in a position to increase our sensitivity to the gap between the putatively natural body and its represented, artificial counterparts; to the body's translation by means of mechanisms of rhetorical displacement; and to structures of visuality inserted between the observer and the representation.

Dress, in some respects, is a more traditional, yet no less timely, co-operating factor in a deluge of contemporary mechanisms of mediation that rely heavily on the artificial, the simulated, the hyperreal, virtual spaces, cyberspaces and the electronic realm, and that serve to problematize with perhaps unprecedented intensity the relationship between the biological and the technological bodies and, concomitantly, the body's relation to both space and time. A detailed analysis of changing perceptions of corporeality brought about by industrialization and attendant interpretations of the concepts of modernity and postmodernity will be carried out in the section of this project devoted to the *collective* body and to the relationship between the *private* and the *public*. For the purposes of the present discussion, it seems sufficient to notice that the breach of bodily boundaries is a recurrent topos in contemporary Western society. Some of the fears and anxieties associated with this tantalizing theme are most obviously dramatized by a plethora of popular horror and science fiction films that, at the same time as they try to perpetuate traditional colonial myths about ultimate frontiers and ultimate settlements, also present emphatic metaphors for the dread of contamination, bodily invasion and bodily collapse into the shadowy realm of the abject. The ambiguous alliance between body and dress could be seen as one of the most inveterate incarnations of the fusion of the natural and the constructed.

As is argued in greater depth in a later chapter dealing with the relationship between fashion, history and authorship, the employment of dress as a widespread form of mediation calls into question conventional concepts of origin and originality by fostering representational modes that make the artificial, the synthetic and the fake indistinguishable from and somehow more authentic and real than the so-called real itself. This ambiguity of attitudes towards reality should not necessarily be taken as evidence for a nihilistic denial of the existence of reality itself. In fact, it may enable us to recognize that, if it is the case that the world now feels less real than ever before, it is also the case that there has never been a completely certain notion of reality, at least since the advent of industrialization, with its ability to manufacture reality by substituting the fabricated for the organic. This recognition may provide useful insights into the specifically mythical dimension of reality and by extension of the bodies and of the representations of the body that fashion that reality as they are fashioned by it. As a moulding agency, dress may seal the body's subjection to invincible collective mythologies; however, its ability to question boundaries and frames and hence to challenge the ideal of a unified identity may concurrently unleash creative potentialities for playful experimentation.

A selective journey into recent views on representations of the body would seem an appropriate starting-point for an evaluation of the part played by dress as a framing structure, a mediating tool, a releasing agent. It is to such an examination that the next section is devoted.

The body is a multi-accentual and polymorphous concept: an uncomfortable compound. According to Adler and Pointon, this is largely due to the body's status as a meeting-point of rhetorical, psychological, physiological and ideological issues:

The body is . . . both an object represented . . . and an organism that is organized
to represent concepts and desires. Two systems of representation intertwine and
overlap. Language is a system of signs produced in a particular set of historical
circumstances and involving repetitions and encodings of the kind to which societies
attribute specific meanings either consciously or unconsciously.[5]

A discourse of the body entails a critical assessment of the multiple interactions of nature, culture and society. The body is pivotal to representations
of emotions and physical activity, of sex, sexuality and eroticism, as supposedly
natural facets of human experience and human intercourse. Yet it is no less
central to the articulation of cultural and social practices as wide-ranging as
economic welfare, consumer culture images, dietary practices and the beauty
and fitness industries. All these discursive structures often hinge on unwritten
laws and naturalized assumptions. These sanction both rules of exteriority
and display – the public projection of the desirable body – and strategies of
internalization designed to reach individual psyches with maximum economy
by recourse to a selective repertoire of socially legitimized images. Dress is
clearly complicit in both, as a vehicle for the externalization of inner drives
and as a code that the subject is expected to introject in order to appropriate
a viable enunciative position.

The body pervades cultural representations throughout history. Yet its
endurance should not be conducive to facile assumptions about the body's
timeless or transhistorical status. In fact, bodies are always historically
situated, and hence sites of ideological contestation. For one thing, the
production and preservation of cultures rest largely on the socio-political
definition of proper and improper bodies. With striking regularity, the
regimentation of desire has been intimately connected with the economic
structuring of property and consumption. There are close analogies between
the fashioning of bodies and the political regimes of the cultures they both
constitute and inhabit: the two are inextricably linked forms of government.

The production and representation of the body, its symbolic articulation
and consumption, its framing, as well as its potential for self-disengagement
from definitive borders, are inscribed in specific historical circumstances:
hence, the body can never be approached as a purely natural entity. As a
fluid object of both representation and analysis, the body is the melting-pot
where discourses of power and sexuality, authority and desire, mix and
collude. Above all, it operates as a constant in the formation of cultural
mythologies. Given its inevitable ideological inscription, therefore, the body
can never be assessed, studied, indeed enjoyed, according to extralinguistic
criteria: its representations are always incarnations of belief-systems and

5. Kathleen Adler and Marcia Pointon (1993), *The Body Imaged*, Cambridge, p.125

6

always bear witness to a society's validation of certain attitudes and stigmatizing of others. Dress actively participates in the emplacement of corporeality as a discursive phenomenon and contributes vitally to processes of cultural mythologization and legitimation. At the same time, it maximizes the body's multiplicity by grafting upon it additional layers, surfaces and personas, thus forging a prismatic construct.

On the one hand, dress is instrumental to the collective orchestration of cultural experience through its ability to cast the body into moulds that correspond to certain socially agreed definitions of an intelligible reality. Through this socialization of perception, standards of both normality and deviation are formulated and related scopic regimes are quantified and accordingly categorized. On the other hand, dress makes the dominant culturescape eminently hybrid, ambivalent and ambiguous through its apparently random, intertextual, irreverent and eclectic appropriation and recycling of disparate motifs and styles. It flouts consistency and stability, challenges hierarchies and boundaries, flattens history into one eternal present, potentially encompassing all pasts and futures, and, last but not least, disrupts the myths of continuity and cohesion traditionally cherished by High Art.

Dress *represents* the body as a fundamentally liminal phenomenon by stressing its precarious location on the threshold between the physical and the abstract, the literal and the metaphorical. What is more, the transition from the material to the metaphorical, and vice versa, is not a smooth passage of either transcendence (in the direction from carnality to disembodiment) or empirical grounding (in the direction from abstraction to incarnation). In fact, no transition is ever conclusive, in so far as the framing strategies enacted by dress invariably involve open-ended processes of disjunction and displacement (temporal, spatial, physical) that may provisionally represent experience but never totalize it. Dress thus emphasizes the haziness and uncertainty of any spaces that the body may strive to inhabit or indeed may be allowed to lay claims on: those spaces are ineluctably associated with a sense of transit and disorientation, with split identities and fretful exploration. The subject dramatized by dress as a composite symbolic formation is a rootless being, floating unpredictably in the limbo of the *beyond*. This is not, however, an irretrievably bleak state of affairs, as it holds scope for contestation, negotiation and redefinition. Boundaries and thresholds may not, after all, indicate sites where something ends, where the subject is forced to confront finally the stark reality of lack, but rather points where something could begin. In highlighting processes of mediation, translation and displacement of corporeality (*the reality of the corpus*), the discourse of dress might be in a position to sharpen our awareness of the implications of living on the borders, of existing in a condition of perpetual wandering: not only its negativity as a state of unrelieved insecurity and irrevocable loss but also its potential for critical and creative relocation and reinscription.

It may seem paradoxical, given the extremely plastic and pliable character of the body – a feature of bodily existence that dress, as suggested in the immediately preceding remarks, patently magnifies – that Western thought should traditionally have tended to approach the body's potential boundlessness not as a source of inspiration for ever-shifting experimental redefinitions but rather as a pretext for the establishment of starkly binarized models. The prioritizing of concepts such as mind, spirit or soul over body, substance and matter, for example, points precisely to a desire to stem the implicit subversiveness of the body as a sprawling tissue of inextricably connected life and death drives by recourse to sanitizing sets of adversarial relationships.

In a pre-deconstructive scenario, based on the assumption that both thought and experience could be articulated according to binary oppositions, within which the first term must automatically be accorded a privileged status over the second, supplementary one, the mind-versus-body model would no doubt hold its ground. Deconstructive criticism, by contrast, has alerted us to the culturally confected nature of any such dichotomies and, concomitantly, to the privileged term's reliance, indeed dependence, on the supplementary one for its very linguistic, conceptual and ideological existence, i.e. its ability to signify at all.

Although the transition from pre-deconstructive to deconstructive approaches cannot be taken for granted, in so far as it is neither smooth nor amenable to generalization, it is still possible to observe the symptoms of a philosophical shift from a corpus of theories within which the body is markedly absent, or present only by virtue of its emphatic marginalization, to certain reassessments of the body's place and functions linked up with recent theories of psychology and ideology, broadly associated with post-structuralism.

Turner argues that the body has been granted no significant part by sociology in our century, and explains this exclusion as a corollary of the discipline's concern with the general and abstract features of industrial society and its prioritization of the technical problems connected with the economic functionings of that society:

> . . . sociology asked a specific and precise question: what are the defining character-istics of urban, industrial society? . . . it was generally assumed that industrial society would converge towards a rationalized, bureaucratic and alienated social order, in which the stability of rural life would be fractured by class conflicts, and the family and the Church would gradually be replaced by more public, rational and

instrumental institutions. . . . It was an economic framework which thus dominated early sociological preoccupations with matters of utility, commodities and equilibrium. . . . Consumer choice, which in principle could have produced a theory of the embodiment of the social actor via the idea of consumer needs and wants, remained largely underdeveloped in economics and sociology.[6]

Sociological approaches of a Marxist orientation dominated by Hegelian influences have equally shown scant interest in the body, their primary preoccupation lying with 'the issue of historicity: how do societies enter history?'[7] Arguably, such a question only makes sense in the context of Hegel's views on historical development as the dialectical unfolding of the Spirit towards higher and higher ends, a crucial stage in this process being a society's emergence into historical self-consciousness. However, were one to doubt the validity of this idealist perspective, it could be opined that no society is ever *outside history*, history consisting not so much of facts, organically related by logical and rational rhythms, as of texts, designed to slot contingent experiences into an intelligible, albeit inevitably fictional, pattern. As will be argued in detail in a later chapter, dress contributes crucially to the debunking of the myth of history as a totalizing metanarrative, by challenging metaphysical notions of origin, teleology and causality. The rehabilitation of the body as a legitimate object of philosophical inquiry and its extrication from the desensualizing ethos of idealism are supported by the discourse of dress, in its capacity, amongst other things, as a vehicle for the interrogation of organic and evolutionary versions of history.

It is precisely in the context of repudiations of Hegel's system, such as the ones advocated by Kierkegaard, Schopenhauer and Nietzsche, that the body comes to be assigned a place of central, if decentred, significance, as an uncompromising reminder of contingency and ephemerality ideally suited to the questioning of idealist dreams of continuity and universality. The positions upheld by those philosophers will shortly be assessed. What is worth examining, before entering a discussion of specific figures, is the attitude displayed towards corporeality by another major twentieth-century discipline, namely anthropology.

According to Turner, anthropology, by contrast with sociology, has by and large devoted more consistent attention to the physical dimension. It must be emphasized, however, that its pivotal concern has generally rested not with the socio-economic, psychological and ideological moulding of bodies in *specific* cultural situations, but rather with the formulation of universal statements about human existence on earth. In this respect, the

6. Turner in Featherstone, Hepworth and Turner, *The Body*, pp.6–7.
7. Ibid., p.8.

discourses of anthropology, however body-oriented they may appear to be, display a universalizing and integrating thrust that may, at times, have served to obscure cultural specificity in the interests of transcendental definitions of human nature and indeed contributed to the establishment of normative values and laws.

> Historically speaking, anthropology has been more inclined to pose questions about the universal essence of humanity, because anthropology in the context of European colonialism was forced to address the problem of human universals (of ontology) in relation to variations and differences of social relationships. The ontological centrality of human embodiment consequently emerged as a focus of universality. . . . the body . . . offered one solution to the problem of social relativism. . . . This line of development can be framed in the question: granted that humanity has a common point of origin in its mammalian species-being, what constitutes the point of disjunction between nature and culture? In short, what is Man?[8]

The ostracizing of the body from classical sociological inquiry and its anthropological sanitization as a universal category for the classification of cultural dominants are ultimately variations on a recurring theme within Western thought, i.e. a widespread uneasiness about desire that can be traced all the way back to Plato's *Symposium* (to mention but one of the most famous, or perhaps notorious, dramatizations of this topos) and its equation of desire with the ethos of individualism, disharmony and envy, as opposed to eros as the fountainhead of friendship and other fruitfully binding energies.

Christianity, for its part, has played no inferior role in emphasizing the necessity of transcending the world of the senses, with a resulting division of society into an explicitly ascetic/monastic élite and the exercise of sexuality as a lay activity: a problematic activity, of course, to be regulated and regimented through practices and rituals such as fasting, designed to keep the body's potential unruliness at bay. The ordering of desire, moreover, corresponds to specific forms of production, consumption and property, most strikingly reflected in the notion of marriage as a contract and in that of the family as a societal microcosm. The interlocking of commercial and bodily politics lies at the roots of the economy of desire exemplified by puritanical/capitalist asceticism, as a form of self-denial based on the sacrifice of immediate gratification to the long-term interests of accumulation. In fully-fledged capitalist dispensations, this kind of work ethic delivers the paradox of a culture wherein desire is not overtly restrained: rather, it is continually manufactured, but in order to minimize, instead of augmenting, opportunities for fulfilment. Desire is promoted so as to be preserved.

8. Ibid., pp.1–2.

This phenomenon is clearly encapsulated by contemporary attitudes to the cultural significance of dietary practices and attendant notions of the ideal body. As Mennel has argued, the association of slenderness and the regulation of food intake with propriety and desirability is a relatively recent phenomenon.[9] The most significant historical shifts in our perception of food have coincided with parallel changes in the economic structures of society, thus reinforcing the link between the physical disciplining of the body and its inscription in particular forms of political government. Moreover, the regulation of the body via the discourse of food frequently evinces telling affinities with a culture's perception of the function of dress.

In the Middle Ages, the oscillation between equally extreme manifestations of fasting and gorging can be related to an emotional volatility engendered by the economic instability of the period. Upon this material base, ideological superstructures are erected whereby the eating habits of an individual or a group come to resonate with complex symbolic meanings. The practice of fasting, or at any rate self-restraint, or related practices such as self-flagellation and the wearing of deliberately uncomfortable materials, and their visible corporeal effects, for instance, become the external manifestation of internal worth. The discourse of food and that of dress, in this respect, could be seen as variations on one central theme of medieval culture, which Breward sums up as follows: 'Within medieval society the body was prioritised as the dwelling-place of the soul, inner character was displayed through outward signs and clothing could not avoid implication in such a problematic moral arena.'[10] It is also worth remembering that in medieval culture, symbols were held not simply to *stand* for ethical, religious and metaphysical meanings but actually to *contain* God's Word, to embody it physically. The body and its clothes are therefore material incarnations of abstract values, corresponding to 'a tendency deeply inherent in medieval popular perception to translate the spiritual into the concretely sensible'.[11]

Up until the eighteenth century, quantity holds priority over quality: the ability literally to stuff oneself is viewed as a signifier of power, the refinement of taste being a virtually irrelevant consideration. Catherine de' Medici, for example, was celebrated on account of her gargantuan appetite and frequent indigestion. The general insecurity and precariousness of living conditions at the time could not possibly have fostered an ethos of delayed satisfaction such as the one we are accustomed to today. Again, the politics of food

9. Stephen Mennell (1991), 'On the Civilizing of Appetite', in Featherstone, Hepworth and Turner, *The Body*.

10. Christopher Breward (1995), *The Culture of Fashion*, Manchester, p.34.

11. Aron Gurevich (1988), *Medieval Popular Culture: Problems of Belief and Perception*, Cambridge, p.194.

consumption are paralleled by analogous views on the role and function of dress. A rapid glance at Renaissance fashion will reveal that in some courtly circles the end of the sixteenth century signals a momentous increase in applied decoration, emphasis on physical bulk and the proliferation of layers of clothing, which makes dress hardly distinguishable from theatrical costume, and thus throws into relief the age's commitment to an ethos of spectacle and display as power's most vital propagators. Paradoxically, the padding out of the body through dress, as a phenomenon comparable to overeating as a signifier of wealth and authority, is conducive to a sense of physical insubstantiality, frailty and tenuousness: what Breward describes as 'the disintegration of both the body's natural contours and any sense of coherent harmony within the design of the components of fashionable dress and its colour and pattern as a whole'.[12]

Mennell notes that it is in the eighteenth century that gluttony comes to be regarded as shameful (Louis XVI's eating habits being accordingly recorded as scandalous) and that appetite is gradually civilized in a fashion that mirrors the increased security, regularity, reliability and variety of food supplies, as well as decreasing disparity in the food intake of different social classes. Emphasis thus shifts from quantity to quality, as shown by the refinement of table manners, the elaboration of culinary skills and the increasingly widespread belief that delicacy and taste require self-restraint. Not surprisingly, it is with the advent of the industrial age and the emplacement of capitalist value systems that these convictions come to place greater and greater pressure upon the socialized body. The growing range of products accessible by eighteenth-century subjects within the culinary realm is comparable to the veritable explosion, made possible by the development of internal markets and of trade with the New World, of materials and accessories available to the prosperous high and middle classes in the domain of dress. Here, too, propriety is often associated with the deliberate avoidance of excess as a marker of refinement and taste. There are also indicators, however, of a schizophrenic attitude to lavish consumption that encapsulates in embryonic form the ambivalent perceptions of conspicuous bodily and sartorial display associated with contemporary culture. Indeed, eighteenth-century critics seem simultaneously willing to condemn vestimentary excess as an unhealthy symptom of 'foppery, expense and anxiety' and to praise it as spectacular evidence of worldly prosperity.[13]

12. Breward, *The Culture of Fashion*, p.51. See also: Roy Strong (1987), *Gloriana: The Portraits of Queen Elizabeth I*, London; Andrew Belsey and Catherine Belsey (1990), 'Icons of Divinity: Portraits of Elizabeth I', in Gent and Llewellyn (eds), *Renaissance Bodies*, London.

13. Arthur Young (1792), *Annals of Agriculture*, London; quoted in Breward, *The Culture of Fashion*, p.135.

It is in the early 1900s, according to Craik, that the split mentalities so closely connected with the discourse of dress in our own time gain unprecedented prominence, largely owing to the coexistence of notions of mass-production and mass-consumption, on the one hand, and the persistence of hierarchies centred on traditional concepts of style and individual talent, on the other:

> The new approach to fashion was schizophrenic. On the one hand, fashion was democratized as more people had access to the images and clothing preferred by the trend setters. On the other hand, fashion producers were setting the styles. Other changes were also occurring in the fashion industry. The aristocracy was supplanted as the elite fashion community and role models. Socialites, artists and movie stars offered alternative sources of inspiration. These role models offered desirable images and behaviour that were no longer based on emulating one's superiors. Individualism and modernity prevailed.[14]

This coexistence of contradictory interpretations and attitudes, generated, to a considerable extent, by the clash between the democratic expansion of the fashion audience and the élitist glorification of the cult of the designer as *genius*, may be related directly to the functionings of (post)industrial society and its ambiguous disciplinary mechanisms. Once more, a parallel may be drawn between the system of food and that of dress: specifically, this time, between a dietary discourse that upholds simultaneously the ideal of self-restraint and that of indulgence and a vestimentary discourse that expects the subject to revel quite uncritically in disparate, often seemingly unreconcilable, body images. The concurrence of contradictory models could be related to the pervasiveness of notions of bricolage, montage and assemblage, in the confection of contemporary marketable products and especially of the body itself as an endlessly recyclable commodity. Chambers describes the effects of this process, with specific reference to fashion, as follows:

> The sights and sounds of the urban scene – advertizing, music, cinema, television, fashion, magazines, video clips – exist in the rapid circuit of electronic production/ reproduction/distribution. They are not unique artefacts but objects and events multiplied by a thousand, a million times over. In the rapid interplay of these signs, sense outstrips the referents. It produces an aesthetics of transitory and tactile reception, of immediate participation and expendable criteria. Contemplation and study can follow, but in a medium in which we have all become experts it is not a necessary requirement.[15]

14. Jennifer Craik (1994), *The Face of Fashion: Cultural Studies in Fashion*, London, p.74.
15. Iain Chambers (1986), *Popular Culture: The Metropolitan Experience*, London, p.185.

The cultivation of disparate body images within contemporary culture is also amenable to investigation with reference to eating habits and disorders, in ways that similarly point to the collage-like character of post-industrial society. The subject is required literally to split itself into diverse, often incongruous personas, don mutually exclusive masks entailing predetermined modes of activity, embrace an ethos of unrelieved impermanence.

The discourse of dieting and the ideal of slenderness, argues Bordo, have operated as normalizing strategies and hence means of producing what, in Foucauldian terminology, constitutes the docile body, through the cultural metamorphosis of the intelligible body, i.e. its philosophical, aesthetic and scientific representations, into an ideologically useful and socially adaptable mechanism.[16] According to Bordo, the individual body is a microcosm replicating the anxieties and vulnerabilities of the macrocosm, namely the social body. Primarily, the contradictions of capitalism and consumer culture – their simultaneous celebration of the myth of autonomous selfhood and promotion of reification – are reflected by the contradictory body images that surround us at all times. For instance, the boyish female ideal could be read as a casting off of the encumbrance of domestic and reproductive stereotypes of femininity, but is also an indicator of fragility and defence-lessness that serves to perpetuate the 'weaker vessel' image, particularly when compared to the resurgent muscularity and bulk of the contemporary male ideal. These inconsistencies are inextricably intertwined with the typically split personality incongruously *nurtured* by capitalism, whereby the producer self is expected to cultivate a work ethic of thrift and efficiency, at the same time as the consumer self is encouraged to desire and indulge. This double-bind mentality is characteristically manifested by women's magazines based on the repetitive juxtaposition of pictures of luscious food and low-calorie diets, emancipating statements to the effect that beauty comes in all shapes and sizes and apotheoses of the size-six outfit.

Bulimia, argues Bordo, is the extreme incarnation of this schizophrenic attitude, in that it combines unrestrained consumption and drastic cleaning-up acts. Anorexia, on the other hand, mirrors self-disciplining work ethics, whilst obesity symbolizes ultimate indulgence. To some extent, therefore, both anorexia and obesity constitute forms of resistance to dominant cultural norms, which demand the coexistence, rather than the mutual exclusion, of self-restraint and self-gratification. However, whilst obesity rejects the values on which mainstream, mass-produced images are founded, anorexia pays homage to their compulsive promotion of thinness-as-beauty. Indeed, it

16. Susan Bordo (1990), 'Reading the Slender Body', in Jacobus, Fox Keller and Shuttleworth (eds), *Body/Politics*, London.

could be argued that anorexia throws into relief the microcosm/macrocosm equation by dramatizing, at the level of the singular body, problems that pervade the collective body, be it on the small-scale plane of family life, or the broader plane of interpersonal relationships within society at large. Anxieties about the bodily eruption of unsolid, unwanted flesh, to be counteracted by the antidote of framing, echo societal fears of contamination by the non-native, the dubiously gendered, the uncertainly socialized other. The delimitation of corporeality effected by dietary practices, moreover, is closely connected with the athletic framing of the body through the cultivation of either the minimalist or the muscular looks, the attainment of which requires not only self-control, self-discipline and self-determination, but also, more radically, a willingness to enter an antagonistic relationship with one's own body.

Arguably, dress does not enact its framing strategies merely as a form of external control, by means of corsets and germane instruments and garments, as those strategies are internalized to the extent that the subject is fashioned from the inside no less than from the outside. As Greenblatt has indicated, fashioning the subject does not simply amount to the 'imposition upon a person of physical form',[17] but refers also to the creation and cultivation of distinctive modes of behaviour and systems of belief. Dress clothes the body from the inside as a self-fashioning discourse. Through a process that is somewhat reminiscent of the Derridean phenomenon of invagination, the body, having turned itself inside out to proclaim its ability to incarnate the moment's ideal through the exteriority of clothing, proceeds to fold back upon itself by reintrojecting the meanings entailed by that clothing and allowing them to exercise their power from within. The body thus becomes the battlefield on which inner and outer dimensions of experience engage in an unresolved, ongoing struggle. As both dietary and vestimentary practices show, there is always an intimate relationship between the political and socio-economic imperatives of the culture within which those practices evolve and dominant definitions of the decorous, civilized body. As Stallybrass remarks: 'To examine the body's formation is to trace the connection between politeness and politics. But because these connections are never simply given, the body can itself become a site of conflict.'[18]

In assessing the role played by the body in twentieth-century Western thought, two main philosophical strands require special attention, namely, post-idealist and existentialist perspectives. In the former category, a crucial

17. Stephen Greenblatt (1980), *Renaissance Self-Fashioning*, Chicago, p.162.
18. Peter Stallybrass (1986), 'Patriarchal Territories: the Body Enclosed', in Ferguson, Quilligan and Vickers (eds), *Rewriting the Renaissance: The Discourses of Sexual Difference in Early Modern Europe*, Chicago, p.123.

role is played by the writings of Kierkegaard, Schopenhauer and Nietzsche, with their rejection of both the Kantian idealization of aesthetic experience and the Hegelian model of history as the benevolent unfolding of reason. In different ways, all three philosophers accord a place to the body that earlier desensualizing approaches had radically denied. Whilst the idealized subjects of Kant's aesthetics and Hegel's spiritual rationalism were posited as a means of harmonizing and reconciling otherwise conflicting and aporetic facets of experience, post-idealist philosophers bring the body back into play precisely to emphasize the fundamentally contradictory character of all physical and intellectual activity.

For Kierkegaard, far from representing a satisfying synthesis of the noumenal and the phenomenal, the aesthetic experience and the body that initiates and receives it inhabit the domain of sensuous immediacy and undifferentiation: a realm that the subject has no choice but to transcend in order to assert itself through existential decisions and actions, if only to discover its unbearable smallness, flimsiness and absurdity in the face of God's absolute infinity. Kierkegaard thus inaugurates existentialism, in a drastic repudiation of Hegel's all-encompassing idealism, with its belief in God as the impersonal absolute and its concomitant positioning of finite human beings and actions as fragments of this spiritual unity, rationally explainable as elements in the total pattern of things.[19]

Schopenhauer's rejection of idealism is also based on a radical debunking of the supposedly cohesive powers of aesthetic experience.[20] The aesthetic, for Schopenhauer, may be a means of negating, albeit only provisionally, the pervasive ascendancy of a blind, irrational and indomitable Will, which reduces human life to an endless circuit (circus) of need, anxiety and boredom, by allowing a temporary transcendence of one's stifling subjectivity. However, it is deprived of any idealized function as the guarantee of ideological consensus and social harmony, since the trigger for sociality, in Schopenhauer's system, is not a profound sense of commonality but simply boredom. It is only as a result of an unhealable feeling of frustration that we seek, cynically and half-heartedly, one another's loveless company. Moreover, if Kant viewed the aesthetic as a vehicle for the consolidation of an otherwise divided subject through the exercise of judgement, Schopenhauer's aesthetic subject is, paradoxically, subjectless. The subject ultimately remains caught up in the mystifying *veil of Maya* of a world of impenetrable phenomena, or *representations*, at all times driven by the Will as the utterly unknowable thing-in-itself.

19. Søren Kierkegaard (1939), *Fear and Trembling*, trans. R. Payne, London.

20. Arthur Schopenhauer (1969), *The World as Will and Representation*, trans. E. F. J. Payne, New York.

The body is uneasily situated on the threshold between the world as Will, its primary energies consisting of an irrational and unconscious will-to-live, and the world as Representation, to the extent that the self is only knowable as a phenomenon, as appearance, as embodied. However, participation in both those realms does not make the body a figure of synthesizing and integrating mediation, but rather the epitome of a radically decentred and misplaced subjectivity. In Eagleton's words: 'the shadowy frontier where will and representation, inside and outside, come mysteriously, unthinkably together'.[21]

Nietzsche's deconstruction of classical logic, based on an acknowledgment of the rhetorical character of all symbolic and linguistic systems, posits reason not only as a spurious metaphysical construct, as was already the case for Schopenhauer, but also as an intrinsically bodily function: a vehicle not for the discovery and dissemination of truth, whatever that may be, but rather for the expression of inherently *biological* needs. Knowledge, argues Nietzsche, is founded on practical, corporeal needs and interests: it does not come to the body from the outside, but is actually produced by it, the metaphysical categories beloved of idealism and rationalism alike (truth, spirit, the mind, the self, etc.) being 'far from a priori or unconditioned. They are instead inscribed on a body's organs only in so far as they serve as resources which contribute to [the body's] expanded reproduction.'[22] Nietzsche's emplacement of the body at the very heart of the philosophical debate about aesthetics is primarily an assault on the puritanical, hypocritical and sanitizing ethos of common sense fostered by German middle-class culture. In *The Birth of Tragedy*, most notably, he discredits the latter's conventional idealization of Classical Greek art as the epitome of harmony, stability, aseptic purity and tranquillity, by arguing that the Apollonian desire for formal order, psychological balance and emotional control coexists at all times with a Dionysian discourse of abandonment, ecstasy, inebriation, the collapse of boundaries and the annihilation of individual identity, in ways that foreground the ascendancy of corporeal functions at their most sensual, erotic and indeed violent. Asserting the life of the body and the language of the senses becomes a means, for Nietzsche, of exposing the mendaciousness of evolutionary world-views proclaiming the incremental betterment and enhancement of human faculties. Indeed, the marginalization of carnality, he argues, has furthered the cause of a slave mentality: asceticism and spirituality have literally eviscerated the human animal, in order to render it compatible with the demands of so-called civilized society. The release of

21. Terry Eagleton (1990), *The Ideology of the Aesthetic*, Oxford, p.170.
22. Scott Lash (1991), 'Genealogy and the Body: Foucault/Deleuze/Nietzsche', in Featherstone, Hepworth and Turner, *The Body*, p.272.

creative energy requires a rehabilitation of physicality and instinctual drives capable of combating the morbid moralizing of mainstream Western thought.[23]

The second field of philosophical inquiry to be taken into account in the evaluation of recent approaches to the body, existentialism, is generally seen to have found its inception in the phenomenological tradition. As a method elaborated by Husserl, phenomenology is in the first place concerned with the identification and inspection of essential mental sets and thought processes, regarded independently of their origins or causes and effects or consequences, since these are felt to be external to the contents and objects of consciousness themselves. Deeply antagonistic to all forms of empiricism, Husserl thus posits philosophy as the scrutiny of universal essences, as opposed to particular acts of sense-perception, as the objective and logical elements of thought shared by all minds.[24] Husserl's anti-empiricist and anti-psychologist approach restrains him from introducing the body, as a notoriously relative dimension, into the question of perception. However, the issue of embodiment has come to play a pivotal part in more recent phenomenological discourses.

Instrumental to the transition from Husserl's positions to later theorizations of the role of the corporeal in the dynamics of perception and knowledge is the work of Heidegger. Anticipating existentialism, Heidegger argues that subjectivity is not a given but rather a process of constant invention and reinvention. Although since Classical Greece *being* has been insulated from *time* by being perceived as an eternal and atemporal presence, to the exclusion of past and future, existence, argues Heidegger, has no such fixed nature. His concept of *Dasein* (literally: being-there) radically upsets traditional notions of stability and continuity where subjectivity is concerned, as it posits existence as a continual process of self-fashioning, legitimation and appropriation, rather than the embodiment of a pre-existing metaphysical substance or essence. Foreshadowing certain recent interpretations of the embodied subject as a precipitate of language and history, Heidegger maintains that although the world is a product of our projections, it is also the case that we are subjected to its impersonal rhythms: the individual is *flung down* or *thrown* into being, in a place and time it did not choose. This uncomfortable state of affairs is due to the human creature's liminal positioning both in and outside material nature. We have wills and consciousness, but are also physical animals and cannot therefore adopt a stance of detached contemplation from a mountain top: *Dasein* is in the world and inseparable

23. Friedrich Nietzsche (1956), *The Birth of Tragedy*, trans. F. Golffing, New York.
24. Edmund Husserl (1970), *Logical Investigations*, trans. J. N. Findlay, London.

from it. As a result, we merge constantly with the objects of our consciousnesses, and our involvement with those objects inevitably threatens the integrity of our boundaries as mental and physical entities alike.[25]

The question of embodiment has been assigned greater and greater significance by later phenomenological and existentialist thinkers:

> That perception and understanding of the world are partly a function of the fact that consciousness is not 'pure', but exists within a membrane of flesh and blood, has led to a situation in which many of the problems seen as otiose by Descartes have been reintroduced as vital to the understanding of how human beings do in fact perceive or constitute the world . . . It was in the work of the French existential-izing phenomenologists . . . (e.g. Sartre and Merleau-Ponty), that the fact that the body actually lives a world, and thus projects 'its' values over a world by intentionality was taken serious account of.[26]

Merleau-Ponty, in particular, maintains that the significance of sense data and impressions does not rest with an object's inherent characteristics, let alone with descriptions of the object delivered by science, but with the form of the object as perceived, although, superfluous to say, perception may be distorted, flawed and misguided. In this, what acquires paramount importance is the way in which the world appears to and is operated upon not by a putatively incorporeal but by an inexorably embodied consciousness.[27]

Related to the issue of embodiment is the concept of the Other, as formulated by Merleau-Ponty and Sartre and subsequently elaborated by Lacan in the area of psychoanalysis, as the factor responsible for the socialization and intersubjectivization of perception. The Other confers meaning on the subject by either facilitating or compelling its definition of a world picture and its place within that representation. The Other could be taken to signify another person, as in Sartre's classic definition of the Gaze of the Other as accountable for the disintegration of the subject's delusions of absolute mastery over its field of vision, or, as in Lacanian theory, the vast net of symbols into which we are born and that will go on operating long after we are gone. Sartre's writings on the Gaze of the Other could be described as a narrative of interference, positing this scopic phenomenon as the undismiss-able reminder of the subject's confined and relative control over its world. Bryson comments on this aspect of Sartre's *Being and Nothingness* (1956) as follows:

25. Martin Heidegger (1962), *Being and Time*, trans. J. Macquarrie and E. Robinson, Oxford.

26. Roger Poole (1990), 'Embodiment', in A. Bullock and O. Stallybrass (eds), *The Fontana Dictionary of Modern Thought*, London, pp.264–5.

27. Maurice Merleau-Ponty (1962), *Phenomenology of Perception*, trans. C. Smith, London.

in its first movement, Sartre enters a park and discovers that he is alone: everything in the park is there for him to regard from an unchallenged center of the visual field. . . . But in Sartre's second movement, this reign of plenitude and luminous peace is brought abruptly to an end: into the park and into the watcher's solitary domain there enters another, whose intrusion breaks the peace and fractures the watcher's self-enclosure. The watcher is in turn watched: observed of all observers, the viewer becomes spectacle to another's sight. . . . the intruder becomes a kind of drain which sucks in all the former plenitude, a black hole pulling the scene away from the watcher self into an engulfing void.[28]

Structures of vision and visuality centred on the recognition of the material, as opposed to bodiless, character of perception and knowledge – of oneself, of others, of the Other – thus point to the ephemerality of the body's boundaries and frames. Above all, they alert us to the fact that what and how we see, what we are able, allowed or indeed made to see, is inscribed in societal formations that, paradoxically, deploy the body's physical faculties at the same time as they strive to translate them into immaterial laws. Crary, in this respect, relates the hegemonic potentialities of visuality to the etymological roots of the terms *observer* and *spectator*:

Unlike *spectare*, the Latin root for 'spectator', the root for 'observe' does not literally mean 'to look at'. . . . *observare* means 'to conform one's action, to comply with', as in observing rules, codes, regulations, and practices. Though obviously one who sees, an observer is more importantly one who sees within a prescribed set of possibilities, one who is embedded in a system of conventions and limitations.[29]

Lacan may have had similar considerations in mind whilst speculating that the world of inanimate objects is not passive but rather endowed with the power to *look back* at the perceiver. What we see is always, to some extent, what we are meant to see: the inanimate world watches us in so far as there is always someone, something that expects us to see in certain ways. As Bryson puts it:

When I look, what I see is not simply light but intelligible form. . . . For human beings collectively to orchestrate their visual experience together it is required that each submit his or her retinal experience to the socially agreed description(s) of an intelligible world. Vision is socialized, and thereafter deviation from this social construction of visual reality can be measured and named, as hallucination,

28. Norman Bryson (1988), 'The Gaze in the Expanded Field', in Hal Foster (ed.), *Vision and Visuality*, Seattle, pp.88–9.

29. Jonathan Crary (1990), *Techniques of the Observer*, Cambridge, Mass., pp.5–6.

misrecognition, or 'visual disturbance'. Between the subject and the world is inserted the entire sum of discourses which make up visuality.[30]

The reinforcement of the dichotomy between mind and body has proved equally useful to the emplacement of unitary vision. Here, the codification of perspective has played a vital role, by positing the notion of an abstract and objective way of seeing, based on the totalizing gaze of one, disembodied and de-eroticized eye/I: 'it followed the logic of the Gaze rather than the Glance, thus producing a visual take that was eternalized, reduced to 'one point of view'.[31] Jay is here alluding to Bryson's distinction between the Gaze and the Glance, put forward in *Vision and Painting*, according to which the former operates as a masterful, vigilant and penetrating weapon, able to freeze the body into a unified icon for vicarious sexual consumption, whilst the latter, as a flickering and ungovernable phenomenon, resists homogenization and highlights the body as the site of polymorphous drives and desires.[32]

The belief in a single, correct way of seeing, corresponding to a single and likewise correct way of representing, is, of course, untenable, since the disembodied eye/I simply does not exist. Vision, however idealized, is necessarily inscribed in contingent material bodies: not to mention the fact that each of a subject's eyes sees *differently*.

The camera obscura, like perspectivalism, contributed to the definition of the status of the observer in the early modern period, as a contraption designed to guarantee objective truth. Everything is processed, known and possessed within this one space, self-enclosed and distinct from external reality, and carefully insulated from the life of the senses. Like perspectivalism, the camera obscura model relies on the dubious premisses of monocularity and desensualization, as a means of enthroning the Cartesian myth of a rationally unified subject and thus replacing all mementoes of the body's unquantifiable materiality with abstract and schematized qualities. However, a crucial shift in the theorization of vision occurs in the early nineteenth century, as the human body attains to possibly unprecedented centrality. The development of physiology, with its awareness of the interrelations between categories of knowledge and physical/anatomical structures, serves to stress the subjective nature of all modes of vision, as well as ongoing interactions between inside and outside. The putative unity of subjectivity is interrogated through the discovery that the nerves of different senses are distinct and that the same external cause will generate quite different

30. Bryson in Foster, *Vision and Visuality*, p.91.

31. Martin Jay (1988), 'Scopic Regimes of Modernity', in Hal Foster (ed.), *Vision and Visuality*, p.7.

32. Norman Bryson (1983), *Vision and Painting: The Logic of the Gaze*, London.

sensations from one nerve to another. The physical subject, as a composite edifice, cannot process the world in one single way, as perspective and the camera obscura claimed, but must rather rely on separate, if complementary, channels, often with unexpected and disconcerting results.

The challenging of the boundaries once deemed capable of separating one body from another and one physical function from another has, since the nineteenth century, clearly escalated, as the impact of science and technology on both individual and collective experiences has gained momentum. The feelings of contingency, indeterminacy and transitoriness typical of much contemporary culture could be seen as an intensification of exactly that challenge. As the body has forced its way (back) into the province of philosophical scrutiny and thus achieved a respectable degree of academic legitimacy, its definition as a discreet and self-contained object of analysis has, paradoxically, coincided with an often reluctant but nonetheless unavoidable recognition of the precariousness of its limits. As the body faces daily prospects of consolidation and no less likely chances of dissolution, it seems pointless to search for meaning in a monolithic system of belief. It may be more cogent, in fact, to assume that any meaning that the body is likely to accrue only proceeds from an acceptance of its duplicity: above all, of its disorienting juxtaposition of a socialized, bounded edge and a subversive, limitless one. It is one of the principal functions of the discourse of dress to underscore simultaneously the body's circumscribed status and its boundlessness – not in order to enlist it definitively in one camp or the other, but rather to highlight the body's location in that uncertain space that Barthes vividly describes as 'the site of loss, the seam, the cut, the deflation, the dissolve'.[33]

33. Roland Barthes (1990), *The Pleasure of the Text*, trans. R. Miller, Oxford, p.7.

The Rim and the Abject

From its inception in the work of Freud, the field of psychoanalysis has been a fruitful, though often frustrating, source for attempts to make sense of the individual and social meanings of the body. In Freud's own commentaries the body is both present and absent, appearing initially as a biological entity, but swiftly overwritten with psychic significance. It interests him primarily as the textual surface upon which the clues to the function of the psyche are inscribed. However, while he retains something of a loyalty to the mind/body dualism of Cartesian thought, his work also contains an implicit critique of such thinking, particularly in his understanding of the ego. In the work of some important psychoanalytic theorists after Freud this critique is developed, though an ambivalence remains in their treatment of the body, repeating the appearance/disappearance vanishing trick that he performs. In this section we will examine aspects of the work of Jacques Lacan and Julia Kristeva, and begin to explore the implications of their theories of the body and the application of some of their ideas to the body/dress relationship.

In his introduction to Lacan Malcolm Bowie comments that:

> Lacan's papers of the nineteen-fifties are often cast in an abstract and unfleshly vein ... he propounds an eroticized science of meaning, modelling devices for which are derived from logic, rhetoric and topology. Lacan's Eros finds its primary expression neither in physical sensations nor in desirous mental states, nor yet in the organs and erotogenic zones that, for other theorists of sexuality, allow the pursuit of pleasure to be mapped and logged on the surface of the human body.[1]

For Lacan, the biological body disappears, or is confined to the order of the Real, and is not accessible other than in the realm of signification. The body can only be represented or conceptualized in the Symbolic and Imaginary orders, and if, as Lacan says, 'the word is the murder of the thing' then the body is murdered by language, its Symbolic presence the marker of its absence. As a result, the importance of the body is in representation, deriving

---

1. Malcolm Bowie, (1991), *Lacan*, London, p.122.

from the mirror stage (*stade du miroir*), in which the infant, experiencing its own body as fragmented because of its uneven physical development, perceives and desires the wholeness of the mirrored image. The fascination of the mirrored image coincides with the child's recognition of lack; the visual image, which is initially not understood because it is 'out-there' as opposed to the 'in-here' of bodily sensation, is gradually comprehended as an image of itself, and the child delights in its visual double for the new sense of power and completeness that it provides. However, because comprehension of 'out-there' means a recognition that there is a division between the subject and the world, self and other, it also represents the first attempts to fill the lack: thus simultaneously the triadic relation of desire is constituted, the dynamic of subject, other and Other. Lacan states that the subject is 'born into the field of the Other',[2] the place from which the subject is recognized, which is both external and internal. The Other can be understood as both the symbolic network governed by language-like rules, and as the internalized form of this, the unconscious. The mirror stage therefore initiates for the subject identification with and dependence on images and representations that will continue throughout its life. Elsewhere, Lacan asserts that 'the unconscious is the discourse of the Other',[3] underlining the connection of many of his ideas, which are crucial to this analysis, indeed crucial to the whole of his thinking. The ego is seen as a tracing of the subject's perceived corporeality, not an outline of the real body but an 'imaginary anatomy'; it is the *meaning* of the body that is introjected by the subject. The 'imaginary anatomy' becomes the point of organization of relations, and as it provides a means by which the self can be perceived by others, it is now both subject and object; the specular image is the basis of being in the world. The name Lacan gives to this moment, in English translation as well as in French (*stade*=stadium), indicates not only the relevance of the visual, but its significance for the subject: it is not simply a developmental phase, but a theatrical stage upon which the drama of subjectivity is constantly enacted: '[it] is no less purely historical when it is actually experienced than when it is reconstituted in thought, nor is it less purely grounded in intersubjectivity.'[4]

The ego is constituted through the complex relations between itself, others and the image of the body. Because of the misrecognition that is a condition of the mirror stage the subject's very sense of an identity is an alienated one, which constantly reminds him of his earliest experience of physical disorder;

2. Jacques Lacan (1977), *The Four Fundamental Concepts of Psychoanalysis,* ed. Jacques-Alain Miller, trans. Alan Sheridan, London, p.199.

3. Bowie, *Lacan*, p.82.

4. Jacques Lacan (1977), *Ecrits: A Selection*, trans. Alan Sheridan, London p.53.

the anxiety associated with the memory of dismemberment strengthens the desire of the individual to secure and possess an integrated bodily 'I'. Perversely, the desire for wholeness and the efforts enacted to secure it emphasize the pull of fragmentation and threaten again the dissolution into broken parts. In neither case, the integrated or the fragmented, is the experience 'real': both bodies are fantasized constructions, produced from private and from collective fantasies of the body's organization. It is not a body so much as a 'heterogeneous mannequin, a baroque doll, a trophy of limbs',[5] a representation of it. The image of the body is a threshold, not (and both) mind or body, individual or social, natural or culturally constructed. This threshold state is unfixed, a marginal condition, and as such the site of the ongoing processes of subjectivity. The effect of the continuing conflict of fragmentation and integration has marked effects that can be observed in a range of ways in human existence, as Lacan comments:

> There is a specific relation here between man and his own body that is manifested in a series of social practices – from rites involving tattooing, incision, and circumcision in primitive societies to what, in advanced societies, might be called the Procrustean arbitrariness of fashion, a relatively recent cultural innovation, in that it denies respect for the natural forms of the human body.[6]

These remarks appear in his discussion of aggressivity, and it seems clear that he is identifying all these practices, including fashion, as manifestations of aggression, as well as suggesting that fashion is simply an advanced version of tattooing or circumcision. The adjective 'Procrustean' is a telling one: Procrustes, in Greek legend, was a robber who forced travellers to lie on a bed that he made them fit by stretching or cutting pieces off their bodies; thus fashion is seen as a system in which, instead of clothing's being constructed to fit a body that is fixed and solid, the body is made to fit the clothes, in the sense of the reorganization of the imaginary anatomy. It is chopped and trimmed, as Cinderella's sisters cut off their toes and heels to fit the magic slipper. This would imply that, far from clothing's providing a boundary for the body, thereby ensuring the presentation of a completed and contained self, it in fact works in reverse, serving to emphasize, or indeed to enact, violence and dismemberment on that body, and to threaten the precarious sense of self by its insistent marginality.

There is an inherent duality in the practices that Lacan names, as well as many others that could be identified as analogous, such as the use of

---

5. Bowie, *Lacan*, p.60.
6. Lacan, *Ecrits*, p.11.

make-up or body-piercing, in that the actions that are performed with the intention of completing or finishing the body are doomed (or actually intended in the realm of the unconscious) to render its incompletion visible. The mechanism by which this process operates can be explained by reference to some of Lacan's later work, specifically the notion of the rim, and the *objet petit a.*

Lacan speaks very directly of the importance of the idea of the rim, and its fundamental implication in the process of realization of subjectivity: 'Everything emerges from the structure of the signifier. This structure is based on what I first called the function of the cut and which is now articulated, in the development of my discourse, as the topological function of the rim. The relation of the subject to the Other is entirely produced in a process of gap.'[7] The basic mode of being, as has already been outlined, is one of lack, splitting, gaps and misrecognition. Lacan here makes a clear connection between the gap, the process of subjectivity, the signifier and the body. In his theorization of the erogenous zones he elaborates on the theme of the margin, stating that erotogeneity occurs when an area of the body has been separated from its physiological function; he suggests that such areas all occur at the margins of the body, in places where a cut (*coupure*) or a discontinuity is apparent:

> The very delimitation of the 'erogenous zone' that the drive isolates from the metabolism of the function is the result of a cut (*coupure*) expressed in the anatomical mark (*trait*) of a margin or border-lips, 'the enclosure of the teeth', the rim of the anus, the tip of the penis, the vagina, the slit formed by the eyelids, even the horn-shaped aperture of the ear . . . Observe that this mark of the cut is no less obviously present in the object described by analytic theory: the mamilla, faeces, the phallus (imaginary object), the urinary flow. (An unthinkable list, if one adds, as I do, the phoneme, the gaze, the voice – the nothing.) For is it not obvious that this feature, this partial feature, rightly emphasized in objects, is applicable not because these objects are part of a total object, the body, but because they represent only partially the function that produces them?
>
> These objects have one common feature in my elaboration of them – they have no specular image, or, in other words, alterity. It is what enables them to be the 'stuff', or rather the lining, though not in any sense the reverse, of the very subject one takes to be the subject of consciousness.[8]

That which marks the cut is the focus of desire, rather than the cut itself, and, as Lacan suggests in his extension of the list of items more commonly

7. Lacan, *Four Fundamental Concepts*, p.206.
8. Lacan, *Ecrits*, pp.314–15.

regarded in psychoanalysis as sites of the erotic, these can be attributes as well as physical entities. In this respect, dress can easily be seen as another possible addition to the catalogue, the placing of clothing on the naked body marks the whole of the surface of the skin as a cut; the entire body becomes a rim, because it is it considered incomplete without the superimposition of clothes. The cut is the place where discontinuity occurs: in textual terms it is where the discourse breaks, where the sliding of the signifier over the signified defers meaning. For the subject its self-division is revealed at this point; the *meaning* of its self, its identity, is likewise deferred; and the body is translated into a web of endlessly sliding signifiers. In this analysis subjectivity stumbles at the edge of the body, the continuous, yet discontinuous, margin of the skin. In physiological terms this is not inaccurate, as the skin is a broken surface, composed entirely of the tiny holes of the pores, its apparent smoothness an illusion of continuity. There is an interesting tacit recognition of this fact in the kind of advertising associated with skin-cleansing products, where a magnified image of the pore is shown, and the danger of blockage of the hole with dirt is emphasized. This connects with Kristeva's elaboration of the notion of the rim, and its part in the maintenance of the clean and proper body: the surface of the skin becomes a site of abjection because of the existence of these millions of, ultimately unpoliceable, holes.

To move beyond the microscopic, the awareness of the existence of the cut produces the desire to fill the space, to plaster over the fissure that betrays the self as fragmented. The subject attempts to plug the gap that speaks of the yawning space at the centre of its being with what Lacan refers to as the *objet petit a*, a substitute object where the small *a* serves to distinguish the contingent 'other' object of desire from the all-pervasive 'Other'. This set of relations is the central triangle that represents desire; it is closed but unfinished, as there is constant movement around it. The drive pushes towards the Other, but, unable to attain it, is directed to the other, *the objet petit a*. The drive, however, is indifferent to its object, as the object reveals another desire, another object that offers satisfaction. The 'object' is always a displacement, a substitute, not really the object but the cause of desire. Dress, as an appendix of the body, is an *objet petit a*, which is desired in order to achieve completion. The object chosen to perform this function will always fail to do so; the gap, by definition, is unpluggable. The object is outside the body; the drive draws itself outwards from the rim towards the object, but also pulls away inwards to the knowledge of its lack. This is clarified in Lacan's diagrammatic representation:

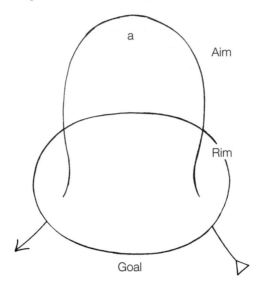

and his comment 'The *petit a* never crosses this gap. This *a* is presented precisely . . . as the object that cannot be swallowed, as it were, which remains stuck in the gullet of the signifier. It is at this point of lack that the subject has to recognize himself.'[9]

Thus the object cannot be fully incorporated or decisively rejected: it hovers at the rim, and as Lacan suggests, while the body can be wholly or partially mirrored, certain of its zones always escape the mirror's grasp, no optical device can achieve purchase on them, 'it is to this object that cannot be grasped in the mirror that the specular image lends its clothes'.[10] He comments in a later essay:

> a, the object of desire, at the departure point where our model places it, is, as soon as it functions there . . ., the object of desire. This means that if it is a partial object it is not just a part, or a detached component, of the device that's here imagining the body, but an element of structure from the very moment of origin, and, if one can put it this way, present in the way the cards were dealt for the game that's in progress. In so far as it has been chosen from among the appendices of the body as an index of desire, it is already the exponent of a function, which sublimates it even before it has been exercised – that of an index finger raised towards an absence of the which the *est-ce* (it is) has nothing to say, unless it says that the absence in question belongs to the place where it speaks (*Ecrits* 682).[11]

9. Lacan, *Four Fundamental Concepts*, p.270.
10. Lacan, *Ecrits*, p.316.
11. Bowie, *Lacan*, p.166.

The wording of Lacan's statement is apposite: clothing can be seen as the *objet a par excellence*; its relation to the body is precisely one of hovering; it is both part of, and not part of, the body; it is detachable; and its presence points to absence, and the absence to which it, like the raised index finger, points is the absence of the body. As an example of this, the 'absent presence' can be observed both in paintings of the clothed body and clothes without bodies. Renaissance portraiture is a common point of reference for commentary on vestimentary codes and the theatricality of power; but such portraits can also be read in Lacanian terms. In some of the well-known pictures of Elizabeth I, such as the 'Ditchley' Portrait (Marcus Gheeraerts the Younger, *c.*1592) her clothing is painted in great detail, the lines of the fabric are stiff, and the shapes exaggerated, and the body, apart from the face, neck and hands, is covered. The body is fragmented: the uncovered parts appear to float, detached from the whole. In the Ditchley picture the stiff edges of the dress function as erogenous zones; rim-like, they mark the places of cut on the royal body: the jewel-bordered end of the bodice points to the genitals, the neckline is a band across the nipples, and the ruff emphasizes the face, upon which the mouth, nostrils and eyes are edged with hard lines. Yet the body is not depicted: through the signifiers of the clothing it is caused to vanish, the 'real' body murdered by the language of the clothing. This is even more obvious when considered in relation to Elizabeth's iconography: the personal body – the body natural – is replaced by the imaginary anatomy of the body politic. This can be extended to the map of England upon which she is standing: it flows from the dress, its edges matching the lines of her skirt, becoming part of her costume. As an *objet petit a*, it stuffs the gap, the fragmented identity of the subject as woman, monarch, mortal, immortal, land and flesh, in order to create the illusion of power and control smoothly boundaried in the person of the queen. It fails because the elements remain discrete, persistently singular in character. The detachable nature of the dress is neatly underlined by the practice of painters of the monarch: very few portraits were painted from life; more commonly, the approved outline of the face was traced, and the painter's only sitting was with the empty dress and unworn jewellery.

In contemporary painting, as Juliet Ash has noted,[12] the depiction of clothes without people has become much more frequent. She interprets the work of Colin Smith, which includes a whole range of paintings of uninhabited garments, as a celebration of their former wearers; but it is also possible to read them in a similar way to the portraits of Elizabeth. In a sense they show the process in reverse: where the queen's body is rendered

12. Juliet Ash (1995), Paper delivered to Art Historians Association Conference, London.

Figure 2. Marcus GHEERAERTS, The Younger, *Elizabeth I* (The 'Ditchley Portrait'), 1592, oil on canvas. Courtesy of the National Portrait Gallery, London.

absent by its clothing, in these pictures the sequence of the process is abbreviated – the body has already disappeared, yet the empty garments indicate its presence. They are indeed floating signifiers, acknowledging that attempts to make reference to a 'real' body of meaning are futile. These are not clothes that have never been worn – the folds and creases suggest fairly recent occupancy; yet they hover in the painted space, objects that cannot be assimilated or rejected, caught in the perpetual dynamic of desire. They are also painful images: dismembered like the separated shirts and dresses, they echo the uncomfortable recognition of lack and the radical fragmentation of the self.

Other practices that we have identified as clothing in its widest sense, such as make-up and body-piercing, are very obviously examples of the functioning of the rim, as those areas usually emphasized are some of the rims that Lacan mentions, the eyelids, earlobes, nostrils and lips. Instead of concealing the cut that the rim indicates, they make it more conspicuous, advertising the fissure and enhancing its erotic attraction. The case of body-piercing is still more pronounced: the crossing over into the mainstream of Western fashion of practices previously considered confined to the limited world of sado-masochistic sex such as the piercing of the navel, the nipples, the rim of the anus and so on, further emphasizes the elements of his analysis. In many non-Western cultures, of course, fabric clothing is often minimal, and adornment of the skin is the primary form of dress. Like clothing made of fabric, make-up, tattooing and piercing confuse the idea of the fixed boundary of the body, raising the question of where precisely these objects are located: are they on the outside of the body, or do they become part of it? We are forced to identify them as marginal phenomena, resident in the flux of subjectivity. There is even a difficulty in naming them: the word 'object' seems unsatisfactory, as does 'practice', which erases the fact of the permanent result. Lacan offers some possible elucidation in his remarks on the libido as an organ rather than a field of forces:

> This organ is unreal. Unreal is not imaginary. The unreal is defined by articulating itself on the real in a way that eludes us . . . But the fact that it is unreal does not prevent an organ from embodying itself . . . One of the most ancient forms in which this unreal organ is incarnated in the body is tattooing, scarification. The tattoo certainly has the function of being for the Other, of situating the subject in it, marking his place in the field of the group's relations, between each individual and all the others. And, at the same time, it obviously has an erotic function, which all those who have approached it in reality have perceived.[13]

13. Lacan, *Four Fundamental Concepts*, pp.205–6.

Figure 3. Colin SMITH, *Wardrobe #16*, oil on canvas, 1996. © Colin Smith 1996.

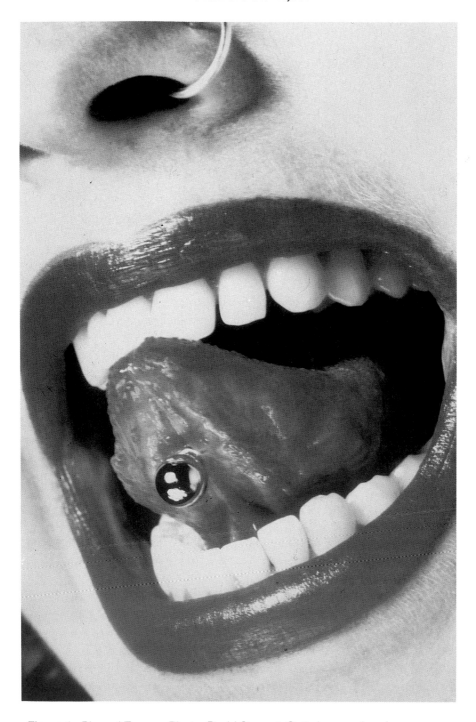

Figure 4. *Pierced Tongue.* Photo: David Stewart, Getty Images, London.

The tattoo cannot be described because it is an unreal organ, embodied, yet free-floating as a part of the social network. These objects, too, participate in the drama of subjectivity in the same ways as garments, reminding us that cohesion, integration and solidity are bound up at all times with the forces of destabilization and self-obliteration. They play the part of a stubbornly auto-erotic character, aware of their dependence on a pre-given structure, yet determined to face that structure with the self-determining audaciousness of an independent force. They are detachable, yet assume the status of organs, becoming the surrogates and derivatives of the phallus, the spectral organ to which all *objets* refer:

> the *objet a* is something from which the subject, in order to constitute itself, has separated itself off as organ. This serves a symbol of the lack, that is to say, of the phallus, not as such, but in so far as it is lacking. It must, therefore, be an object that is, firstly, separable and, secondly, that has some relation to the lack.[14]

Lacan's analysis also suggests the masochism of this process: the subject is continually reminding himself of his unfinishedness, his fragmentation. The masculine pronoun is perhaps more inappropriate than usual in this sense, as in Western culture particularly, it is the female subject who is seen to be the willing victim of the fashion system. This perhaps unsurprising, given the close relationship between the *objet petit a* and the phallus in Lacanian thought: 'The moment of cut is haunted by the form of a bloody scrap – the pound of flesh that life pays in order to turn it into the signifier of signifiers, which it is impossible to restore, as such, to the imaginary body; it is the lost phallus of the embalmed Osiris.'[15]

In his theorization of sexual difference Lacan departs little from Freud: for both of them woman is constituted by lack, and the phallus is the signifier of that which she lacks. For the woman, then, the necessity of attempting to complete the unfinished self is even more urgent, and doubly futile. Lacan, recognizing this paradox, suggests that women contrive an ingenious method of circumventing their failure to cancel their lack: through self-decoration they attempt to reconstitute themselves as objects rather than subjects of desire; if they cannot possess the phallus, they can become it in relation to men. By logical derivation, women become for men the *objet petit a*, with all its inherent unsatisfactoriness, and the desire to replace the inadequate (female) object with another, more beautifully adorned, object is naturalized into a nearly essentialist position.

14. Ibid., p.103.
15. Lacan, *Ecrits*, p.265.

In psychoanalytic terms then, we are offered an explanation for the 'arbitrariness of fashion' as a system that goes beyond a simple Marxist or feminist analysis of fashion as a mere function of capitalism or patriarchy. It suggests ways in which capitalism or patriarchy can actually co-opt the psyche in their operations, and why the seductions of fashion are so difficult to resist. The purchaser and wearer of clothing is not simply a brainwashed adherent of a transparently exploitative system, but a participant in a complex process of self-determination. Items of clothing are objects of desire that hold the promise of completion, the last piece necessary to close the gap; but because they are inherently condemned to failure, the subject's desire turns to another piece, a new object to fulfil that desire.

The Abject

. . . all identities are unstable: the identity of linguistic signs, the identity of meaning and, as a result, the identity of the speaker. And in order to take account of this destabilization of meaning and of the subject I thought the term 'subject in process' would be appropriate. Process in the sense of process but also in the sense of a legal proceeding where the subject is committed to trial, because our identities in life are constantly called into question, brought to trial, over-ruled.[16]

The precariousness and instability of identity and meaning are thrown into relief by the equivocal function of clothing as a structure simultaneously capable of framing the subject and dispersing it across multiple surfaces, of co-operating with psychological and ideological programmes of containment and yet defying their totalizing thrust. The ensuing discussion proposes an analogy between the discourse of dress and the Kristevan concept of *abjection*, based on their shared emphasis on a manifestly anti-binary approach to subjectivity and signification, resulting in the coexistence of operations of exclusion and inclusion, self-differentiation and self-dissemination.

The psychoanalytical/philosophical notion of abjection is inextricably intertwined with Kristeva's endeavour to trace the flight path of those phenomena of linguistic and subjective nebulousness that, though repressed by the signifying systems within which the socialized being is inscribed, are nonetheless central to multifold forms of human creativity and indeed return to haunt the patterns of organized discourse through their 'incandescence':

In order to research this state of instability . . . I proposed to take into account two modalities or conditions of meaning which I called 'the semiotic' and 'the

16. Julia Kristeva in Interview with Susan Sellers, *Women's Review*, no.12, p.19.

symbolic'. What I call 'the semiotic' takes us back to the pre-linguistic states of childhood where the child babbles the sounds s/he hears, or where s/he articulates rhythms, alliterations, or stresses, trying to imitate his/her surroundings. In this state the child doesn't yet possess the necessary linguistic signs and thus there is no meaning in the strict sense of the term. It is only after the mirror phase or the experience of castration in the Oedipus complex that the individual becomes subjectively capable of taking on the signs of language, of articulation as it has been prescribed – and I call that 'the symbolic'.[17]

However, the semiotic, though primarily associated with the flow of drives (*pulsions*) that constitutes the pre-oedipal child's language before its articulation into stable symbolic terms, can still be discerned in adult discourse in non-verbal qualities of language, for example tone, rhythm and laughter, and in forms of rhetorical displacement, disruption and contradiction, as well silences and gaps. The semiotic disrupts the relatively crystallized categories of symbolic language by creating an excess over precise meanings and interpretations through an anti-teleological decentring of the unitary constructs of received opinion. The jumble of diffuse impulses that constitute the semiotic *chora* display a carnivalesque disregard for all criteria of unity and stability supposed to delimit bodily processes and functions. The Kristevan body is as heterogeneous, open-ended, dynamic, protean and intertextual as the *dialogical*, experimental text that, following Bakhtin, Kristeva posits as a major form of resistance to the ordering agencies of the symbolic. The body is conceived of as a discordant assortment of states and drives wherein no stillness or equilibrium is ultimate, since momentary stasis itself invariably preludes yet more motility. The semiotic, with its unformalized undifferentiation and lack of any neat distinctions between subject and object, shuns socialized patterns of signification, their reliance on principles of separation, the *thetic*, and binary polarizations of subject and object, signifier and signified. The resurfacing of the *chora*'s pulsational energies in adult life is symptomatic of the ongoing influence on psychic development of the pluralities, uncertainties and ambiguities of the pre-symbolic body, and hence represents a *temporary semiotization of the symbolic*.

If the symbolic requires us to put on putatively consistent *costumes* as enunciative subjects, the semiotic, by contrast, infringes upon that dramatic unity by promoting the adoption of a virtually limitless range of roles and of alternating, indeed conflicting, forms of *apparel*. The symbolic assumption of identity is based on a clear demarcation between self and other, as well as on the translation of the physical being into a disembodied signifier. The semiotic, for its part, is inimical to inviolable boundaries and constantly

17. Ibid.

draws us back to both the sorrows and the delights of material reality – not least, to the materiality of language itself. The symbolic's vulnerability to the intrusions of the repressed semiotic is largely due to the indecisive, shadowy character of the very process of transition from the pre-linguistic to the linguistic stage. Crucial to this rite of passage, as hinted at earlier, are acts of self-differentiation. Yet the subject's ability to embrace a notion of separate personhood is only a precarious endowment, embroiled in a meandering process, fraught with uncertainties and doubts: the subject may only recognize itself as an independent entity *in relation* to some other entity; and because of this relationality, its very autonomy comes seriously under scrutiny: 'sometimes I take myself to be me, sometimes I confuse myself with my mother'.[18] (The term 'mother' is here being employed as an instance of what, in a broader frame of reference, could be described as the other, the image or representation from which the subject aims at distinguishing itself, in order to be *itself*.)

The discourse of dress complicates these already intricate operations, in so far as the subject, when confronted with dress as the other, is called upon to define itself in relation and in opposition to this other. This act of self-differentiation constitutes the first step towards the acquisition of identity as a clothed, i.e. framed, body. Yet this preliminary configuration of selfhood is unstable; for at one point, the subject may take itself to be *itself*, an entity independent from the framing structures that are supposed to differentiate it and, simultaneously, from which it is supposed to differentiate itself; whilst at another point, it may confuse itself with them, with the *other*. Whereas totalizing strategies of socialization and sublimation of the corporeal are held capable of resolving, or at least containing, this narcissistic instability (am I myself or am I the other?), dress precludes any final and irrevocable integration into the symbolic, by constantly reintroducing into the latter's prescribed modalities reminders of an archaic and intractable entanglement with materiality. The semiotic potentialities of dress are underscored by its linguistic and rhetorical features. According to Bové, the resurgence of the semiotic in poetic discourse gives rise to a 'new language ... defined in opposition to traditional language where logically connected clauses and denotation are primary. Instinctual language highlights connotations and creates patterns that are more rhythmical than logical.'[19]

Like Kristeva's *poetic language*, the language of dress presents us with a scenario where virtually everything is of the order of connotation, rather

18. Ibid., p.20.
19. Carol Mastrangelo Bové (1984), 'The Politics of Desire in Julia Kristeva', in *Boundary 2: A Journal of Postmodern Literature*, Part 12, p.219.

than denotation, where arbitrarily concocted patterns and the principle of *non sequitur* gain primacy over logical links and associations. This analogy between the Kristevan semiotic and the language of dress is further corroborated by the latter's disregard for notions of self-regulating autonomy and homogeneous identity. The domain of fashion knows no stasis: what it proposes, in fact, is a gallery of permutable and fluctuating selves, following one another in rapid and random succession. Moreover, communication is only one and by no means the main aspect of the language of clothes, just as the communicative function is of peripheral importance in the realm of the semiotic. The discourse of dress, by analogy with 'the poetic word', is therefore 'polyvalent and multidetermined, adheres to a logic . . . exceeding that of codified discourse and fully comes into being only in the margins of recognized culture',[20] by promoting the coexistence of 'nonexclusive opposites'.[21]

If a grasp of the concept of the semiotic, given its emphasis on the revival of suppressed bodily attributes of discourse, is crucial to an understanding of the process of abjection, so are the phenomena of *projection and introjection*. Kristeva views these complementary occurrences as psychosomatic events that involve the externalization of the body's interior and a parallel internalization of outer material reality. In Gross's words, this amounts to 'the mapping of the body's interior on its exterior and its exterior on its interior'.[22] It may be worth recalling that in the Kleinian frame of reference – to which Kristeva's theories are tangentially indebted – projection alludes to the expulsion of part objects that the subject perceives as *bad*, dangerous and unyielding, whilst introjection indicates the incorporation of *good*, comforting and ego-supporting elements. Related to these two processes is the phenomenon of *projective identification*, whereby the subject proceeds to introject external entities that it has already filled with parts of itself, i.e. upon which it has already exercised forms of projection. A particularly intriguing manifestation of this psychological event is the case of heroic identification, as the subject's attempt to merge with an idealized figure. Central to all these processes are the conflicting, yet interdependent, concepts of fragmentation, the subject's aggressive dismantling of dreaded part objects, and reparation, the guilt-motivated reassembling of the fragments into a new whole. All products of human creativity could be seen as containers

---

20. Julia Kristeva (1980), *Desire in Language: A Semiotic Approach to Literature and Art*, trans. Thomas Gora, Alice Jardine and Leon Roudiez, New York, p.65.

21. Ibid., p.71.

22. Elizabeth Gross (1990), 'The Body of Signification', in J. Fletcher (ed.), *Abjection, Melancholia and Love*, London, p.84.

into which the subject's splintered body images may be placed in order to restore a sense of unity and coherence.

Dress is implicated in complex dynamics of both projection and introjection. It visibly embodies the effects of those processes of ejection of internal states and absorption of external ones through which the subject aims at fashioning a satisfying identity. Following the ambiguous logic of projective identification, moreover, it could be argued that what we term *choice*, in our adoption of specific garments, styles and hence personas, really amounts to the introjection of external objects that we have invested with idealized versions of ourselves. The *collage* or *patchwork*-like character of the discourse of fashion itself could be seen as a dramatization of the inevitable coexistence of rupturing and reparative drives: in dress, perhaps more graphically than in other comparable forms of productivity, the fragments tend to retain an independent character even as they are joined together within a patterned whole – since they could, in principle, participate in a limitless range of alternative combinations – and thus operate as reminders of the fundamental disunity upon which any identity rests. At the same time, dress *contains* the body: completes it, delimits it and gives intelligible shape to its sprawling affects and energies. This confining function, however, requires the enactment of constant adjustments and variations, as no one type of clothing may fulfil indefinitely, or indeed for long, its disciplining and redeeming vocation. This is largely due to the transitory character of the type of satisfaction yielded by the incorporation of *any* idealized image or role: the introjection of the treasured, integrated and unimpaired object does not secure permanent pleasure but actually breeds anxiety, as it ineluctably intimates the possibility of loss in both the internal and the external worlds.

For Kristeva, the ability to negotiate and come to terms with the unsettling consequences of both projection and introjection is inseparable from the phenomenon of abjection, in so far as this plays a vital part in enabling the subject to build metaphorical bridges between bodily experiences such as sensations and perceptions and their linguistic substitutes, i.e. signifiers, between inside and outside, between self and other. Kristeva is specifically concerned with the corporeal mechanisms of repulsion, revulsion and expulsion whereby socialization is effected, particularly the elimination and banishment of what a given culture perceives as unclean, disorderly, improper, asocial or antisocial. If the developing subject is to accomplish an effective entry into the symbolic and thus achieve a cultural identity and an enunciative position, a boundary needs to be traced between the *clean* and *proper* body and its opposite. A necessary precondition for the subject's admission to the order of language is therefore its ability to abandon its corporeality, its perception of itself as a physical entity, since language requires the substitution of decarnalized signifiers for the concrete body. As a product of language, the speaking self is merely a pronoun, a shifter whose status is irrevocably relational and contingent on its discursive context. The transition from the imaginary/the semiotic to the symbolic, in other words, coincides with acts of self-dispossession or self-renunciation whereby the subject is supposed to relinquish its material identity in exchange for a linguistic position that alone may release it to the possibility of social intercourse. The disavowal of corporeality is a figurative death, as encapsulated in the Lacanian dictum 'the Word is the murder of the Thing': it is a salutary death, to the extent that the alternative would be a dislocation of identity conducive to schizophrenia; but it is nonetheless a dramatic surrender to an ideology of drastic disembodiment. For Kristeva, however, the ostracizing of physicality is never final: the recognition of its necessity is inseparable from a parallel acknowledgment of its only partial attainability. Indeed, whilst for Lacan the symbolic is inescapable and determines everything else, in Kristeva's writings, the symbolic is not quite so all-powerful. The return of the expelled abject, haunting the subject through multiple mementoes of its own indomitable materiality such as the daily cycles of absorption and elimination, incorporation and evacuation, points precisely to the conditional character of all processes of symbolic socialization. Failure to retain access to the material, bodily qualities of language or to develop our sensitivity to the resurgence of semiotic energies traversing, pluralizing and criss-crossing accepted symbolic structures would debilitate the self and inhibit creativity. As John Lechte observes: 'Not to have entered the symbolic at all, that is, not to have separated from the mother – as in extreme psychosis – is to be close to living death. On the other hand, not to be alerted to the material basis of the symbolic which the concept of the semiotic evokes, is to remain at the level of a static, fetishized version of language.'[23]

By analogy, it could be suggested that in a Lacanian frame of reference dress would represent a primarily decarnalizing agency, intent on the translation of the physical body into a web of endlessly sliding signifiers; in the context of Kristeva's theories, on the other hand, dress, whilst still performing this symbolic function, may simultaneously be taken to hint at a return of the material, since the relationship between clothes and the body is, unavoidably, an emphatically *physical* phenomenon. Clothes are projected, introjected, indeed abjected, not simply at the metaphorical level of self-formation, but also at a material level, displaying features comparable to those of intrinsically bodily phenomena, such as eating, drinking, shedding tears, vomiting, bleeding, laughing, ejaculating, breathing.

23. John Lechte (1990), *Julia Kristeva*, London, p.27.

As a socializing tool, literally intended to cover up *improper* aspects of bodily existence, dress may seem to take sides with the symbolic. It frames, separates and sanitizes the body, by giving its fluid outline a definite, culturally acceptable shape and thus anchoring it to a shared repertoire of codes and conventions. Yet dress simultaneously articulates imaginary yearnings that defy symbolic orderliness and reach back into the semiotic bundle of free-floating drives. Much as the subject may adopt this or that form of clothing as a means of gaining a place in the symbolic as an immutable site of signification, its vestimentary envelope will inexorably carry traces of its primordial fantasies of self-realization and pre-linguistic expression, which challenge the requirements of the adult domain of laws and institutions. Dress lingers at the border of selfhood as an apparently unifying system, which, however, concurrently hints at prospects of breakdown and dissolution, at the impermanent status of symbolic identity as an arbitrary construct. Dress may be equated to cleanliness, order and propriety and, indeed, recurring definitions of fashion in terms of *taste*, *style* or *decorum* would appear to corroborate this correlation. At the same time, its penchant for a reactivation of pre-symbolic fantasies harks back to the carnivalesque dimension of potentially disruptive semiotic forces. Its association with pre-symbolic experiences is reinforced by its metaphorical resemblance to a Lacanian mirror, i.e. a guarantee of cohesion and plenitude based not on the reality of corporeal unity but on the dream of a total communion between the physical apparatus and the specular image, i.e. on misrecognition. The identities supplied by clothes are correspondingly fictional, fallacious and phantasmatic; yet they do provide a temporary illusion of stability by enabling a jubilatory transmutation of the chaotic and fragmented body into a seductively co-ordinated self-image.

Identity, then, may only be forged out of a disavowal of those physical functions that, as was pointed out by Freud in *Civilization and its Discontents* and in *Totem and Taboo*, are deemed impure by society, because of their close association with the pre-oedipal subject's polymorphously perverse and hence menacingly unstable sexuality. But Kristeva goes somewhat further than Freud, by arguing that the forms of corporeality on which the symbolic lays its heaviest ban and of which the subject must therefore be radically purged can never be totally erased. Their dismissal is supposed to grant the subject a fixed self, yet their subliminal survival inevitably exposes the provisional character of any psychosomatic constellation: stability may at any point be disrupted by the dissolving agency of bodily functions that keep hovering on the precarious threshold between self and other. This laceration of the mythical seamlessness of subjectivity is especially evident in that puzzling moment in which the subject recognizes the ongoing presence of *defiling* elements even in the ostensibly most aseptic scenario. According to Gross, this manifestation of the abject 'is, as it were, the unspoken of a stable speaking position, an abyss at the very borders of the subject's identity, a whole into which the subject may fall. . . . The subject must have a certain, if incomplete mastery of the abject; it must keep it in check and at a distance in order to define itself as a subject.'[24]

As the object of primary repression, the abject 'draws us toward the place where meaning collapses'[25] in re-enacting the horror and nausea experienced by the pre-oedipal infant in its early attempts to separate itself from the mother, and thus shatters the subject's narcissistic self-delusions. The abject is hence a vestige of the metaphorical death that, as mentioned earlier, we are expected to assume upon entering language: 'the death that I am provokes horror'.[26] Our demise as intact material entities entails a readiness to embrace our radical otherness to ourselves; paradoxically, it is only by accepting this figurative extinction that we may be born again as culturally groomed creatures:

> I expel myself, I spit myself out, I abject myself within the same motion through which 'I' claim to establish myself. . . . 'I' am in the process of becoming an other at the expense of my own death. During the course in which 'I' become, I give birth to myself amid the violence of sobs, of vomit. Mute protest of the symptom, shattering violence of a convulsion that, to be sure, is inscribed in a symbolic system, but in which, without either wanting or being able to become integrated in order to answer it, it reacts, it abreacts. It abjects.

As in the phenomenon of abjection, in the discourse of dress, the subject is called upon to carry out a self-defining task that involves a relinquishment of corporeality in the service of abstract symbolic codes. The body *dies*, as dress takes over in its enunciative role: it dematerializes into a network of intersubjective and transpersonal values and expectations that explode all narcissistic mythologies of plenitude. However, as was emphasized above, abjection as a process of expulsion does not ultimately preclude the possibility of a return of the abject, of spectral tokens of those residues of otherness that mockingly undermine finite subjectivities. If the abject, in this respect, resembles a black whole, swallowing any nostalgic relic of self-containedness into its imploding whirlpool, its resurrection also holds the pleasurable potential of a playful excess over precise meaning, by joining forces with the semiotic's experimental proclivities. Dress, analogously, operates as an

24. Gross, 'The Body of Signification', p.87
25. Julia Kristeva, *The Powers of Horror*, trans. L. Roudiez, New York, p.2.
26. Ibid.

incarnation of the abject, in its ability to remind the subject of the precariousness of its boundaries. Yet, at the same time, it may open up prospects of constant self-reinvention by traversing and pluralizing the symbolic's rigid and supposedly monolithic structures with fluid drives reminiscent of pre-symbolic carnality. The creative process triggered by dress entails continual readjustments and re-negotiations, in that it both produces and annihilates subjectivity, supplies viable roles and instantly questions their authenticity, offers apparently impregnable masks and, in the same movement, exposes their cardboard vulnerability. Abjection is likewise paradoxical in its ability to encompass everything that we do not consciously wish to acknowledge and that, nevertheless, retains a powerful emotional fascination: very possibly, because abjection makes us and unmakes us at the same time, promises a bounded identity and the illusion of wholeness and depth, whilst dispersing our being across a flat surface marred by absences and gaps:

> the abject simultaneously beseeches and pulverizes the subject . . . the abjection of self would be the culminating form of that experience of the subject to which it is revealed that all its objects are based merely on the inaugural loss that laid the foundations of its own being. There is nothing like abjection of self to show that all abjection is in fact recognition of the want on which any being, meaning, language, or desire is founded.

In conjuring the subject as a socialized substance, dress, like the abject, simultaneously disintegrates identity by intimating that the objects that the subject adopts in order to assert its distinctness – in this instance, ego ideals on the mental plane and actual garments on the physical one – do not demonstrate a presence but an absence, not a possession but a lack. How would the ethos of fashionable *glamour* ever manage to perpetuate itself, were it not for this substratum of deprivation?

Kristeva's concept of abjection is closely related to the Lacanian image of the *rim*, the interface between the inside and the outside of the physical body, specifically associated with the erotogenic zones and with liminal fissures and hollows through which the material products inducing abjection, e.g. tears, blood, milk, faeces, urine, sperm, are passed. As Gross observes:

> These corporeal sites provide a boundary or threshold between what is inside the body, and thus part of the subject, and what is outside the body, and thus an object for the subject. This boundary must be traversed by the incorporation and/ or expulsion of erotic objects. Objects are, in this sense, neither fully contained within the subject's body nor ever entirely expelled from it.[27]

27. Gross, 'The Body of Signification', p.88.

Clothes are similarly describable as part of the subject and as objects for the subject, which are not accommodated within the body and yet cannot be conceived of as totally separate from it. Their deployment as erotic objects may depend exactly on the degree to which they are incorporated or expelled: incorporation may lead to autoeroticism and narcissism, expulsion to a dismissal of the symbolic tenets that the language of dress is deemed capable of incarnating. These are not, of course, the only options. In fact, the subject is more likely to amalgamate forms of incorporation and expulsion, i.e. introject those attributes of dress that will enable it to project certain internalized representations on to the external world, thus retaining its chances of identifying and interacting with what it has excluded. Like the Lacanian *objet petit a*, dress thus posits itself as an object that the body can neither fully domesticate nor conclusively marginalize. Clothes may be disassociated from the body as dispensable appendages and hence safely expelled, yet their separability from the physical apparatus is hardly gratifying: in fact, it suggests that clothes may not be securely contained within the subject's frame and that they may therefore defy the body's unitary shell as threateningly alien agencies. Cohesion, integration and solidity are bound up at all times with destabilizing forces and prospects of self-obliteration. There may be ways of engulfing the straying object into the body's stream: if the object could be absorbed through the body's rim, for example, its claims to autonomy could be colonized and harnessed to the symbolic self's territorial aspirations. Regrettably, perhaps, the liminal object is not a nameable substance but an active process: it cannot be pinned down and categorized because it is ceaselessly engaged in dynamics of projection, introjection, depletion and ejection. In the specific context of dress, this resistance to compartmentalization is typified by fashion's interminable recyclings, mutations and recombinations. The object-in-process simply cannot plug the gap upon which our existence as symbolic, sexual, gendered, enunciative and desiring subjects is predicated. To resort again to a possible comparison between dress and the *objet petit a*, it could be argued that clothes are both a part and not a part of the body: being both attached to and detachable from it, they promise to stop up a lack, yet make that lack all the more prominent and thus imperil the body's subsistence as a free-standing category; assure the erection of inviolable boundaries, yet testify to their ultimate implausibility. It is in this stubborn commitment to indeterminacy, fundamentally, that dress bears close affinities to the *rim*, the *objet petit a* and, above all, the *abject*:

> we may call it a border: abjection is above all ambiguity. Because, while releasing a hold, it does not radically cut off the subject from what threatens it – on the

contrary, abjection acknowledges it to be in perpetual danger. But also, abjection itself is a compromise of judgement and affect, of condemnation and yearning, of signs and drives. Abjection preserves what existed in the archaism of pre-objectal relationship, in the immemorial violence with which the body becomes separated from another body in order to be – maintaining that night in which the outline of the signified thing vanishes and where only the imponderable affect is carried out.[28]

Dress lulls us into the fantasy of a utopian region where 'signs' and 'drives' may not be at war with each other, where separation is not a prerequisite for being, through its stimulation of imaginary/symbolic intensities; at the same time, its symbolic role associates it not with 'affect' and 'yearning' but rather with 'judgement' and 'condemnation' and requires it to transmute the 'outline of the signified thing' into a fully-fledged sign. It is not, however, from a definition of dress as *either* a pre-symbolic *or* a symbolic system that a recognition of its creative potentialities may be derived; in fact, it is its flair for revamping pre-symbolic forms of signification *within* the symbolic itself that discourages its consigning to either of two mutually exclusive domains and fosters, by contrast, an understanding of the coexistence, rather than segregation, of opposites, contradictions and antithetical stances. Beside food and corporeal waste, Kristeva views the 'corpse' as one of the major and most horrific manifestations of abjection. And it is with the corpse that dress shares its central abject characteristics: 'it is something rejected from which one does not part, from which one does not protect oneself as from an object'.[29] Standing at the borders of life, bodiless clothes, like the corpse, teeter at the brink of the gaping gulf severing the quick from the dead:

> There is something eerie about a museum of costume . . . We experience a sense of the uncanny when we gaze at garments that had an intimate relationship with human beings long since gone to their graves. For clothes are so much part of our living, moving selves that, frozen on display in the mausoleums of culture, they hint at something only half understood, sinister, threatening; the atrophy of the body, and the evanescence of life . . . Clothes without a wearer, whether on a second-hand stall, in a glass case, or merely a lover's garments strewn on the floor, can affect us unpleasantly, as if a snake had shed its skin.[30]

28. Kristeva, *The Powers of Horror*, pp.9–10.
29. Ibid., pp.3–4.
30. Elizabeth Wilson (1989), *Adorned in Dreams*, London, pp.1–2.

2

Shielding and Sprawling Garments

This chapter will concentrate on the duplicitous character of dress as a boundary, i.e. its ability to function both as an isolating frame or screen and as a cohesive structure, mediating between the individual and the collective bodies. A brief outline of some of the principal implications carried by the image of dress as a screen will be followed by an investigation of theoretical positions variously concerned with the cultural fashioning of boundaries. Barthes's theories, particularly as formulated in *A Lover's Discourse* and *The Fashion System*, will be employed as a means of assessing the relationship between dress and the body in erotic terms. The erotic, as used in this context, does not refer exclusively to the sexually stimulating powers of dress – a virtually commonplace object of study – nor does it allude to the disembodying ideals preached by Platonic models that posit Eros as an aesthetic tool for transcending brute materiality in the interests of superior ethical values – the aesthetic, as is often the case in Western philosophy, being only a means to an end. In fact, mapping out the body/dress relationship as a *love* relationship entails both an understanding of certain ideological aspects of amorous discourse that resist reduction to the status of metaphors or metonyms for overt sexual intercourse and, at the same time, raise the question of corporeality as an attribute of inanimate no less than animate matter.

Foucault's writings will provide a framework for the investigation of the complementary dynamics of discipline and transgression, particularly where sexuality is concerned. Finally, Deleuze and Guattari's concept of deterritorialization and the germane figures of the body-without-organs, nomad thought and schizoanalysis will be employed to extend the aforementioned discussion of questions of discipline and transgression in relation to the regimentation of desire and the image of the uncontainable body. Special attention will be devoted, in this respect, to the notion of becoming-animal, as an appropriate transition to the exploration of the phenomenon of contagion, to be addressed in Chapter 3 as a crucial aspect of fashion's collective body.

Dress as an image, or representation, operates as a *screen* on different levels. It is capable of acting as a sort of shield, a structure indicating and determining a division or separation, and, at the same time, as a surface on to which other images may be projected. As shield, dress constitutes a protective barrier meant to insulate private fantasies, which are themselves inarticulable in so far as they are incompatible with the laws of the public spectacle, from symbolic codes and conventions, such as power relations and concomitant forces of production, reception and consumption. However, private fantasies are never self-contained, since they constantly interact with others' fantasies or the fantasies of the Other. Hence the armour supplied by dress as shield is a flimsy one indeed. This is largely due to the fact that nobody can unequivocally associate personal dress with personal fantasies as fully rounded wholes, and thus exploit clothing as a self-differentiating structure. No garment incarnates unproblematically a specific symbolic content, instantly recognizable and decodable. Individual and collective responses to clothes, therefore, cannot be woven on one single narrative, but rather result from the coalescence of fragmentary and frequently conflicting elements, deriving from many disparate mental images and corresponding fictive permutations. Dress may act as a kind of catalyst through which some of these diverse elements become amalgamated, are projected on to one another, and thus are made to converge into a unified imaginary scene. But no sooner has this process been triggered than the dream of self-differentiation fizzles out, as the imaginary scenario is fundamentally predicated upon principles of undifferentiation, fusion, merging.

It is at this point that dress as a screen ceases to connote a dividing shield and comes to function as a projection surface. Clothes acquire the status of a culturally legitimated imaginary scene, allowing points of contact between more or less suppressed personal fantasies and the cultural ensemble, mediating between them and remodelling private yearnings according to the requirements of a collective web of tropes and myths. The vestimentary imaginary is never, however, of the nature of a return to a pre-symbolic state. In fact, it is deeply embedded in the symbolic: hence projection is always, inevitably, accompanied by phenomena of introjection. Whilst the subject projects its more or less repressed fantasies on to the collective screen, it simultaneously introjects the desirable images displayed on this screen; conversely, whilst the screen projects its images on to the viewing subject, it simultaneously introjects the latter's gaze and thus incorporates it into the domain of culturally legitimated scopic regimes.

Love, Dress and the Body

It is common and perhaps clichéd to think of the relationship between the body and dress in sexual terms, given the close association of clothing with the phenomena of exhibitionism, narcissism, scopophilia, fetishism and other related psychological mechanisms based on the production or stimulation of pleasure and affectivity through looking/being looked at. What seems less popular is the concept of the body/dress relationship as an amorous one, i.e. as a discourse that, being inscribed in no dominant metanarratives, escapes totalization. As will be discussed in more detail later, the definition of the connection between clothes and flesh in erotic terms requires a clear differentiation between love and sex. According to Barthes, love is unspeakable, except within the domesticating framework of the canonical love story, whilst sex has an accepted status in everyday discourse; paradoxically, love, not sex, is branded as obscene: 'it is no longer the sexual which is indecent – it is the sentimental – censured in the name of what is in fact only another morality'.[1] This idea echoes Foucault's assertion that, since the Victorian period, sex chatter has been all-pervasive in our society, and indeed has been encouraged as a controlling mechanism analogous to the confessional mode.[2] If, like the discourse of sexuality, dress may operate as a disciplinary instrument or situating device, like Barthes's demonized love, it may also constitute a dislocating mechanism.

It could be argued, therefore, that in its culturally sanctioned guise the body/dress relationship is sexual, to the extent that clothes frame the body and translate its sexual drives into filtered, acceptable forms. As an amorous relationship, on the other hand, the nexus of body and dress problematizes identity, structures and limits. The following commentary will attempt to trace parallels between the body/dress relationship and the main features of the lover's discourse, based on these preliminary assumptions: the partnership of the corporeal and the sartorial holds potential meanings everywhere and therefore inhabits a universe of signs wherein everything is endlessly interpretable; it shatters individual identity by turning the subject into a fictional persona within a narrative and making it interchangeable with a vast array of intertextual alter-egos; it epitomizes the ethos of endless recycling and circulation typical of commodity fetishism; it is centred on fragments of meaning that revel in anarchy and randomness and yet, for this very reason, invoke disciplinary measures that result in either institutionalization or marginalization.

1. Roland Barthes (1990), *A Lover's Discourse*, trans. Richard Howard, London, p.177.
2. Michel Foucault (1978), *The History of Sexuality, Vol. I: An Introduction*, trans. Robert Hurley, London.

In Barthes's text, the discourse of love is overtly dramatized by means of a critical method that aims at enacting and simulating it rather than describing it in a metalinguistic fashion. This stance could be related to the Lacanian notion that there is no Other of the Other, since the symbolic order is with, in and around us at all times and there is no way of transcending it by means of putatively detached metalanguages.[3] Barthes's simulative techniques could also be viewed in relation to postmodernist positions, such as Lyotard's proclamation of the death of metanarratives[4] or Baudrillard's assertion that the whole of reality has been taken over by the order of simulation, the simulacrum, the hyperreal.[5] Either way, one thing seems clear: for Barthes, as for Barthes's lover, meaning is everywhere: 'The incident is trivial . . . but it will attract to it whatever language I possess. . . . Countless minor circumstances thus weave the black veil of Maya, the tapestry of illusions, of meanings, of words.'[6] Any object may be 'fetishized',[7] and the lover is capable of transferring its being 'inside it altogether',[8] regardless of the patently futile nature of the situation: 'Everything is solemn: I have no sense of proportions.'[9] Unintentional and motivated signs are confused, in a dizzying alternation of moments of clear-sightedness and spells of interpretative obsessionality, occasionally culminating in the absurd dream of putting an end to decoding – an aim which is incompatible with the lover's ceaseless erring.

In dress, too, meaning is everywhere, i.e. dispersed across multiple surfaces. Interpretation is never conclusive; indeed, fashion underscores the significance of reading as an unlimited and unlimiting experience. The discourse of dress, like that of love, pivots on the dissemination of sense over numerous planes rather than on its anchoring to a privileged site. Surfaces, it turns out, may be more significant than the depths they are supposed to camouflage, as it is from the superficial envelope that its contents derive value and the ability to charm. As Glynn observes:

Why are the nicest presents always gift-wrapped? Why do shops spend a fortune on decorating their parcels with quite unnecessary bows and loops of ribbon? Why is it that the brown-paper parcels are more exciting in direct ratio to the number

3. Jacques Lacan (1977), *Ecrits: A Selection*, trans. Alan Sheridan, London.

4. Jean-François Lyotard (1984), *The Postmodern Condition: A Report on Knowledge*, trans. Geoff Bennington and Brian Massumi, Manchester.

5. Jean Baudrillard (1983), *Simulations*, trans. Paul Foss, Paul Patton and Philip Beitchman, New York.

6. Barthes, *A Lover's Discourse*, p.69.

7. Ibid., p.71.

8. Ibid., p.75.

9. Ibid., p.37.

of unassailable knots? In order to double the anticipation, to force the eager hands to fight for what they hope to possess, to cut through knots and rip aside bows until at last the secret trinket is revealed. To many people the fact that the contents of the package may be a saucepan or a diamond necklace seems to matter much less than the tremendous fun and stimulation of undoing things.

Similarly, the most obviously exciting adjuncts to clothing are the fastenings. As with a present, appearance is all, and the more deliciously superfluous the bows, the more obdurate the knotted belts, the more and the longer the zip fasteners, the better the contents are going to seem when they are finally handed over.[10]

Silk satin bows making a showy appearance on otherwise relatively simple evening gowns are possibly the most obvious instance of ornamental items designed to maximize the desire for discovery of the body's hidden gifts. Lace trimmings, posies and symbolic embroidery placed in strategic locations such as the bodice are familiar characteristics of wedding dresses, which similarly instigate the unwrapping itch. Designers as diverse as Victor Stiebel (1940s), Norman Hartnell (1950s), Bellville Sassoon (1960s), David and Elizabeth Emanuel (1970s), and John Galliano (1980s) have experimented with these types of sartorial decoration. The location of the bow is of crucial importance. Sometimes a ribbon looped around the waist culminates in an ostentatious bow placed above the navel. At other times, the bow displays itself as an almost prosthetic body part draped over the backside. Both anatomical sites are traditionally invested with portentous symbolic signifi-cance and therefore represent privileged points of entry for the exploration of the erotic body. They also suggest the necessity to both bind and bound the female figure precisely where its putatively unruly sexuality is most likely to spill out.

But the gift-wrapping approach can also work in less explicit ways to no less momentous effect. A dark, sombre, even intentionally subdued formal suit may be accessorized by recourse to an unexpectedly flamboyant tie, scarf or handkerchief. Such surprising splashes of colour in an otherwise restrained and unassuming outfit function in much the same way as the ribbon applied to a wrapped-up present. The parcel itself is sealed, anony-mous, possibly amorphous. It could contain anything and everything. The parcel itself is uncanny in its silence and mysteriousness: something about its deliberate secretiveness may even make it slightly off-putting. But the ribbon reaches out to us. It seductively provokes us to undo it, to fiddle with the knot, or to tear the whole contraption out, if we are so inclined. Items of clothing such as scarves, especially if they are conspicuously juxtaposed to conservative garments, appeal precisely to the gift-wrapping

10. Prudence Glynn (1982), *Skin to Skin: Eroticism in Dress*, London, p.136.

mentality. They are apparently dispensable additions to the more substantial gear they accompany. But they are also, vitally, so many invitations to *unwrap* the authorized, clothed body.

Paradoxically, what the final disclosure of the putatively hidden gift may deliver is not a fulfilling presence but an absence: not, of course, as the lack of a body underneath the clothing in a literal sense, but very possibly as a recognition of the lack of the redeeming faculties that that body, prior to its unveiling, is expected to possess and that the keen unwrapper is intent on appropriating as a means of alleviating its own sense of loss. The body's casing may ultimately prove more meaningful, indeed better equipped to signify, than its contents, any epiphany being, after all, only the prelude to yet more fretful hankering after revelatory experience.

The word 'discourse' is itself of central importance, in this respect, as it foregrounds the sense of restless exploration, inconclusiveness and delirious self-fashioning and refashioning – peculiar to the language of love and the production of vestimentary trends alike – and thus precludes the possibility of firmly locating the sources and destinations of meaning: '*Dis-cursus* – originally the action of running here and there, comings and goings, measures taken, 'plots and plans': the lover, in fact, cannot keep his mind from racing, taking new measures and plotting against himself. His discourse exists only in outbursts of language, which occur at the whim of trivial, of aleatory circumstances.'[11]

The ephemeral and transitory nature of all body/dress associations is characteristically encapsulated by the fickleness and capriciousness with which successive generations of consumers relate to changing trends. According to Rudofsky:

> Whichever way we look at clothes, one factor stands out – our inability, or unwillingness, to settle for a type of dress of more than passing interest. Our dissatisfaction with the body and its coverings expresses itself in ceaseless change. Each new dress becomes something like an accomplice with whom we enter a most intimate, if brief, relationship. The first stirrings of timid desire for the adoption of a fad; the intense devotion to it while it lasts; the sudden boredom and physical revulsion for an outlived vogue – all these are the perfect analogy to the phases of courtship: craving for the loved object, and its rejection after wish fulfilment.[12]

This account bears remarkable affinities to Barthes's delineation of love's peculiar curve: 'when the lover encounters the other, there is an

11. Barthes, *A Lover's Discourse*, p.3.
12. Bernard Rudofsky (1972), *The Unfashionable Human Body*, London, p.13.

immediate affirmation (psychologically: dazzlement, enthusiasm, exaltation, mad projection of a fulfilled future: I am devoured by desire, the impulse to be happy): I say yes to everything (blinding myself). There follows a long tunnel: my first *yes* is riddled by doubts, love's *value* is ceaselessly threatened by depreciation'.[13] '. . . I perceive suddenly a speck of corruption [which] suddenly attaches the loved object to a *commonplace* world.'[14]

The unformalizable diffusion of meaning across disparate levels of experience – the sublime and the ludicrous, the apparently significant and the ostensibly paltry – radically undermines both humanist and structuralist valorizations of ideas of origin and telos as privileged sites of signification. Barthes's employment of the device of alphabetical ordering contributes precisely to the debunking of logical sequences of cause and effect and thus to underscore the artificiality and volatility of all structuring mechanisms: 'It is the very principle of this discourse . . . that its figures cannot be *classified* . . . to discourage the temptation of meaning, it was necessary to choose an *absolutely insignificant* order.'[15] Here, the lover's discourse patently mirrors the discrediting of traditional concepts of causality and teleology operated by fashion: both contest the entire notion of continuity and the very ideal of purposefulness in history and in narrative alike.

The challenge to traditional perspectives on the value of structural and semantic hierarchies runs parallel to the collapse of all barriers conventionally separating the categories of writer, reader, critic, narrator, character or fictional persona. Barthes features as a reader, both of other texts, as highlighted by the book's intertextual configuration, and of his own writing, in the very process of its coming into being. He is both detached from and entangled with his multiple narrative personas, thus playing the role of a middle voice, which does not totally comply with either the active I fostered by humanism and bourgeois ideology or the passive I that post-humanist theories describe as spoken by language. The lover is an agent in a play of endless and feverish speculation, anticipation and interpretation. Yet its language is not something it speaks of its own volition, the lover being, above all, a *discursive site*, any more than its actions are willed. The lover acts according to a predetermined script: 'Waiting is an enchantment: I have received orders not to move.'[16]

The body/dress combination likewise produces intricate bundles of narrative and dramatic identities: the subject is both an active force operating

13. Barthes, *A Lover's Discourse*, p.24.
14. Ibid., p.25.
15. Ibid., pp.7–8.
16. Ibid., p.38.

choices and a patient: '[Fashion gives] the human person a double postulation: [it confers] either individuation or multiplicity, depending on whether the collection of characteristics is considered a synthesis or whether, on the contrary, we assume that this being is free to be masked behind one or the other of these units.'[17] Hence dress simultaneously promotes the myth of a unified identity and atomizes the subject into a plethora of alternative masks. Paradoxically, it is the unified self fostered by the principle of individuation that may turn out to be a psychological and ideological trap, as the consumer required by the clothing industry is fundamentally hybrid and prismatic, the splintered subject engendered by the principle of multiplicity that may open up vistas of irreverent play.

Comparably, the lover's discourse constitutes both a challenge to the myths of unity, autonomy and self-determination propagandized by the bourgeois ethos in its humanist version and a mode of cultural production potentially complicitous with the endless reshuffling of ideas as commodities inherent in post-industrial dispensations: 'On the one hand, a bourgeois economy of repletion; on the other, a perverse economy of dispersion, of waste, of frenzy.'[18] But love could also be seen as late capitalism's scapegoat: in certain important respects, it is the epitome of commodity fetishism; yet it is 'ignored, disparaged, or derided', and thus pushed into a condition of 'extreme solitude',[19] as though to suggest that love's frenzy is inimical to the dominant culture's sanity and rationality, or at any rate a peripheral and isolated phenomenon within it. Love would seem to serve a function akin to that of Writing in deconstructive criticism: the marginalization of Writing and concomitant prioritizing of Speech have traditionally enabled Western metaphysics to claim that a distinction may be drawn between a putatively reliable and immediate form of signification and a distorting, displacing and ambiguous one. Hence, though Writing embodies paradigmatic features of all linguistic activity, primarily the inescapability of the rhetorical dimension, it has been treated as the repository of intractable negativity, alienation and lack, so as to efface the reality of absence that defines any process of symbolization.

In a different context, Baudrillard argues that prisons exist in order to conceal the carceral nature of society as a whole, just as Disneyland is presented as a holiday alternative to real American culture in order to hide the theme-park character of that culture in its entirety.[20] In the body/

17. Roland Barthes (1990), *The Fashion System*, trans. Matthew Ward and Richard Howard, Berkeley and Los Angeles, p.255.
18. Barthes, *A Lover's Discourse*, p.85.
19. Ibid., p.1.
20. Baudrillard, *Simulations*.

dress relationship, along similar lines, we are constructed as quintessential consumers; and although this role is clearly not a marginal facet of cultural experience but actually exemplifies an extensive system of production and reception, the discourse of clothing is repeatedly belittled as a trivial pursuit, as if to suggest that transient infatuation with non-essential commodities is a superfluous aspect of that system rather than its governing principle.

Love is mocked and discredited for being based on unreliable premises, such as its hankering after unattainable objects and its masochistic tendency to derive pleasure from this hopeless quest. Yet the ideological systems that categorize love along these lines adopt analogous strategies to secure their own cultural and economic functionings. Isn't love's eternal self-perpetuation and recurrence, after all, akin to the endless circulation of the commodity in post-industrial culture? The exclusion of love as an unproductive and pathological factor could serve the purpose not so much of asserting the positive values of a supposedly sane and productive society as of disguising the fact that such a society as a whole is caught up in a chain of pathological unproductiveness, dressed up as wholesome efficiency. Like the commodity system, love is centred on insatiability and indefiniteness: 'This can't go on! Yet it goes on . . . . Reasonable sentiment: everything works out but nothing lasts. Amorous sentiment: nothing works out but it keeps going on.'[21] Metonymic displacement and errantry are the central mechanisms: 'Though each love is experienced as unique and though the subject rejects the notion of repeating it elsewhere later on, he sometimes discovers in himself a kind of diffusion of amorous desire; he then realizes he is doomed to wander until he dies, from love to love.'[22]

Metonymic displacement likewise plays a major role in the discourse of clothing, not only as a crucial advertising ploy but also as a central trait of the dress/body relationship. In both cases, metonymy is based on the attachment of value to minute and often apparently insignificant details, echoing Barthes's lover's tendency to fetishize fragments of the loved one's body: 'eyelashes, nails, roots of the hair, the incomplete objects'.[23] Paradoxically, whilst the utilization of metonymic devices in fashion photography and specifically in adverts serves to turn the body into a splintered and powerless object, dissected for rapid consumption by the viewer's voracious gaze, the investment of minutiae with autonomous meanings in the body/dress partnership may simultaneously assist a critical interrogation of myths of subjective

21. Barthes, *A Lover's Discourse*, p.140.
22. Ibid., p.101.
23. Ibid., p.71.

plenitude and impregnability. If the body derives meaning from the garments it wears, such a meaning can never be ascribed to the unruptured totality of dress as a seamless container, but must rather be detected in the interplay of a plethora of Lilliputian items.

The concept of meaning as an unsited structure, fluidly moving in and out of small details, is central to the textual organization of *A Lover's Discourse*, based as this is on the principle of *figures*, or 'fragments of discourse'.[24] These cluster into a situation or scene the moment they can be recognized as amenable to such a strategy of aggregation by either someone inclined to identify with their psychological import or by an ideology devoted to the disciplining of the incoherent. The organization of love's fragments may, therefore, take two radically different forms. On the one hand, a reader may recognize minute scraps or shreds of Barthes's lover's anxious consciousness and 'lunatic chores'[25] and possibly identify with them, without seeking to unify those elements into a reassuringly synthetic whole. In fact, orderlessness may constitute a crucial trait of the reading/recognizing experience no less than of the writing one. On the other hand, the reader who subscribes to the domesticating tenets of classic realism would strive to order the fragments into a coherent pattern. This move may branch off into two discrete directions: the institutionalization and compartmentalization of love into a self-contained narrative; or, as previously mentioned, its marginalization and ridiculing as an *atopic* phenomenon, i.e. something for which there is no place within the reign of the symbolic.

The former option is conducive to: 'the love story, subjugated to the great narrative Other, to that general opinion that disparages any excessive force and wants the subject himself to reduce the great imaginary current, the orderless, endless stream which is passing through him, to a painful morbid crisis of which he must be cured, which he must "get over".'[26] This colonizing of the lover's random soliloquy into a coherent pattern proceeds from the symbolic structuring of socialized subjectivity: 'only the Other could write my love story, my novel'.[27] As will be argued in more depth in a later chapter concerned with the relationship between fashion and history, the ordering impulse described by Barthes is paralleled, within the discourse of dress, by numerous texts characterized by a veritable obsession with turning fashion into a *history* of costume by recourse to grand metanarratives linking dress

24. Ibid., p.3.
25. Ibid., p.23.
26. Ibid., p.7.
27. Ibid., p.93.

to the *Zeitgeist*, or else outlining periodic changes according to criteria of predictable permutation.[28]

In the narrative sanitization of the lover's discourse, boundaries are erected around the subject so as to deprive it of the very right to an enunciative position: its potential refusal to accept the ordering laws of the symbolic is met with the threat of exclusion from language itself:

> Today . . . there is no system of love: and the several systems which surround the contemporary lover offer him no room (except for an extremely devaluated place): turn as he will toward one or another of the received languages, none answers him, except in order to turn him away from what he loves. Christian discourse, if it still exists, exhorts him to repress and to sublimate. Psychoanalytical discourse (which, at least, describes his state) commits him to give up his Image-repertoire as lost. As for Marxist discourse, it has nothing to say. If it should occur to me to knock on these doors in order to gain recognition somewhere (wherever it might be) for my 'madness' (my 'truth'), these doors close one after the other; and when they are all shut, there rises around me a wall of language which oppresses and repulses me – unless I repent and agree to 'get rid of X'.[29]

And:

> Discredited by modern opinion, love's sentimentality must be assumed by the amorous subject as a powerful transgression which leaves him alone and exposed; by a reversal of values, then, it is this sentimentality which today constitutes love's obscenity.[30]

As was mentioned earlier, the paradox delivered by this state of affairs is that love, not sex or sexuality, comes to be branded as unspeakable and subversive. Indeed, as Foucault has shown, the discourse of sex, once considered taboo, is now widespread; and its pervasiveness is not truly emancipating, for the tendency to talk more or less openly about sex does not simply enable the release of repressed energies but also makes the subject vulnerable to heightened forms of societal control and regimentation, thus operating as a variation on the confessional model promoted by traditional religion. Sex-talk offers ideology a useful means of gaining access to its subjects' most intimate concerns and hence identifying psychological and behavioural categories that may be safely harnessed to dominant discursive

28. See, for example: Tony and Claes Lewenhaupt (1989), *Crosscurrents: Art–Fashion–Design, 1890–1989*, trans. Jorgen Schiott, New York; A. L. Kroeber and J. Richardson (1940), *Three Centuries of Women's Dress Fashions*, Berkeley and Los Angeles.

29. Barthes, *A Lover's Discourse*, p.211.

30. Ibid., p.175.

practices. Love, on the other hand, remains unformalized and may therefore subvert accepted meanings and doxastic assumptions. Love is *obscene*, in the sense of the term as deployed by Barthes, namely, as referring to something that happens offstage.

Just as dress, whilst contributing substantially to the subject's symbolic socialization, simultaneously problematizes the dividing structures on which such a process relies, similarly the discourse of love is enmeshed in linguistic codes, conventions and stereotypes and yet articulates a deep dissatisfaction with the symbolic: 'the Whole cannot be inventoried without being diminished: in *Adorable*! . . . *Adorable* is the futile vestige of a fatigue – the fatigue of language itself. From word to word, I struggle to put into other words the ipseity of my Image;'[31] '. . . one cannot speak *of* the other, *about* the other; every attribute is false, painful, erroneous, awkward: the other is *unqualifiable*'.[32] Moreover, the symbolic order and the attendant sensation of loss are of the order of an *always-already*: 'the lover's anxiety . . . is the fear of a mourning which has already occurred, at the very origin of love, from the moment when I was first 'ravished'. Someone would have to be able to tell me: 'Don't be anxious any more – you've already lost him/her.'[33]

Both the discourse of love and that of dress operate at one and same time as incarnations of the symbolic order's laws and as potentially anti-symbolic forces. They thus participate concurrently in the logic of neurosis, based as this condition is on the creation of alternative realities that are still, however, inscribed in the symbolic, and also in that of psychosis, as the total abandonment of reality. 'Sometimes the world is unreal (I utter it differently), sometimes it is disreal (I utter it with only the greatest difficulty if at all). . . . In the first moment I am neurotic, I unrealize; in the second, I am psychotic, crazy, I disrealize.'[34]

In psychosis, the subject surrenders totally to a denial of the real, to a fantasy world that respects no symbolic organization of meaning. In neurosis, conversely, certain conventions are maintained, if only perhaps as distorted versions of types of conduct generally described as normal. The neurotic subject does not relinquish reality altogether, but replaces it with alternative realities, no less patterned than symbolic reality itself, as the rigorous carrying out of neurotic rituals bears witness. The text of bliss, however apparently crazy, reveals typically neurotic traits: it preserves something of a hold on reality, some adherence to conventions of sorts, in order to create a tension between reality and fantasy. Were it to repudiate reality completely, there

31. Ibid., pp.19–20.
32. Ibid., p.35.
33. Ibid., p.30.
34. Ibid., pp.90–1.

would be no tension, and without tension there could be no pleasure – hence the tantalizing paradox of a text that is conformist and mobile at once: 'the texts . . . which are written . . . from the center of madness, contain within themselves, *if they want to be read*, that bit of neurosis necessary to the seduction of their readers . . . Thus every writer's motto reads: *mad I cannot be, sane I do not deign to be, neurotic I am*.'[35]

Like the text of bliss, love and dress hark back to the Imaginary: 'the amorous relation has made me into an atopical subject – undivided: I am my own child; I am both mother and father (of myself, of the other)'.[36] These experiences involve 'rediscovering the *infant body*'[37] but cannot retrieve it totally, as they must accept a constant oscillation between conflicting orders without any guarantee of a final resting-place: the entry into language has annihilated concrete selfhood, and turned the I into a dematerialized shifter: 'I cannot *write myself*. What, after all, is this "I" who would write himself? . . . the word "suffering" expresses no suffering';[38] 'writing compensates for nothing, sublimates nothing, . . . it is precisely *there where you are not*'.[39] Compelled into socialized modes of being that engulf individuality in the whirlpool of intersubjective commitments, the subject is alienated from itself; as fashion continually reminds us: 'the world is full of indiscreet neighbors with whom I must share the other. The world is in fact just that: *an obligation to share*.'[40] The awareness that dress does not individualize induces a recognition of the delusory nature of all dreams of distinctiveness, both in the circumstances of the body/dress relationship and in the vestimentary staging of subjectivity, in spite of the lure of the following figures:

1. 'Special Days'
fete / festivity
The amorous subject experiences every meeting with the loved being as a festival.[41]
2. 'Blue Coat and Yellow Vest'
habit / habiliment

Any effect provoked or sustained by the clothing which the subject has worn during the amorous encounter, or wears with the intention of seducing the loved object.[42]

35. Roland Barthes (1990), *The Pleasure of the Text*, trans. R. Miller, Oxford, pp.5–6.
36. Barthes, *A Lover's Discourse*, p.99.
37. Ibid., p.180.
38. Ibid., p.98.
39. Ibid., p.100.
40. Ibid., p.110.
41. Ibid., p.119.
42. Ibid., p.127.

The de-individualizing function of dress as a cohesive tissue rather than a separating frame is, after all, the obvious corollary of the manufacturing of desire according to imitative mechanisms:

The loved being is desired because another or others have shown the subject that such a being is desirable: however particular, amorous desire is discovered by induction. . . . (Mass culture is a machine for showing desire: here is what must interest you, it says, as if it guessed that men are incapable of finding what to desire by themselves.)[43]

Once again, it seems worth stressing that the reifying thrust of the fashion system does not exhaust the discourse of clothing, since the apparent blocking off of imaginative competences ironically coexists with opportunities for experiment. So, for example, although dress is often dismissed as an empty code, it may prove capable of releasing space for creative invention precisely because of that emptiness: in this respect, it is analogous to the 'love-you' formula. The latter, argues Barthes, may seem merely hollow and stereo-typical; but paradoxically it is its vacuousness that allows the play of language to go on, as the subject fills the formula with its own meanings, however sadly incommunicable they may be; the very blankness of the formulaic register exempts us from the task of trying to anchor love down to supposedly fuller signs, which would inevitably prove equally spurious – only more pompously so.

As proffering, I-love-you is not a sign, but plays against the signs. The one who does not say I-love-you . . . is condemned to emit the many uncertain, doubting, greedy signs of love, its indices, its 'proofs': gestures, looks, sighs, allusions, ellipses. . . . The 'signs' of love feed an enormous reactive literature: love is represented, entrusted to an aesthetic of appearances (it is Apollo, ultimately, who writes every love story). As a counter-sign, I-love-you is on the side of Dionysus.[44]

One final incongruity may be added to the list of ambiguities, ironies and duplicities on which the discourses of love and dress seem to thrive, namely the paradox of a relationship wherein subject and object, agent and patient, hunter and prey become bafflingly interchangeable, and conventional roles are quizzed and reversed:

in the ancient myth, the ravisher is active, he wants to seize his prey, he is the subject of the rape . . . in the modern myth (that of love-as-passion), the contrary

43. Ibid., pp.136–7.
44. Ibid., p.154.

is the case: the ravisher wants nothing, does nothing; he is motionless (as any image), and it is the ravished object who is the real subject of the rape; the object of capture becomes the subject of love; and the subject of the conquest moves into the class of loved object.[45]

Just as the lover, though apparently active, is turned by the paralysing effects of passion into an inert captive, so in the body/dress relationship, the ostensibly inanimate and hence powerless item of clothing is transformed into an agent by its ability to furnish the body with signifying powers that the unclothed subject would lack.

Clothing's ambiguity is encapsulated by its ability to operate as a framing device and a cohesive structure at one and the same time. Frequently, it is very difficult to categorize definitively an item of clothing or a style as *either* framing *or* cohesive, because the two functions coexist. When we wear tight-fitting clothes, for example, we may be aiming at framing our bodies in explicitly noticeable ways. A skin-tight outfit insulates the body, wraps it up impenetrably. But it also exhibits more of the body's anatomy than a loose garment does. It is an ironical means of increasing our dermal layers, as if to evoke tantalizing images of the 'real', underlying skin. Blatantly framing styles affectively connect our bodies even as they appear to divide them from one another. On the other hand, flowing, 'baggy' and marginally shapeless clothes may seem to operate as a cohesive tissue in so far as they blur the body's boundaries and thus enable it to diffuse itself through its environment. But 'sprawling' outfits are not necessarily randomly assembled. They, too, embody specific styles and are therefore ways of framing the body despite their penchant for connectivity. For instance, *Bohemian* fashion reworks various historical and ethnic styles with an ongoing emphasis on fluid, loosely draped fabrics and capacious cuts that often flout the conventions of Western tailoring. Bohemian clothes are generous and comfortable, and they adapt to bodies of all shapes and sizes without seeming concerned with framing them. Such a style is cohesive in two ways: it clouds the individual body's frontiers, thus suggesting its co-extensiveness with its surroundings; and it collapses territorial frontiers by blending together motifs drawn from disparate cultures. But Bohemian fashion also functions as a framing mechanism. This is borne out by its predilection for proliferating layers of clothing (ensembles consisting of multiple skirts, tops, waistcoats and boleros abound in this style): the body is shaped by a steady accretion of packaging and wrapping surfaces. Moreover, Bohemian fashion literally *tailors* certain cultural definitions of ethnicity through the often arbitrary

45. Ibid., p.188.

appropriation of styles that would no doubt have meant something quite different in their original regions: dress aids the framing not only of the individual body but also of the collective corpus.

One of the most obvious incarnations of the ambivalence of dress as simultaneously framing and cohesive is supplied by the notorious *corset*. It is virtually commonplace to state that the corset has framed women's bodies to tragic extremes at various junctures in history. What is possibly less obvious but no less crucial is the fact that the corset, in bounding the body, also connects it to its surroundings: it defines the body in terms of the amount of space that that body is entitled to occupy in relation to other bodies, thus encoding the physical form as a function of its environment. (This inter-weaving of insulating and connecting strategies also reminds us that the body image does not end with the skin. In fact, it is largely determined by the body's relation to the space that encircles it. This space is only precariously quantifiable, because there is always an indeterminate zone between the body image and the rest of the world, which may be narrowed or expanded depending on social circumstances.) The corset also operates as a cohesive structure because, like all underwear, it stimulates intersubjective feelings and desires. It is intimately associated with notions of propriety and restraint, on the one hand, and erotic pleasure and fetishism, on the other. The corset *contains* the body in order, paradoxically, to turn it into a public spectacle to which others may *relate*: a body attired only in underwear could, equi-vocally, be regarded as clothed and unclothed at the same time. Furthermore, underwear generally and the corset in particular are not merely frames, because one of their main roles is to *mediate* between the body and outer garments – i.e. between the natural flesh and the encultured image of the body that others will perceive. A foundation garment is not expected to fit well just as an end in itself: it must either follow, exaggerate or subtly modify the body's natural curves to help outer garments display themselves to maximum effect. The cultural meanings of underwear are inseparable from corresponding meanings in the realm of outerwear. The successful accomplishment of certain fashionable silhouettes demands the harmonious co-operation or coalescence of two. For example: 'the ultra-feminine silhou-ette of the 1947 New Look required a severely sculptured midriff. Fashion-conscious women achieved this by wearing the stiff belt-like 'waspie', a much diminished lace corset either worn alone or with a roll-on.'[46]

The ambiguity of dress is reinforced by the fact that it is virtually meaningless to speak of clothing, or of the garment, in the singular, since

46. Smitheram, M. (1996), 'Underwear', in A. De La Haye (ed.), *The Cutting Edge*, London: V & A Publications, p.181.

various levels of signification are continually implicated in the discourse of dress. This pluralization is highlighted by Barthes in *The Fashion System*, with specific reference to the rhetoric of fashion magazines, wherein three types of garment must be distinguished: 'image-clothing' (the photograph or drawing); 'written clothing' (the text accompanying the image as a description that does not simply comment on the image but actually constructs a narrative in its own right); and 'real clothing' (the concrete item that the first two types 'are supposed to represent'). The multiplication of signs and hence interpretative arenas within the system of fashion is further complicated by the facts that none of the three levels just mentioned is ultimately reducible to any of the others, and that although there are important correlations amongst all three, there is no way of homogenizing them into one seamless whole:

> we might suppose that these two garments [image-clothing and written clothing] recover a single identity at the level of the real garment . . . that the described dress and the photographed dress are united in the actual dress they both refer to. Equivalent, no doubt, but not identical; for just as between image-clothing and written clothing there is a difference in substances and relations, and thus a difference of structure, in the same way, from these two garments to the real one there is a transition to other substances and other relations . . .[47]

The relations referred to by Barthes throw into relief the necessity for an exploration of the language of dress that addresses simultaneously the individual function of clothing as an insulating shield and its collective value as a connecting tissue. Following Saussure's bipolar model of *langue* and *parole*, Barthes draws attention to the difference between the 'structural, institutional' system of dress in general (language in its entirety, conceived synchronically and paradigmatically) and the 'actualized, individualized' garments worn by a particular subject (the individual utterance produced diachronically at the level of the syntagm).[48]

The plural status of dress is, relatedly, due to the fact that garments derive their meanings not from one single order but from various cultural planes, and depend not on self-contained sets of evaluative or psychological criteria but on dynamic relationships between different 'commutative classes'.[49] So, on one level, clothing is defined in relation to the 'world', by being assigned 'a certain function, or more generally, a certain suitability',[50] measured

47. Barthes, *The Fashion System*, pp.3–4.
48. Ibid., p.18.
49. Ibid., p.20.
50. Ibid.

against social and ideological expectations characteristic of a given culture as a whole and hence not specifically associated with vestimentary codes. On another level, clothing is not assessed by the yardstick of external opinion but rather, self-reflexively perhaps, by that of the fashion system itself: 'in many utterances, the magazine simply describes the garment without correlating it to characteristics or worldly circumstances . . . in this sort of example we have only one class at our disposal, the clothing'.[51] In this case, the significance of dress emanates not from its relevance to cultural requirements and ideals in a broad sense, but to the subject-specific laws of the fashion system, for example the garment's conformity to dominant trends, its departure from them, or indeed its potential for the setting of new fashions.

Fabrications

In this section, Barthes's evaluation of different materials and their physical properties will be outlined as a general introduction to the exploration of the part played by the garment, as a corporeal reality in its own right, within the body/dress relationship. Barthes emplaces the concept of *coenaesthesia* as a leading thread in his assessment of the multiple attributes of cloth and fabric, thus emphasizing the need to think in terms of a coalescence, rather than mutual exclusion, of bodily effects:

> Here is a group of variants whose function is to make certain states of the material signify: its weight, its suppleness, the relief of its surface, and its transparency . . . no variant is in fact literal: neither the weight nor the transparency of a fabric can be reduced to isolated properties: transparency is also lightness, heaviness is also stiffness; in the end, coenesthesia leads back to the opposition between *comfortable* and *uncomfortable*; these are in fact the two great values of clothing whether, as was the case in the past, we signify what is heavy in association with authority or whether, as is the case today, we give a general privilege to comfort and thereby to lightness; this privilege explains why today the *heavy*, having unpleasant connotations, is rarely noted; or further, why the *transparent*, being associated with the euphoric, is singled out as a desirable sensation far from its opposite the *opaque*, which . . . is the norm: this play of oppositions is somewhat troubled by an implicit system of sensual (as well as historical) taboos. These variants of substance should in principle concern only the fabrics, fibers, woods, stones, and metals of which the garment and its accessories are made . . . but . . . by synecdoche, written clothing invariably transfers the nature of the substance onto the piece . . .[52]

51. Ibid., p.21.
52. Ibid., pp.123–4.

Indeed, it could be argued that this transposition of attributes – and of the sensations they may evoke – does not simply affect the overall ensemble of garments worn together at any one time but the body itself if, as will be argued later, the casing supplied by dress is more intimate an appendage than a superficial reading may indicate. Barthes underlines this intimacy by positing clothing not as an addition to but actually a kind of deputy or surrogate for the body:

> as a substitute for the body, the garment, by virtue of its weight, participates in man's fundamental dreams, of the sky and the cave, of life's sublimity and its entombment, of flight and sleep: it is a garment's weight which makes it a wing or a shroud, seduction or authority; ceremonial garments (and above all charismatic garments) are heavy; authority is a theme of immobility, of death; garments celebrating marriage, birth, and life are light and airy.[53]

Such symbolic associations are not, however, devoid of paradoxes: sartorial images of authority, for instance ceremonial gowns for academics, priestly vestments, courtroom apparel, do not advertise themselves as symbols of 'death' but, in fact, its opposite, i.e. the immortality of the traditions they incarnate. Furthermore, garments supposed to celebrate life often only *appear* to be light: marriage gowns and even the tiny baptismal robes designed for the new-born project their illusions of luminous evanescence through ponderous layers of cloth and lace. Leigh Hirst's *Untitled, from the Series 'Feast'*, effectively encapsulates this ambiguity. The imaginary garments it depicts make explicit reference to nuptial symbolism, by means of colours, floral motifs, lacy ornamentation and, most obviously, the formal attributes of the wedding cake. If tradition associates life-exalting occasions with light materials and fabrics, Hirst's picture conveys the exact opposite. The sensation of airiness conventionally associated with wedding garments is here completely absent. Dress, in the photograph, is a weighty, stiff and somewhat constraining structure. Disregarding the tactile and visual properties peculiar to the delicate textiles favoured by tradition, the image encases the body in an *architectural* frame of monumental solidity. It is the body, in fact, that is rendered weightless to the point of becoming transparent, as though its cake-like accoutrements had emptied it of all materiality. Various effects are achieved and various messages relayed through this technical composition. Firstly, the photograph suggests that there is no real opposition between fashion and architecture, although Western culture has insistently encouraged us to regard the former as transient and the latter as enduring. After all, architectural and sartorial structures perform similar functions in deploying

53. Ibid., p.126.

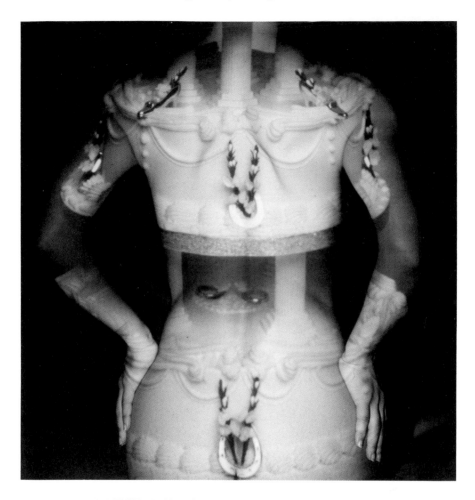

Figure 5. Leigh HIRST, *Untitled*, from the series *Feast*, 1997, C-type print. © Leigh Hirst 1997.

their different strategies for framing the body. Garments and buildings alike *clothe* the human form. Secondly, the architectural themes derived from the structure of the wedding cake transform the woman's body into a statuesque configuration, sustained by props reminiscent of the columns of a classical temple. This device serves to lend dress a feel of classical timelessness: the volatility of fashion is redeemed by the metamorphosis of clothing into a durable edifice. However, the photograph emphasizes that this transformation can only be achieved at the expense of the body, for in the process of translation of the ephemeral into the permanent, the bod itself all but vanishes. The figurative connotations of the wedding cake are also worthy of consideration. The wedding cake symbolizes the pact of peace, analogous to the breaking of the bread, between two parties brought together by marriage. But, more importantly in this context, it also symbolizes the connection, beloved of Freudian psychoanalysis, between food and sex. Hirst's picture equates the body with an edible object, thus stressing stereotypical images of woman as an object for consumption, and simultaneously giving visible shape to the cultural processes that fashion the body by regimenting its relationship with food. In portraying garments that are quite literally sculpted out of food, the image incisively and succinctly unites two of the most powerful forces through which the body is routinely encultured.

'Suppleness'[54] is an equally intriguing quality, not least owing to its changing connotations throughout history: now valued in contrast with stiffness, but once seen as a sign of impregnability most obviously typified by armours and other protective clothing, this variable maximizes the idea of unpredictability and hence stimulating possibilities of intermittent contact between dress and the body.

It is worth noting, in this respect, that chafing, rubbing, stroking, brushing and other related forms of tactile experience are inevitable components of the body/dress association that might prove, upon close examination, rather more complex physical and psychological phenomena than mere irritation or momentary pleasure. All those terms, after all, allude quite explicitly to sexual activity, as do words such as caress, embrace, hug, hold, which are repeatedly employed in fashion writing and which, in general parlance, are often used to describe the ways a garment relates to the body on which it hangs. 'Relief', as manifested in decorative practices such as 'indentations or bosses' as well as in the general 'surface . . . of the fabric'[55] and *'protruding and hollow'*[56] elements, is a property to which Barthes does not devote much space: yet its erotic potentialities are strong. It is 'transparence' that holds the most overtly titillating connotations, in the context of *The Fashion System*: this variable exhibits remarkable affinities to the concepts of intermittence and errancy formulated in both *A Lover's Discourse* and *The Pleasure of the Text,* and is indeed central to Barthes's theoretical corpus as whole:

> it consists of two poles: a full degree (the *opaque*) and a zero degree which corresponds to the total invisibility of the garment (this degree is obviously unreal, since nudity is taboo); like the 'seamless', a garment's invisibility is a mythical and utopian theme (The Emperor's New Clothes); far from the moment we validate the transparent, the invisible becomes its perfect state.[57]

54. Ibid.
55. Ibid., p.127.
56. Ibid., p.128.
57. Ibid., pp.128–9.

In so far as the subject cannot reveal the concrete body, for this has been decarnalized by language, it either dreams of the body's invisibility, as an escape from the schizophrenic state entailed by both having and being a body and not having/being it, or opts for compromise formations. On the one hand, it aims at totally becoming the opaque clothing that erases the body visibly and thus accepts decarnalization altogether. On the other, it toys with the interplay of concealment and revelation through transparence, as if to intimate that although the body is symbolically metamorphosed by and into language, it may still be brought back, if not as a real entity in its own right, at least as an accomplice in its play with dress.

Be that as it may, of the two terms *opaque* and *invisible*, one represents a quality so constant it is never noted, and the other a quality which is impossible; notation can only apply to intermediate degrees of opacity: openwork and transparent (or veiling); between these two terms there is no difference in intensity, only in aspect: openwork is a discontinuous visibility (fabric or crochet), transparence is an attenuated invisibility (gauzes, mousselines) . . . Here is the table for this variant:[58]

[opaque]/openwork/transparent/[invisible]

with holes   veiling
           veiled

The plastic meaning of a garment depends a great deal on the continuity (or discontinuity) of its elements, even more than on its form. On the one hand, we could say that in its profane way the garment reflects the old mystical dream of the 'seamless': since the garment envelops the body, is not the miracle precisely that the body can enter it without leaving behind any trace of this passage? And on the other hand, to the extent that the garment is erotic, it must be allowed to persist here and disintegrate there, to be partially absent, to play with the body's nudity.[59]

Linen, cotton, silk, wool, velvet, leather . . . how do we go about selecting the materials and fabrics of which our clothes are constituted? To what extent do we simply make decisions on the basis of the binary opposition between formal and casual wear, or on that of seasonal requirements? And to what, in choosing this or that material, do we – unconsciously, perhaps – don a new skin? The latter possibility is implicitly supported by Barthes when he argues that 'all species of materials end by being catalogued under an

58. Ibid.
59. Ibid., pp.136–7.

opposition of the type . . . light/heavy',[60] since this reduction of the system to the variant of weight highlights the fact that certain materials will invest the wearer with an identity that may be light (fine, refined, even ethereal, on the one hand; lightweight, frivolous, tenuous, on the other) and others with a heavy image (coarse, uncouth, even gross, on the one hand; authoritative, awe-inspiring, solemn, on the other). In so far as the variant of weight is the most overtly material of all, its dominance foregrounds the bodily status of the garment as an alternative skin rather than an artificial envelope. Lurie advocates this idea by stating that:

> To some extent, fabric always stands for the skin of the person beneath it: if it is strikingly slick or woolly, rough or smooth, thick or thin, we unconsciously attribute these characteristics to its wearer . . . Primitive hunters dressed in the hides of the beasts they had killed in order to take on the magical nature of the bear, the wolf or the tiger.[61]

Lurie's proposition about clothing's ability to 'stand for' the body's skin could be radicalized in the light of the possibility that the body might *need* the skin supplied by dress because it cannot signify by itself. In a post-structuralist scenario, this is due to the disembodying effects of the subject's admission to the symbolic. Yet, the idea that it is clothing that gives the corporeal the instruments through which to signify can be traced further back. Hegel, for instance, argued that 'It is clothing which gives the body's attitude its relief, and for this reason it must be considered as an advantage, in the sense that it protects us from the direct view of what, as sentience, is devoid of signification'.[62]

It is not sufficient, however, to observe that dress allows the body to signify, as this would seem to imply a universalistic concept of the body as a transcendental, uniformly shared, quality. We need to address the question of which particular body, or rather bodies, dress enables or indeed encourages to signify. Barthes identifies three main types of body: 'The first solution consists of proposing an ideal incarnate body; i.e., that of the model . . . a pure form, which possesses no attribute . . . and by a sort of tautology, it refers to the garment itself'; the second is based on 'a yearly decree that certain bodies (and not others) are in fashion'; 'The third solution consists of accommodating clothing in such a way that it transforms the real body and succeeds in making it signify Fashion's ideal body: to lengthen, fill out, reduce, enlarge,

---

60. Ibid., p.172.
61. Alison Lurie (1982), *The Language of Clothes*, London, p.232.
62. W. F. Hegel (1944), *Esthetique*, Vol.III, Part 1, Paris, p.147.

take in, refine . . . Fashion can convert any sentience into the sign it has chosen, its power of signification is unlimited'.[63]

The difficulty of establishing why certain materials and fabrics may be invested with greater erotic potential than others, both in the context of interpersonal relationships and in the case of the individual partnership of body and dress, is fundamentally due to the fact that no type of material can be unproblematically associated with one single set of symbolic connotations. Therefore, if changing trends and subjective preferences are largely responsible for associating this or that fabric with sensuality or sensuousness, it would also seem to be the case that all the most enduring materials may be assigned quite different meanings and functions, depending on which particular properties one chooses to concentrate on. Wool, for example, could be thought of as a sensible, practical and down-to-earth material, compared, say, with velvet, brocade or taffeta. Its properties of insulation, absorbency and resilience are well known. Yet there are obviously remarkable differences in the sensuous and possibly enticing qualities of cashmere, for instance, with its luxuriousness, softness to the touch and ability to provide warmth without the encumbrance of weight, and coarser types of wool such as the ones used for heavy-duty knitwear, tweeds, and indeed blankets and carpets. Silk, on the other hand, is traditionally associated with a delicate look and feel; but is also, paradoxically, the toughest of all natural fibres, ranked in strength with nylon. Cotton, though victim of a drastic fall in popular demand in the mid-1960s owing to the increase of available synthetic fibres, has rapidly regained status since, and the cult of the 100%-cotton garment is now widespread. And what to make of linen? Although it has more lustre than cotton, its relatively inelastic nature may evoke images of the unyielding body. Maybe cost is what makes it attractive, or maybe it is its tendency to wrinkle and hence its ability to endow the body of its wearer with characteristics of fashionable nonchalance and *coolness*.

It would be inappropriate, in the present context, to enter a detailed examination of each of the materials referred to in the preceding paragraph or indeed countless others, given the prodigious variety of available fabrics, fibres and textiles, both artificial and natural, as well as the increasingly complex experiments undertaken by fabric technology. As an illustrative case study, the following section will focus on one particular cloth, i.e. velvet, to try and highlight the multiplicity of associations, reverberations and interpretations that any one type may yield and, relatedly, both its symbolic and tactile functions in the body/dress relationship. More opulent, glorious and lustrous than perhaps any other fabric known to humankind, velvet

63. Barthes, *The Fashion System*, pp.259–60

seems ideally suited to appeal to the world of the senses. Yet its utilization in religious, imperial and military garb and imagery throughout the centuries discourages a purely sensuous reading of its properties. Like other *fanciful* cloths, velvet has more than a merely physical nature: it carries a wealth of symbolic meanings laden with ideological and economic implications. Fabrizio de' Marinis observes:

Velvet has clad kings and condottieri, saints and virgins, noblewomen and courtesans with its surreal dazzle. It has inspired great painters as they immortalized those figures who have made history age after age in their precious works. The Church has long used velvet for important ceremonies and for the ceremonial garb of popes. Kings and emperors, wrapped in sumptuous velvet, have decreed wars and signed peace treaties, given birth to states and nations or signed their death warrants. From the sumptuous apparel of Renaissance queens, to the less sumptuous outfits of Greta Garbo and Joan Crawford . . . velvet has established the rules and canons of elegance . . . perhaps because of the magic of its soft and intriguing structure, as pleasing to the finger as to the eye, [it] has continued to live and to adjust to new eras. And so from the oriental 'Alambras', we find velvet on the throne of the Medici. We glimpse it in antique paintings, under the armor of Renaissance warriors such as Malatesta, Federico da Montefeltro, and Bartolomeo Colleoni. It surrounds nude women and coy cupids. And at the birth of every new school, such as Art Nouveau or Bauhaus, the fabric is once again brought to the forefront with determination by the 'maîtres a penser', revived and redesigned. Even the Beatles, in the Sixties, when they sang 'Let It Be', in London for the first time, were wearing four close-fitting jackets in black velvet.[64]

De' Marinis thus highlights two central characteristics of the material under consideration: its pervasive magnetism not only across history but also across disparate media and cultural circles and, at the same time, its ability to embody abstract signifiers of authority, grace, spiritual worth, status symbolism, marketability and eroticism in an intensely material fashion, thanks to its emphatically three-dimensional textile structure. Velvet is fundamentally versatile in both the paradigmatic and the syntagmatic senses. In the relationship between dress and the body, a cloth so pregnant with cultural subtexts may trigger more complex sensations than merely tactile ones, by cladding the body not simply with a garment but also with layers of tradition and history, wherein the rise and fall of role models in a variety of political, aesthetic and commercial domains is of particular significance. If, as was suggested earlier, materials and fabrics assume the status of a

---

64. Fabrizio de' Marinis (1994), 'The Realm of the Senses', in Fabrizio de' Marinis (ed.), *Velvet – History, Techniques, Fashions*, Milan, pp.9–10.

substitute skin, the one provided by velvet, given the wealth of allusions it summons up, is probably of the order of an elaborately stratified shell.

Of course, it could be argued that all materials have a history, documentable by reference to an extensive and voluminous archive of discursive reference. And indeed, as was noted earlier, the case of velvet is here being employed as illustrative of broader phenomena of multi-accentuality where the reading of materials is concerned. However, it is worth stressing that it is precisely when confronted with a product that so ostentatiously displays its polysemy that the subject may become aware that in selecting a particular kind of apparel, it is automatically initiating two further actions: on the one hand, the subject restores materiality to its decarnalized being by weaving itself into an eminently tangible envelope; on the other, it attests to its own symbolic immateriality by becoming embroiled in a sprawling net of disembodying icons, models and emblems. In the case of velvet, these figures may be as diverse as the famous 'blue velvet dress worn by Greta Garbo in a number of scenes in the film *Inspiration*' and destined to become, indeed, 'an endless source of inspiration' or 'Joan Crawford's little velvet bolero jackets';[65] the orientalized styles promoted in the Thirties, such as 'the "Nabab" velvets by Chatillon Mouly Roussel and the "Nocturne", "Tahiti", "Morocco", and "Mameluck" velvets by Ducharne', designed to entice the public 'with their exotic and seductive names' and 'rich deep colors';[66] the luxurious outfits associated with Dior's 'New Look' in the late Forties; the 'smooth printed velvets' of the Sixties, usually characterized by 'representative graphics and . . . a daring array of colors', as evinced by Emilio Pucci's and Ken Scott's collections;[67] the more recent adaptations of velvet, for example through elasticizing processes, to the requirements of practical garments, particularly sportswear, as a means of combining a sense of informality with classic concepts of 'elegance and refinement';[68] and, last but not least, the kaleidoscopic images delivered by the postmodern proliferation of types of velvet and techniques for their manufacturing, some new, others appropriated from past traditions (corduroy, stretch velvet, velveteen, velour, gauffered velvet, etc.) and of areas of the clothing industry that may make creative use of this protean cloth: velvet, far from being confined to the production of formal apparel, pervades casual wear, so-called ethnic styles and everyday accessories:

---

65. Aurora Fiorentini Capitani and Stefania Ricci (1994), 'Velvet in Fashion – From the Thirties to the Present', in de' Marinis, *Velvet*, p.117.

66. Ibid., p.120.

67. Ibid., p.134.

68. Ibid.

With respect to previous historical periods, the twentieth century was to furnish an image of velvet that was far more varied than ever before, well suited to different and versatile possibilities. Velvet was used in its traditional role as a prestige fabric, reserved to the most exclusive creations of high fashion, but it was also used in alternative formulas – suffice it to think of synthetic furs – which made it a sporting and democratic fabric, well suited to all times of the day and all occasions.[69]

The plastic qualities of velvet make it particularly interesting, in the context of an assessment of the body/dress relationship. Indeed, this cloth's obvious three-dimensionality – and hence its ability to interact with the body of the wearer as a bodily substance itself in more overt ways than flimsier materials – is a property of velvet that fashions have been intent on maximizing at least since the Renaissance. Increasingly, weavers and designers studied ways of exploiting the dynamic potentialities of a cloth that, depending on the cutting of the pile and on the application of pattern and ornament, such as the use of bas-relief impressions or of gold and silver thread, could add special effects to the body's postures and gestures by playing with varying intensities of weight and light: 'The fabric was therefore designed with emphasis given not only to the pattern but also to its overall appearance, with due considera-tion given to the fact that it was being worn by a body in movement, so that the lighting and the shades of color changed as it moved.'[70]

In a Barthesian frame of reference, it may be particularly worth noticing that, at certain junctures in history, velvet could be used in especially appealing ways as a means of producing, or else mimicking, visual effects based on the lure of the cut, the gap, the suture, indeed intermittence. So, for example, when, in the sixteenth century, 'slashes in clothing . . . incurred the wrath of magistrates . . . velvet manufacturers succeeded in imitating those cuts, producing fabrics that were both in accordance with the sumptuary laws and the dictates of elegance. The false slashes had the appearance of small tufts that were much larger than the normal pile of velvet . . .'.[71]

Discipline and Transgression

The sumptuary laws referred to above suggest another field of investigation of dress as boundary – its function in mediating between the individual body and the collective body of state and society. As such it can be analysed as a

69. Roberta Orsi Landini (1994), 'The Thousand Faces of Velvet for Clothing', in de' Marinis, *Velvet*, p.109.
70. Ibid., p.81.
71. Ibid.

site of power, though not simply one where individuals conform, or do not conform, to state strictures or the imperatives of fashion. It can be seen as a place of dense concentration of significance, a complex transfer point of power relations, and in Foucauldian terms as having an important role in the dynamic of discipline and transgression. Although Foucault, unlike Barthes, rarely discusses clothing directly, his concentrated focus on the body as the axis of social life provokes his reader to ask questions about those bodies and their material adjuncts. Foucault's bodies are surely not naked; yet he tantalizingly stops short of including any analysis of their coverings, or indeed uncoverings, and their place in the shifting matrix of power. The reader is forced to extrapolate from implications in the rich discussions of body-politics, and here we intend to examine a few of the key notions – discipline, transgression, sexuality and knowledge – to provide a perspective on the social role of dress.

The example of the sumptuary laws precedes, chronologically, what Foucault identifies as a fundamental change in the operation of power, the move from a society of spectacle to one of surveillance, in his own words from punishment to discipline. The body is, for him, the pivotal point of this change, and it is inseparably tied to the function of the gaze. In the pre-seventeenth century period the exertion of power on the individual is accomplished through spectacle: the individual looks upon various displays of state power such as pageantry or royal processions, where the body of the monarch is its locus, and the surplus of that real body's power constitutes the body politic. By contrast, the subject, who, often simultaneously, sees public exhibitions of torture and execution along with pageantry, is marked by lack of power. Thus he or she comes to know that the surplus power has the right to overflow into his or her lack of it, and that the state has the right to his or her body in terms of pain and violence; it can be tortured, branded, mutilated, imprisoned or killed. With the advent of the modern period these practices begin to shift, and the body comes into a new regime. Although this change takes place over a long period of time, Foucault observes that its beginnings can be seen in the seventeenth century, particularly in judicial procedures that effectively remove the body from view:

One no longer touched the body, or at least as little as possible, and then only to reach something other than the body itself . . . The body now serves as an instrument or intermediary: if one intervenes upon it to imprison it, or to make it work, it is in order to deprive the individual of a liberty that is regarded as a right and a property . . . Physical pain, the pain of the body itself, is no longer the constituent element of the penalty.[72]

72. Michel Foucault (1977), *Discipline and Punish*, trans. Alan Sheridan, London, p.11.

What replaces the bloody and battered body of punishment is what Foucault names the 'discipline-mechanism', a complex series of systems of surveillance in which being observed or being conscious of the possibility of being observed produces conformity to the demands of power. His model of power is not one of a monolithic block bearing down on the powerless, constantly repressing, but a method that actively produces effects, a flexible and pervasive system in which the individual is inevitably and inescapably involved: 'Our society is not one of spectacle, but of surveillance . . . We are neither in the amphitheatre or on the stage, but in the panoptic machine, invested by its effects of power, which we bring to ourselves as we are part of its mechanism.'[73]

In this new 'scopic regime' the modern body is mere flesh, a remnant of its previous signifying potential. The developing philosophic concerns of the Enlightenment project take consciousness as the primary definition of the human condition, and the body is relegated, at best to being the corporeal vehicle of the Cartesian thinking self, at worst to being the dead weight of impeding earthly animality whose desires must be regulated and controlled. The body here can be seen as the clothing of consciousness, or of the soul, purely material substance that both enables and restricts, providing a suggestion of the form and limit of the individual and a means of relation to the social group. In this it has another similarity to dress, in that it is regarded as deceptive and deceiving; the body, like garments, speaks of the individual, but also betrays him; it does not speak the truth, because its crudity cannot embody the complexity of the conscious self. It also deceives others, because it covers and recasts individual identity, misleading the observer about the nature of the 'true' self. One of the offshoots of this paradox is the interest in the classification of physical features that reaches its apotheosis in the work of the nineteenth-century physiognomists, the attempt to make the body, and particularly the face, legible as criminal, insane, hysterical, noble or honest. Everyone is worth looking at, because the shift in power from spectacle to surveillance involves an interesting shift in the nature of the gaze, as Foucault comments,

> For a long time ordinary individuality – the everyday individuality of everybody – remained below the threshold of description. To be looked at, observed, described in detail, followed from day to day by uninterrupted writing was a privilege. The chronicle of a man, the account of his life formed part of the rituals of his power. The disciplinary methods reversed this relation, lowered the threshold of describable individuality and made of this description a means of control and a method of domination.[74]

73. Ibid., p.217.
74. Ibid., p.191.

This lowering of the threshold brings everyone within the scope of the gaze, and every detail of their physical activity becomes relevant to the production of the case history. The modern body becomes the object of *knowledge*: within the residual dead flesh is the potential for investigation, that which can described, organized, trained and made available for use.

Foucault attempts to redefine the relations of power and knowledge, suggesting that we should abandon the notion that knowledge can only exist where power is suspended, and realize that power and knowledge directly imply one another, that power relations produce a field of knowledge, and that knowledge presupposes and in fact constitutes power relations. The modern body is typified by his notion of docility, which is where the elements of knowledge and control come together; as Foucault says, it joins ' the analysable body to the manipulable body. A body is docile that may be subjected, used, transformed and improved.'[75]

One of the ways in which the body can be made docile is through clothing. Dress renders it analysable, either forcibly through required clothing, or voluntarily through self-selected garments; it becomes manipulable through the effects of being dressed. The four elements that Foucault refers to are apparent in different areas of vestimentary practice, though all the functions are closely interrelated. By taking an example that corresponds quite closely to the fields of discipline that Foucault himself explores, the uniform, it is possible to see how these four elements are manifested.

i) Certain types of uniform clothing speak clearly of subjection: for example, the clothing of the criminal, the pauper and the insane in nineteenth- and early twentieth-century institutions. These indicated that the individual no longer had the right to be regarded as such: he or she had fallen beneath the level of morality, sanity, or economic independence required to be seen as a free and self-determining citizen. The right to individuality and its self-expression was therefore removed and the right of power to distinguish difference as it saw fit imposed in its place. However, this is not to suggest that the subjected were undifferentiated, but that they were *known* in other ways; through observation and the maintenance of records of behaviour, each became a case, a file of the most minute detail of movement, gesture, eating, sleeping and exercise. Dress here nullifies the subject, preventing the establishment of an identity independent of that which the institution wishes to create, reminding him constantly of his relation to that institution and enrolling him in the dominant discourses of decency, morality or appropriate gender. It also marks out the inmate from the superintendent, suggesting by contrast the inmate's lack of entitlement to assume responsibility, while

75. Ibid., p.136.

simultaneously indicating that the guard's power is not his own. However, there is not a simple opposition of subjection and freedom, which is indicated by the relaxation of the rules of institutional dress. Within the context of the prison, just as much as outside, self-selected clothing is a tool of subjection. This would seem counter-intuitive, as the common-sense view of clothing might be that it individualizes in a humanist sense, allowing the free expression of the individual's personality, differentiating him or her positively against the mass of other people, and in many cases resisting what is seen as the restriction of authority. However, apparently 'allowing' a person to choose their own dress renders them as equally, if differently, 'knowable' to the observing eye as someone clad in uniform. As Elizabeth Wilson notes on the reasoning behind abolition of uniforms for women prisoners: '. . . the better the authorities knew the individual woman in question the more successful their surveillance of her would be . . . if female prisoners dressed as they pleased they would "reveal" their personalities more fully than had been possible in a uniform .[76]

She also remarks that such 'privileges' were seen to promote a more acceptably heterosexual culture in the prisons, so that in wearing civilian clothes and make-up the woman prisoner co-opts herself into a system of maintenance of 'proper' femininity.

ii) Another kind of uniform, which is the marker of the body that has been subsumed into a larger body like the army or the police force, indicates the body as usable. Here people are distinguished from the mass, set apart by their dress. The uniform here speaks of a double valency, in that those uniformed are both subjects of power and also agents of power over the non-uniformed. A complex structure obtains, in which uniform can be seen not to be 'uniform' at all, but a subtle machinery of differentiation, as it is carefully distinguished by details that indicate rank and status. Uniform is not meant to make everyone look the same, but to produce a hierarchy in which those who need to know can make the necessary distinction. To the untutored eye all men in a regiment would appear similar; but the members of that regiment would be able to discern instantly another soldier's rank, length of service, or role within the organization. Power is enforced in an outward direction, as it presents itself as an unreadable blank of absolute similarity to the section of the population who are to be impressed by it. It is also enforced inwardly, as each member is a single case contained within the grid of organizational relations.

iii) The transformation of the body takes place in both these examples as

76. Elizabeth Wilson (1992), 'Fashion and the Postmodern Body', in Juliet Ash and Elizabeth Wilson (eds), *Chic Thrills: A Fashion Reader*, London, p.11.

the flesh is re-created and re-presented within its casing of signifying fabric. A third type of regulated and regulating dress is the religious habiliment of nuns, priests and officers of the Church. Like army or prison dress, it suggests both subjection and use; the person wearing it has accepted obedience to power, though in this case it is the supernatural power of God. It also implies the absolute subjection of the flesh, the abolition of the distracting desires of the guilty body and the transformation of that body from abject tissue to a clean and empty vessel to be filled with spiritual power. The separating nature of clothing is starkly apparent, as each outfit screens the body from others and from itself, attempting to make it vanish from view. The body is marked as non-sexual, removed from certain social interactions; yet by the fact of its absence it produces an effect of definition on those interactions.

iv) All these examples ultimately bespeak the improved body. The mad, the criminal and the pauper become clean, ordered and controlled. The soldier is drilled and trained in a programme of movements alien in their exaggeration or attenuation to the functioning of the natural body, and the shine of the boots and the crease of the trousers are inspected as rigorously as marching and presentation of weapons. The same unnatural exaggeration of tiny movements that is expected of the body is also expected of the fabric of the uniform. The body of the pious can only be improved by its mortification, and by its banishment from the field of vision. The improvement of the individual bodies through the mechanisms that foster docility improves the social body, giving it the gloss of order and propriety.

This discussion of the uniform serves to throw into the sharpest relief the function of dress in discipline, as one of its most visible manifestations. It is possible to see how this analysis could equally be applied to any type of clothing. The corset, for example is often used as an illustration of Foucault's ideas,[77] particularly because it demonstrates the multiple possible meanings of fashion in relation to the female consumer. Unsurprisingly perhaps, as the uniform and the corset exist at the extreme visible edge of discipline in dress, they are both a particular focus of the correlate condition, transgression, which will be discussed in greater detail below.

The recurrent ideas in this analysis are differentiation and separation, which runs counter to the usual view of uniform as something that makes bodies similar. Our argument is that, from a Foucauldian perspective, both these practices are shown to be possible, and that they are not mutually exclusive. It is possible to gather groups of people but to establish an internal structure to the group, enabling it to be managed at a microcosmic level. In a very obvious sense this alludes to Foucault's detailing of the principles of

77. Ibid., p.10.

discipline; he comments: 'In discipline, the elements are interchangeable, since each is defined by the space it occupies in a series, and by the gap that separates it from the others . . . It individualizes bodies by a location that does give them a fixed position, but distributes them and circulates them in a network of relations.'[78]

Clothing is a vital aspect of the erection and maintenance of boundaries, but what Foucault's remark suggests is that what matters is not so much the marking of the individual body, but of the *spaces between*, policing of the social body is carried out through supervision of these created spaces:

> In the first instance, discipline proceeds from the distribution of individuals in space. To achieve this end, it employs several techniques. Discipline sometimes requires *enclosure*, the specification of a place heterogeneous to all others and closed in upon itself. It is the protected place of disciplinary monotony. . . . But the principle of 'enclosure' is neither constant, nor indispensable, nor sufficient in disciplinary machinery. This machinery works space in a much more flexible and detailed way. It does this first of all on the principle of elementary location or *partitioning*. Each individual has his own place; and each place its individual. Avoid distribution in groups; break up collective dispositions; analyse confused, massive or transient pluralities. Disciplinary space tends to be divided into as many sections as there are bodies or elements to be divided. Its aim was to establish presences and absences, to know where and how to locate individuals, to set up useful communications, to interrupt others, to be able at each moment to supervise the conduct of each individual, to assess it, to judge it, to calculate its qualities or merits. It was a procedure, therefore, aimed at knowing, mastering and using. Discipline organizes an analytical space.[79]

In this section Foucault is specifically describing the operation of discipline through architecture and the arrangement of the built environment; but many of his terms suggest that this can be extended to the analysis of dress. The space of clothing, for example, is precisely one of enclosure; dress is heterogeneous and closed in upon itself; what it encloses is the body, and it refers inwards to that body. But as Foucault observes, the element of enclosure is not the sole means of control; it is not sufficient that each individual is enclosed by garments, but the way in which that clothing differentiates the space between him or her and the next individual is also vital in the flexible operation of power. It must also refer outwards. Dress divides social space into as many segments as there are bodies; but it also subdivides the particular body into further segments according to the composition of the clothing – for example the difference between under and outer garments, or between

78. Foucault, *Discipline and Punish*, p.145.
79. Ibid., p.141–3.

fabric clothing and additions like shoes or hats, or between uniforms and medals or insignia of rank. The subdivision at this level indicates the radical splitting of the subject: far from being the integrated ideal of Enlightenment philosophy, he is layered and sectioned, and each of the separate segments is subordinate to differing requirements and effects. This corresponds to what Foucault calls the 'microphysics of bio-power', the control of the infinitesimal movement of all parts of the human body through the agency of observation. The boundary is imposed in order to banish the fluidity and liminality of the margin, to make the space-between intelligible and controllable rather than threatening and destabilizing. The boundary, however, is not rigid and permanent. Foucault emphasizes the flexibility of such forms, which while retaining their deep structural functions, are adaptable to circumstance, allowing attempts at transgression to be assimilated. From this perspective, society can be seen to be organized through clothing into a series of observable boundaries; those erected on the single body by separate items of dress, those existing between bodies, and those serving to distinguish groups of bodies from other groups.

The model of architectural discipline that Foucault provides is an appropriate one for the analysis of dress. Architecture has been described as 'fashion's "other",[80] and there are numerous points of comparison between buildings and bodies: both breathe air, excrete waste, and have a skeleton, a skin and a nervous system of electricity. Buildings are, in a sense, bodies, and both are machines. Descartes makes an explicit analogy: 'I considered myself, firstly, as having a face, hands, arms and the whole machine made up of flesh and bones, such as it appears in a corpse and which I designated by the name of body,'[81] and this has been a frequent description, especially in the twentieth century, when technological advances have appeared to produce an even closer correspondence. Buildings are also regularly thought of as mechanical: Le Corbusier famously described a house as a machine for living in. It is not an analogy that is ignored by fashion designers, photographers or commentators. Designers and fashion editors frequently talk about the 'construction' of clothes, particularly *haute couture*; underwear before the 1960s was referred to as 'foundation' garments; the outer layer of a building is called 'cladding'. In fashion photography situated in an urban landscape the connection is often clearly apparent: in a kind of pathetic fallacy the landscape becomes part of the signifying web. There is no distinction drawn between the dress of the model and the building; both are dressed

80. Paulette Singly and Deborah Fausch (1994), 'Introduction', in D. Fausch, P. Singley, R. El-Khoury and Z. Efrat (eds), *Architecture: In Fashion*, New York, p.7.

81. Rene Descartes (1968), trans. F. E. Sutcliffe, *Discourse on Method and the Meditations*, Harmondsworth, p.1.

Figure 6. Thierry MUGLER, Wall Street, New York, May 1980 – *Boites Mugler.*
© Thierry Mugler 1980.

and dress each other. In the work of the designer and photographer Thierry Mugler severe and opulent outfits of satin and leather, fur and lamé are juxtaposed with the gigantic architecture of buildings like the Chrysler skyscraper, the Paris Opera and the monumental structures of Communist states.[82] The movement from the 'natural' to the constructed is emphasized in every element of the photograph: the body of the model appears as statue-like, no longer soft and ephemeral; the organic origins of the leather and satin are now obscured by their transformation into strongly coloured, stiffly geometric shapes; and the stone, glass and steel of the buildings bear no relation to their natural constituents. All are presented as 'improvements' in the Foucauldian sense, and their relation to discipline is stark, even to the quotations from military uniforms on the outfits.

There is also an important connection between architecture, clothing and power in the notion of modernism. Though Elizabeth Wilson offers modernity as a possible model for the interpretation of fashion[83] she refers only to art, and ignores any relation to architecture, which was, and is, perhaps the most obvious manifestation of modernism in culture, being the largest in physical terms. The aesthetic principles of modernist architecture are commonplace in contemporary fashion: indeed, Mies van der Rohe's dictum 'less is more' has been repeated so often as style advice that its origin as a comment on the artistic philosophy of building has been all but lost. In the modernist aesthetic decoration is no longer regarded as necessary or beautiful – one of the foundation texts of architectural modernism is entitled 'Ornament and Crime'[84] – the building is stripped to its function, and the bare frame is idealized in a manner reminiscent of classical drawings of the ideal form of the human body. The basis of modernism in architecture is an explicit opposition of the modern to fashion, it embraces the 'new' as an expression of the changing condition of twentieth-century existence, but eschews 'novelty' as the childish (feminine) desire for the latest trend regardless of its beauty or value. Many of the early essays of the modern movement make direct, and unfavourable, comparisons between the ugliness of women's dress, which is seen as enslaved to the whims of changing taste, and the beauty of the new architecture, which aspires to the condition of universal and timeless beauty. Le Corbusier wrote of the difference between classics and trash: 'Trash is always abundantly decorated: the luxury object is well-made, neat and clean, pure and healthy, and its bareness reveals the quality

82. Thierry Mugler (1988), *Thierry Mugler: Photographer*, London.
83. Elizabeth Wilson (1985), *Adorned in Dreams: Fashion and Modernity*, London.
84. Adolf Loos (1908), 'Ornament and Crime', in Ulrich Conrads (ed.), *Programs and Manifestoes on 20th Century Architecture*, trans. Michael Bullock, Cambridge, Mass.

of its manufacture',[85] and both he and Adolf Loos refer constantly to the frivolity and superfluity of feminine decoration in their early manifestos.[86] Like William Morris, that other polymath of design, they too designed clothing for women that reflected their artistic principles: Le Corbusier in particular left numerous sketchbooks of women's fashions of both past costumes and his own designs. There is a clear, and strongly gendered, moral element in this aesthetic, with its language of purity, cleanliness and health that is based in a notion of truth or honesty. It is a logical result of a junction of post-Reformation thought, which regards decoration as lies, and of the fetishization of the machine in the industrial age. The machine is not deceitful: it is efficient, reliable and obedient, in fact it is the ideal body, transformed and improved and in sharp distinction to the sullied and wilful flesh. More contemporary representations of the 'bad machine' are backward readings, where the attributes of the flesh are re-inscribed on the inorganic.

This yoking of moral and aesthetic 'truth' to simplicity can account for a strand of dominant thinking in contemporary clothing; from everyday dress to the higher echelons of fashion, simple design is equated with intelligence, efficiency and natural beauty. The frills and furbelows of a Versace dress occupy a completely different moral and aesthetic space from the simple sculptured lines of one designed by Giorgio Armani. The Versace design refers to the body, the excess of decoration draws attention, it is essentially spectacular; while the Armani dress effaces the body and is supposed to displace attention to the other, unfleshly qualities of the wearer. The two garments also speak differently of power: the former might be seen as something to be worn by woman-as-possession, whose relation to power is only as adjunct, the chosen object of a powerful man. His power is concealed on his own body, but displayed through dress, on hers. By contrast the Armani dress is usually seen as that of an independent woman, who possesses power in her own right, yet reveals it through a similar strategy of concealment. In the gendered terms of the early modernists she has discarded the feminine enslavement to the 'trash' of decoration and moved into the sphere of the masculine modern, with its 'timeless' values of simplicity and classic beauty. She is not-to-be looked-at, asserting her control of the appropriating power of the gaze.

To relate this back to Foucault's analysis of the display of power, it can again be seen in relation to architecture: the buildings that speak of power

85. Le Corbusier (1924), 'L'Art decoratif d'aujourd'hui', *L'Esprit Nouveau*, 24, in *The Decorative Art of Today*, trans. James. A. Dunnett, Cambridge, Mass., p.85.

86. See for example, Le Corbusier (1931), *Towards a New Architecture*, trans. Frederick Etchells, London; Adolf Loos (1982), 'Ladies' Fashion' in *Spoken Into the Void: Collected Essays 1987–1900*, trans. Jane Newman and John Smith, Cambridge, Mass.

are not those that are decorated. The Houses of Parliament, though we know they are the seat of government, do not impress us with their neo-Gothic detail: in fact, Westminster looks more like a fairy castle by the river Thames than a structure that inspires fear and respect. This is because it conforms to Foucault's older paradigm of power, that of spectacle, and we no longer have the same optical discipline in relation to it. The paradigm that we now occupy is that of surveillance, which explains why a building like the Ministry of Defence, or the new MI5 headquarters at Vauxhall Cross, implies power much more distinctly. It is not simply because we know what they contain: these buildings resist the gaze, they are not for us to look upon, to be able to read, but for the reverse, to observe and to read us. Exactly the same is true of the garb of state power; compare for example the state opening of Parliament and an American presidential cavalcade. The Queen's dress, regalia and transport are rich in ornament, colour and lustre: all are covered with what are in effect hooks for the eye upon which the gaze catches. It is an interesting sight, even beautiful, but it no longer signifies power, it is history – what power once looked like. The presidential procession is like the modernist building, all its surfaces are smooth, shiny and reflective, our gaze returns to us deflected from the bullet-proof glass and mirror shades of the security guards. No purchase is possible, and we are watched by it and placed by its gaze: 'Power has its principle not so much in a person as in a certain concerted distribution of bodies, surfaces, lights, gazes; in an arrangement whose internal mechanisms produce the relation in which individuals are caught up.'[87]

Postmodern clothes and buildings offer yet another variation on the dynamics of the gaze: the Pompidou Centre or the 'deconstructionist' clothes of Martin Margiela are confusing and disturbing because they are inverted, the inside is on the outside, the visual equivalent of a body with its organs externalized, an embarrassment to the modern subject's dream of the banished flesh, and in a Lacanian sense an almost unbearable reminder of the fragmentation it struggles to overcome, a literal example of the finished-yet-unfinished movement that is the narrative of identity.

The insistence of the flesh, despite the attempt of modernity to marginalize it, raises the question of another significant relationship in our exploration of dress and its mediating place between the individual and collective body – that of the body and the text. In the introduction to the first volume of his great unfinished project on the history of sexuality, Foucault foregrounds the confession as the means by which the body and its activities are displaced into language through meticulous self-examination and directed articulation

87. Foucault, *Discipline and Punish*, p.202.

of thoughts and actions. The self becomes the observer of the self, ensuring the division of subjectivity that produces guilt in relation to its actions and serving to enmesh it further in the toils of power. As Francis Barker suggests:

> It always-already prejudices the independence of the free subject, short-circuiting that subject's potentially subversive desire by establishing inside it a self-disciplinary fixation predicated on the outlawing of the body and its passions as the absolute outside..of the divided subject. It draws a shifting but unbreakable limit around subjectivity as the domain of propriety and speech, not as a code of manners, but as a deep structural effect of this form of the subject's locatedness in being and signification.[88]

Desire is transformed into discourse, but not as a direct translation, for the discourse is governed by rules of expression that carefully juxtapose speech and silence, not in any binary sense but as equal tokens in the text which is produced. The subject substitutes for its corporeal body the body of the text, and its fleshliness is dissipated, then reassembled in a new order in language, distanced from itself and placed at the edge of its conscious being. For Foucault, confession exceeds its specifically devotional context, and becomes the mode of expression, of speaking of the self in every area of life. If all speaking of the self is confession, then as well as seeing the flesh made word, we can also see the flesh made fabric through clothing: dress is the text that first clothes and then displaces the body. The dress-as-language metaphor is the most frequent figure in the discussion of clothing; Alison Lurie, drawing on Barthes's work, extends the metaphor across her whole book,[89] but she consistently reads clothes as speaking *of* the body in fairly simple manner rather than, as Foucault might suggest, *instead* of it. The body and the text separate in the writing process; desire and meaning drift apart from one another. Through clothes we indeed write ourselves into discourse, but that discourse is confession, and the price of the ability to write is the self-consciousness that divides and ultimately contributes to the securing of our subjection.

In a twist that reverses the positions of Lacan's view of the *objet petit a*, or Kristeva's of the abject, it is now the body, and not dress, that hovers at the edge of identity, neither fully present nor conclusively absent. The failure to banish the body completely from the scene of discourse is clear in the case of dress. The wearing of clothes is the emblem of the obedient and improved (absented) body, yet this forces the subject to recognize his or her

---

88. Francis Barker (1995), *The Tremulous Private Body: Essays on Subjection*, Ann Arbor, p.54.
89. Lurie, *Language of Clothes*.

subjection, the place he or she has taken in the shifting grid of knowledge, and to become nostalgic for the flesh. This, we would suggest, is at the root of the uncanny feeling experienced in the presence of empty clothes. We long, not for the bodies that once occupied them, but for our own bodies, which we do not possess, and have never possessed, hostage as they are to the scopic regimes we inhabit. Again, this is not to say that power deprives us of our bodies in the simple sense of complete removal of our control over them, but that the dynamics of power relations are such that we cannot ever establish a final boundary between the individual and the social meanings. Foucault's examination of the confession and the production of discourse in the place of the body is an example of his contention that what appears to be repression passively exerted is thoroughly bound up with the active production of meaning. He strongly contests what he calls 'the repressive hypothesis'[90] in the field of sexuality: 'Pleasure and power do not cancel or turn back against one another; they seek out, overlap, and reinforce one another. They are linked together by complex mechanisms and devices of excitation and incitement.'[91] For him, sexuality is not something natural and inherent that struggles against the restraining efforts of power, but that which is produced at myriad points of contact, and via processes that are in themselves erotic, as this quotation suggests: 'The power which thus took charge of sexuality set about contacting bodies, caressing them with its eyes, intensifying areas, electrifying surfaces, dramatizing troubled moments. It wrapped the sexual body in its embrace.'[92]

The wearing of clothes, then, is not the *expression* of the inherent sexuality of the body, as the language-of-clothes argument posits, but part of the *production* of a sexuality, which is both of the body and in some sense independent of it, an attribute that hovers at the nexus of body and society. Equally, dress does not silence the 'true' sexuality of the body, that which comes from the imagined primal state of uncomplicated existence, precisely because that state has never existed. Clothes are part of the sex-chatter, the proliferation of discourses that Foucault proposes has replaced the relatively unitary practice of the Middle Ages, whereby the singular notion of penance has scattered and broken apart, multiplying into such various fields as demography, biology, medicine, psychiatry, psychology, ethics, pedagogy, political criticism[93] and, we would add, fashion.

Sexuality emerges from the friction of discourses, as sexual sensation emerges from the friction of bodies. Dress is enabled to give the body sexual

90. Foucault, *The History of Sexuality*.
91. Ibid., p.48.
92. Ibid., p.44.
93. Ibid., p.33.

meanings that it does not necessarily possess by virtue of the existence of the dictates of power; as Foucault says, it intensifies, electrifies and dramatizes, making the ordinariness of the flesh extraordinary and thereby establishing a linkage that power is able to exploit. This can perhaps be seen by exploring the example of the corset, which has had a lively history, moving from functionality to fashion, to notions of decency, to being seen as unnatural, and as erotic. Though the body in a corset is the same in physical terms as the body without, it is *not* the same body. The corset, likewise is the same piece of fabric worn or unworn, but also not the same in its different contexts. The meaning of both body and garment is produced by their juxtaposition, and that meaning changes according to the context in which it is worn. The erotic is not an attribute of any of the three elements of body, garment or context, but comes into existence at their junction. The disciplining of the corseted body in a late-twentieth-century setting differs radically from that which obtains in the late nineteenth century, because it is voluntary, no longer undertaken at the behest of propriety. Some of the social meanings have fallen away as the garment has passed out of common use, and its extraordinariness is able to recharge an erotic current because it is made to appear personal. In the nineteenth century a woman wore a corset for more general reasons of fashion, or social status, and though it has been argued that she may have derived her own satisfaction from it,[94] the meaning produced was one of conformity to a masculine power structure that dictated passivity for the bourgeois woman, rather than one of explicit eroticism. A contemporary man seeing a woman in a corset is able to believe that she is wearing it for him, that she is aware of its disciplinary message and prepared to present herself as passive in relation to him: the power relation has changed from a general to an individual one, and one that is directly erotic.

In a passage that could have come from Barthes or Lacan, Foucault, again speaking of architecture, describes 'the calculation of openings, of filled and empty spaces, passages and transparencies'[95] that characterizes the disciplinary institution. It could be argued that for Foucault, as well as for Lacan and Barthes, the erotic charge emanates from the gap, and that the 'opening' in discipline is exactly coterminous with the lack that produces desire or the gape of the garment that provokes sexual feeling. Just as the space or opening in the prison might be thought to offer freedom to the body enclosed, but is in fact a node of visibility and control (it is not a secret place, its existence is widely known, and it has usually been placed there precisely for the purposes of observation): so likewise in clothing or

94. David Kunzle (1982), *Fashion and Fetishism*, Princeton, NJ.
95. Foucault, *Discipline and Punish*, p.172.

oñ the body, the gap is not a secret place, it is an obvious, and even an advertised, focal point, even if, as where two pieces of clothing meet, the gap is temporarily closed. Even so, this does not constitute the acquiescence of the body or its clothes in a pre-arranged and permanent discourse, as the vital element of the power relation is the dynamic nature of the interaction. Contestation of the boundaries is what keeps power alive and prevents it from becoming inert and therefore useless. Transgression is discipline's double, not its opposite: both actively produce one another in complex processes, often on a minute scale. This double relation can be seen in the transgressive attempt to create spaces other than those offered ready-made in the structures of power, or to utilize them in ways not predicted by those in control.

One example of this is the 'coding' behaviour of sub-cultures, particularly in clothing, which is a correlation of what Foucault calls the 'reverse discourse'.[96] The medical surveillance of sexuality in the late nineteenth and early twentieth centuries concerned itself strenuously to classify and define the type of the deviant personality, and among its definitions of the lesbian was the preference of a woman for masculine clothing. Once this entered into more public discourses via the specialized language of law and medicine, it meant that a lesbian now had the possibility of using that definition for her own purposes, namely to show herself and to recognize other women as lesbians. The reverse discourse is no more permanent than the dominant discourse, however, and in this example it is possible to trace the path of definition by masculine dress from the medico-legal specialists through the encoding by the lesbian community and into the very public arena of general knowledge, and finally into the mainstream of fashion. At the penultimate stage, masculine dress is no longer subversive in the way that it was when it was understood by fewer people, and assumed the status of direct confrontation. At this point it crosses firstly into the extreme edge of high fashion and then into general currency, where its threat is defused so completely that Princess Diana is seen wearing a tuxedo and bow tie to a public event.

As might be expected, the transgressive sexuality of the lesbian becomes differently encoded at the same historical moment, now in a parodic version of the dominant notion of heterosexual femininity. This image too has, by the mid-1990s, been recuperated into the fashion mainstream, as Reina Lewis observes in her article on the neutralization of some of the imagery in the work of the lesbian photographer Della Grace.[97] Transgression, like

96. Foucault, *History of Sexuality*, p.101.
97. Reina Lewis (1994), 'Dis-Graceful Images: Della Grace and Lesbian Sado-Masochism', *Feminist Review*, No.46, p.85.

discipline, cannot be a permanent condition: it can only ever be local and temporary, dependent on the changing configurations of systematic relationships; and clothing is no exceptional case. Despite clothing's appearance of involvement in movements of liberation, free expression and newness, it is perhaps best described in Foucault's summary of society: 'loudly castigating itself for its hypocrisy . . . speaks verbosely of its own silence, takes great pains to relate in detail the things it does not say, denounces the powers it exercises, and promises to liberate itself from the very laws that have made it function'.[98]

Sprawling Bodies

In shielding the individual body from its milieu, yet simultaneously connecting it to other bodies, dress problematizes corporeality in at least three ways: as a symbolic structure, it denies the body's physicality by translating it into a decarnalized system of signs; as a surrogate for the physical apparatus, it reintroduces materiality into language in a metaphorical fashion; as a bodily structure in its own right, inseparable from the tangible and sensuous properties of the fabrics of which it is literally constituted, it infringes upon the symbolic's boundaries as a reminder of stubborn materiality indisposed to sublimation. The sensuous properties of different kinds of cloths and materials, as discussed in the context of the preceding tour into the polysemic language of velvet as an illustration of the multi-accentual connotations of *all* vestimentary media, vividly underscore the materiality of dress. Following Deleuze and Guattari, it could further be argued that different types of materials allude metaphorically to divergent philosophical approaches and their varying emphases on concepts of *system* and *flux*. Different materials may be seen as embodiments of two distinct, albeit inevitably interacting, types of space: the *smooth*, as the locus of fluidity, fusion and boundlessness, and the *striated*, as that of order, classification and categorization. Smooth space is associated with *nomad thought*, an intellectual operation that seems to supply a fitting metaphor for the functionings of fashion; as Massumi points out in his Foreword to *A Thousand Plateaus*:

> It does not repose on identity; it rides difference . . . Rather than analyzing the world into discrete components, reducing their manyness to the One of identity, and ordering them by rank, it sums up a set of disparate circumstances in a

---

98. Foucault, *History of Sexuality*, p.9.

shattering blow. It synthesizes a multiplicity of elements without effacing their heterogeneity or hindering their potential for future rearranging.[99]

The smooth and the striated are not mutually exclusive, for: 'the two spaces in fact exist only in mixture: smooth space is constantly being translated, transversed into a striated space; striated space is constantly being reversed, returned to a smooth space'.[100]

Fundamentally, the coexistence and reciprocal transformability of the two types of space point to the inseparability of disciplinary and transgressive practices, as it is impossible to establish with any degree of finality to what extent the smooth is regimented by the striated and to what the striated is exploded by the smooth, any more than dress may be unequivocally construed as either a bounding structure or a vehicle for the unlimiting of embodied subjectivity: 'Is a smooth space captured, enveloped by a striated space, or does a striated space dissolve into a smooth space, allow a smooth space to develop?'.[101] Analogously: is the ambiguously bounded physical body framed by clothes, or do clothes further problematize the body's precarious borders?

Amongst the various models offered by Deleuze and Guattari as a means of illuminating the concrete articulations of the smooth and the striated and the relations between them, is the 'technological model', wherein the multifold cultural implications of both spaces are assessed by reference to fibres, fabrics, weavings and materials of various kinds.

A fabric presents in principle a certain number of characteristics that permit us to define it as a striated space. First, it is constituted by two kinds of parallel elements; in the simplest case, there are vertical and horizontal elements, and the two intertwine, intersect perpendicularly. Second, the two kinds of elements have different functions; one is fixed, the other mobile, passing above and beneath the fixed . . . Third, a striated space of this kind is necessarily delimited, closed on at least one side; a fabric can be infinite in length but not in width, which is determined by the frame of the warp; the necessity of a back and forth motion implies a closed space . . . Finally, a space of this kind seems necessarily to have a top and a bottom . . .

Felt [on the other hand] is a supple solid product that proceeds altogether differently, as an anti-fabric. It implies no separation of threads, no intertwining, only an entanglement of fibers obtained by fulling . . . An aggregate of intrication

---

99. Gilles Deleuze and Felix Guattari (1988), *A Thousand Plateaus – Capitalism and Schizophrenia*, trans. Brian Massumi, London, pp.xii–xiii.

100. Ibid., p.474.

101. Ibid., p.275.

 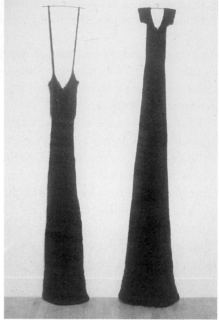

Figure 7. Emily BATES, left: *Dress*, 1993, human hair, spun and knitted; right: *Depilator*, 1994, human hair, spun and knitted. Photo: Shirley Tipping.

of this kind is . . . smooth, and contrasts point by point with the space of fabric (it is in principle infinite, open, and unlimited in every direction).[102]

To resort to some of the central concepts explored thus far, fabric could be said to lie on the side of the symbolic, the institutionalization of desire, the text of pleasure, the notion of dress as an insulating casing, anti-fabric on that of the imaginary, the lover's atopic discourse, the text of bliss, the notion of dress as a cohesive structure capable of collapsing individuality into collectivity, self into other.

Certain materials physically denote clothing's implication with smooth, non-hierarchical, amorphous, unbounded space, and hence the open-endedness of sartorial and, by extension, broadly cultural meanings and interpretations. Others aim at highlighting the function of dress as a regulatory discourse through their imposition on the body's continuum of affects of a compart-mentalizing grid. Fabric and anti-fabric are the two extreme points of a spectrum amenable to a formidable range of variables: it is vital to take into

102. Ibid., p.475–6.

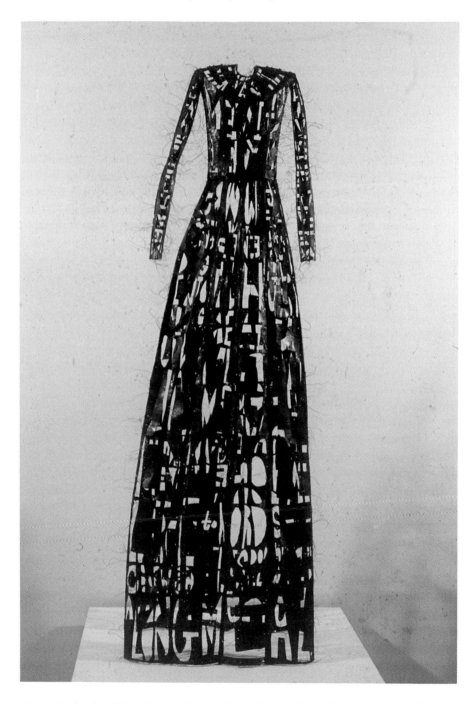

Figure 8. Lesley DILL, *Hinged Copper Poem Dress #3*, 1997, copper, steel. Private Collection, Atlanta, Georgia; Courtesy of George Adams Gallery, New York.

consideration, in this respect, not only the smooth potentialities of the striated and vice versa, but also the varying degrees of resistance to conversion into its opposite which either pole may exhibit.

> There are many interlacings, mixes between felt and fabric . . . In knitting, for example, the needles produce a striated space . . . Crochet, on the other hand, draws an open space in all directions – but still has a center. A more significant distinction would be between embroidery, with its central theme or motif, and patchwork, with its piece-by-piece construction, its infinite, successive additions of fabric. Of course, embroidery's variables and constants, fixed and mobile elements, may be of extraordinary complexity. Patchwork, for its part, may display equivalents to themes, symmetries, and resonance that approximate it to embroidery. But the fact remains that its space is not at all constituted in the same way: there is no center; its basic motif ('block') is composed of a single element; the recurrence of this element frees uniquely rhythmic values distinct from the harmonies of embroidery (in particular, in 'crazy' patchwork, which fits together pieces of varying size, shape, and color, and plays on the texture of the fabrics). . . . An amorphous collection of juxtaposed pieces that can be joined together in an infinite number of ways.[103]

If patchwork could be regarded as a felicitous metaphor for the operations of fashion and its combinatory games, dress in general, through its literal manipulation of materials, may be seen to dramatize the interplay of smooth and striated spaces, of movement, change and flux, on the one hand, and system, pattern and stasis, on the other. The language of clothing manifestly participates in both these dimensions, one of its most distinctive characteristics being precisely the ability to delimit and thus systematize the body and still unlimit subjectivity into an extensive cast of *dramatis personae*. The interaction of smoothness and striatedness in the manufacture and utilization in clothing of different materials offers an allegory of the ambivalent status of dress as both a controlling mechanism and a field of inventive play. It is not simply a question of acknowledging that the same material may be interpretable as *both* smooth *and* striated, rather than either one or the other, but also, perhaps more importantly, of recognizing the coexistence of smooth and striated elements in any one vestimentary ensemble. Indeed, if it is the case that dress is presumed capable of dissolving the individual body by connecting it to the Other, i.e. transforming singular bodies into microscales of fibres destined to become entangled with countless other corpuscles, it is also the case that it does so by enveloping the physical within fabrics based on principles of hierarchical organization. Conversely, if dress is supposed to structure the body, i.e. turn it into a striated space, it inevitably

103. Ibid., p.476.

performs this operation by relying on amorphous agglomerations and random juxtapositions.

The latter, as a process of dispersal and dissemination, is vividly reminiscent of Deleuze and Guattari's broader philosophical project, namely schizo-analysis. This is fundamentally a rejection of the process of oedipalization, aimed at redefining the unconscious as a libidinal flow, or the release of desire prior to any forms of representation and production, and hence at *deterritorializing* any normative structures centred on criteria of unity and totality, such as the family, or the state. Freudian psychoanalysis, in the context of this debate, is seen to epitomize modern Western culture's commitment to strategies of regimentation of desire, ultimately responsible for the constitution of ideology at the levels of being, creating and consuming, which pivot on principles of condensation. Indeed, the Freudian mapping out of psychic development in accordance to the oedipal triangle *Mummy/Daddy/Me* is an eminently economical way of representing the trajectory of desire and thus predictably outlining its orbit. At the same time, this schema is also symptomatic of the economic priorities fostered by bourgeois capitalism. Schizoanalysis questions the reductive, territorializing agenda carried by the Freudian model, by proposing an alternative to conventional theorizations of the body as a hierarchically structured organism, in the guise of the Body without Organs (BwO). This, argue Deleuze and Guattari, 'is not at all a notion or a concept but a practice, a set of practices. You never reach the Body without Organs, you can't reach it, you are forever attaining it, it is a limit'.[104]

The constitution of this sprawling, uncontainable body, constantly in the process of filtering the disparate energies that circulate through its margins, is facilitated by dress, if the latter's main function is understood in terms of a maximizing of the body's threshold characteristics, plurality and fluidity. Moreover, as in the discourse of clothing, in the deterritorialized world of the Body without Organs, the only prospect of consistency may be glimpsed in processes of collage, patchwork, more or less random assemblage and disassemblage:

> The question . . . is whether the pieces can fit together, and at what price. Inevitably, there will be monstrous crossbreeds. The plane of consistency would be the totality of all BwO's, a pure multiplicity of immanence, one piece of which may be Chinese, another American, another medieval, another petty perverse, but all in a movement of generalized deterritorialization in which each person takes and makes what she or he can, according to tastes she or he will have succeeded in abstracting from a

104. Ibid., p.149–50.

Self, according to a politics or strategy successfully abstracted from a given formation, according to a given procedure abstracted from its origin.[105]

The crossbreeding mentioned in the above quotation also alludes to Deleuze
and Guattari's figure of *Becoming-animal*, as a metaphor for phenomena of
production and reproduction that irreverently repudiate the primacy of
natural filiation and, as will be discussed in Chapter 3 of this project, bear
intriguing affinities to the *contagious* processes through which fashion
disseminates itself.

105. Ibid., p.157.

3

The Collective Body – Fashion, History, Commodities

This chapter proposes to examine the collective body produced by the discourse of dress, through its acts of mediation between the private and the public spheres, with a focus on the relationship between fashion and history. Central to the ensuing investigation will be the idea that fashion manifestly challenges conceptions of history based on principles of linearity and progress, and that the history-of-costume model of investigating changes in dress could productively be replaced by a method resembling Foucault's concept of *archaeology*. It will also be suggested that the more or less radical readjustments in the curve of fashion's themes and creations are not so much dependent on individual genius and other related transcendental icons as on a collective, decentred and contingent dissemination of ideals and desires, analogous to the phenomenon of *contagion*. Akin to the figure of the sprawling and deterritorialized Body-without-Organs discussed in Chapter 2, with its propensity to enfeeble the myth of the body as an organic and singular apparatus governed by an oedipal economy of desire, the concept of contagion alludes to mass phenomena that are not attributable, ultimately, to any obvious parent or origin; nor are they explainable in terms of natural growth and mimetic ramification. In the discourse of dress, the historical frame inevitably breaks up, as putatively insulating boundaries are converted into vague and questionable margins. Any effort to fashion a bounded individual endowed with some degree of signifying depth ultimately yields the picture of an unlimited and superficial culturescape, inhabited by composite subjects: everyday versions, perhaps, of the ancient shaman, the Dionysian reveller, the mythical vampire, the cyborg. As a commodity form unremittingly enmeshed in economic and ideological considerations and expectations, dress invites an assessment of this fuzzy state of affairs that could be summarized in the following question: is the *hybrid* delivered by the explosion of notions of evolutionary linearity and hierarchical reproduction an inert incarnation of post-industrial society at its least creative, or does it hold creative potentialities? Without wishing to deify dress as the final repository of

95

creativity, or indeed ignore its reifying bias, this discussion will try to evaluate the plausibly *recreative* – in both senses of the term – attributes of its discourse.

Repeated attempts to associate shifts in trends with the emergence of new authors could be read as means of forging a history of fashion compatible with quasi-Hegelian models of organic and dialectical development, and thus formalizing and justifying the random rhythms of fashion's cycles. Similar objectives would seem to motivate the thrust of many a text intent on connecting dress with the *Zeitgeist*, as evinced, for example, by Tony and Claes Lewenhaupt's *Crosscurrents*. Here, parallels are drawn between the clothing characteristic of a particular era, from Art Nouveau to the present day, and the visual arts, sculpture, architecture, furniture, cosmetics, accessories and design generally, in order to suggest that apparently separate fields of human productivity are inextricably, albeit imperceptibly, interconnected, and that there are therefore unifying, totalizing traits at the heart of any period, whose highlighting will serve to illuminate the dominant spirit of the time. In underlining affinities between the curvilinear sculpturing of 'the Art Nouveau woman of 1895' and the Brothers Thonet's 'light bentwood chairs'[1] of the same period, say; or between the 'cubistic and geometric ideals' of the fashion of the twenties and the 'geometric simplicity', combined 'with a feeling for the grandiose', of the 'Concert Hall in Stockholm from 1926';[2] between 'tough' men's suits, popular in women's fashion in the mid-nineteen-sixties, and 'the futuristic functional design' of contemporaneous 'telephones, lamps, and ashtrays';[3] or indeed between clothing's and architecture's ways of 'playing with styles'[4] in postmodern culture, *Crosscurrents* endeavours to weave the discourse of dress into a grand metanarrative wherein every element is rationally linked to every other.

Similarly, Kroeber and Richardson systematize changes in fashion, with the aim of making them appear regular, by measuring variations in particular features of female evening wear: the length of the skirt; the height of the waistline; the depth of the neckline; the width of the skirt; the width of the waist; the width of the neckline.[5] As Barthes observes, this kind of project has the effect of suggesting that, on the one hand, 'history does not intervene in the Fashion process' and 'does not produce forms' and that, on the other,

1. Tony and Claes Lewenhaupt (1989), *Crosscurrents*, trans, Jorgen Sciott, New York, p.11.
2. Ibid., p.65.
3. Ibid., p.153.
4. Ibid., p.189.
5. A. L. Kroeber and J. Richardson (1940), *Three Centuries of Women's Dress Fashion*, Berkeley and Los Angeles.

change is 'regular' and 'tends to make forms alternate according to a rational order':

> for example, the width of the skirt and the width of the waist are always in inverse relation to each other: when the one is narrow, the other is wide. In short, . . . Fashion is an orderly phenomenon, and this order is derived from Fashion itself: its evolution is on the one hand discontinuous, it proceeds only by distinct thresholds; and on the other hand it is endogenous, since it cannot be said that there is a genetic relation between a form and its historical context.[6]

In fact, it could be argued that clothing's peculiar tempos and cadences are inexplicable by reference to concepts of stability and regularity, for if it is the case that change is somewhat foreseeable, both on the functional level of material deterioration and replacement and as a concomitant of the ideological manufacturing of desire, it is also the case that this element of predictability is at all times surrounded by a halo of uncertainty and doubt, as there is no way of anticipating with confidence which particular turn the search for the new might take. Barthes, in this respect, describes the rhythm of change in fashion as eminently equivocal, as 'simultaneously unpredictable and systematic, regular and unknown, aleatory and structured'.[7]

More pertinent to a study of the relationship between dress and time than any regularizing model would seem certain approaches to history advocated by postmodernist criticism and theory. Fashion debunks the dream of a total history and totalizing narratives, it overtly flouts the demand for any clear points of origin, any closure, *telos*, or coherent and ideologically logical resolutions, owing not only to its penchant for ceaseless recycling but also to its patently anti-chronological admixture of past and present, the old and the new. The subversive potential of this demystifying process should not be underestimated, if, as Hutcheon maintains: 'To challenge the impulse to totalize is to contest the entire notion of *continuity* in history and its writing.'[8] Dress emphasizes temporal dislocation by exposing the arbitrariness of time-honoured principles of causality and purpose and the artificiality of rhetorical mechanisms and methodologies committed to making history into a homogeneous whole. Its version of time, in fact, hinges on the engendering of a network of interacting heterogeneous discourses. Relatedly, fashion self-consciously transforms both the past and the present – and, indeed, the future – into varyingly erratic and fortuitous narratives; it does

6. Roland Barthes (1990), *The Fashion System*, trans. Matthew Ward and Richard Howard, Berkeley and Los Angeles, pp.295–6.

7. Ibid., p.300.

8. Linda Hutcheon (1989), *The Politics of Postmodernism*, London, p.66.

not deny the existence of historical events, but does foreground the status of all histories as products of 'narrativizing acts'.[9]

The detemporalizing drives of the discourse of dress could be attributed to a fundamental *aporia*, whereby fashion both flattens all conceivable time-scales into an unadulterated new present that savagely repudiates the past and self-deludingly ignores contemplating the future, and yet robs the new of its novelty and the present of its presentness, by submitting the new to a logic of calculated obsolescence and the present to an unspoken obligation to encompass the past. The imperative to produce something novel makes the product, when it materially surfaces, somewhat predictable – structurally, if not at the level of its immanent characteristics- in that it was always already expected to appear onto the scene as a fresh intervention: how, then, can it be truly new, if novelty requires surprise? Similarly, all present trends being varyingly indebted to past themes and repertoires of images, fashion is in the business of simultaneously celebrating its reappropriating powers by placing the past under erasure and of implicitly acknowledging the past's omnipresence. Paradoxically, however, this structural belittling of the powers of the new and the present coincides with an ongoing pursuit of difference, based on the ability to capitalize on minimal variations of a purely diachronic order, as well as on a proclivity to anaesthetize collective memory.

> Fashion tames the new even before producing it and achieves that paradox of an unforeseeable and yet legislated 'new'; in short, we can say that Fashion domesticates the unforeseen without, however, stripping it of its unforeseen character: each Fashion is simultaneously inexplicable and regular. . . . pure Fashion is never anything but an amnesiac substitution of the present for the past. . . . In fact, Fashion postulates an achrony, a time which does not exist; here the past is shameful and the present constantly 'eaten up' by the fashion being heralded.[10]

It is as a corollary of fashion's compulsive 'achrony' that its cycles, although they addictively appeal to concepts of timelessness and universality, highlight the relative, temporary, makeshift and uncertain character of all narratives. If there is any stability anywhere, it only lies in the recognition that this has always been the case, that the role of dress does not lie in grasping and embodying the ineffable *Spirit of the Age* but rather in organizing and constructing lifestyles through the largely impromptu assembling and editing of available fragments, of thematic threads and perspectives. Some may be tempted to think of the fashion system in terms of a grandiose plot or conspiracy of the kind beloved of many a postmodern writer; this approach,

9. Ibid., p.67.
10. Barthes, *The Fashion System*, p.289.

however, would ultimately constitute yet another attempt to totalize history by subordinating the random and the inchoate to metaphysical notions of a quasi-transcendental *Plan*. As White observes, in this respect, 'the conventional historian's conceptions of history are at once a symptom and a cause of a potentially fatal cultural illness'.[11] The hybrids and variants ceaselessly churned out by the fashion industry simply cannot be viewed as aberrations in a culture otherwise governed by principles of self-identity and uncontaminated seamlessness. They do not deviate from a norm, they do not pervert a belief-system: they incarnate it. Hence, despite their apparent triviality, those protean forms may assist us in the exposure of the fallacy of attitudes to history based on the ideal of an intelligible progression towards a crystalline goal, by underlining the infectious inmixing of heterogeneous factors and thus throwing into relief the spurious status of historical linearity as both a 'symptom' of a culture impaired by its pathological yearning for rational explanations and a 'cause' of this fruitless hankering after closure.

Fashion's denaturalizing tactics may be primarily observed in its demystification of the traditional comprehension of the relationship between the present and the past, in so far as the discourse of dress self-consciously narrates in the present events of the past, narrates the present via the past, and thus enacts an open-ended dialogue between presence and absence, 'about the conjunction of present action and the past absent object of that agency',[12] which does not purport, in a Hegelian vein, to supply dialectical resolutions, but rather juxtaposes disparate temporal levels. The question it invites, therefore, is, quite simply: what do we really know about the past? Or, in Hutcheon's formulation:

> How can the present know the past it tells? We constantly narrate the past, but what are the conditions of the knowledge implied by that totalizing act of narration? Must a historical account acknowledge where it does not know for sure or is it allowed to guess? Do we know the past only through the present? Or is it a matter of only being able to understand the present through the past?[13]

Dress produces constant connections between the past and the present, but not in order to justify the relevance of the past to the present, or vice versa: rather, it founds its linkages upon such arbitrary and anachronistic premises that we are impelled to recognize a fundamental discontinuity

11. Hayden White (1978), 'The Burden of History', in idem, *Tropics of Discourse: Essays in Cultural Criticism*, Baltimore and London, p.30.
12. Hutcheon, *Politics of Postmodernism*, p.71.
13. Ibid., p.72.

between the two temporal dimensions and hence the gap between what we know, or think we know, and what we actually experience.

Towards an Archaeology of Dress

> . . . where the history of ideas tried to uncover, by deciphering texts, the secret movements of thought (its slow progression, its conflicts and retreats, the obstacles that it has overcome), I would like to reveal, in its specificity, the level of 'things said': the condition of their emergence, the forms of their accumulation and connexion, the rules of their transformation, the discontinuities that articulate them. The domain of things said is what is called the archive: the role of archaeology is to analyse that archive.[14]

Foucault's elaboration of the possibility of an investigative method that explores relations within and between discursive fields offers an attractive means of looking at the 'history' of clothing without recourse to the kinds of models outlined in the preceding section that insist on continuity, development and the location of origins. Foucault is aware of the possibilities of employment of his method – in his closing remarks in *The Archaeology of Knowledge* he briefly suggests fields in which his model might be applied, and his inclusion of painting is instructive:

> . . . [archaeological analysis] would not set out to show that the painting is a certain way of 'meaning' or 'saying' that is peculiar in that it dispenses with words. It would try to show that, at least in one of its dimensions, it is discursive practice that is embodied in techniques and effects. In this sense, the painting is not a pure vision that must then be transcribed into the materiality of space; nor is it a naked gesture whose silent and eternally empty meanings must be freed from subsequent interpretations. It is shot through . . . with the positivity of a knowledge (*savoir*).[15]

The comments on painting have many resonances for a possible archaeology of dress; his setting aside of the view that visual embodiment is simply speaking without words enables us to dismantle the position commonly articulated that regards clothing as a relatively simple language, for example in this remark by Alison Lurie, 'by the time we meet and converse we have already spoken to each other in an older and more universal tongue'.[16] This

14. Michel Foucault (1972), *The Archaeology of Knowledge*, trans. Alan Sheridan Smith, London, back cover.
15. Ibid., p.194.
16. Alison Lurie, (1982), *The Language of Clothes*, London, p.3.

is not to deny that clothing and language are intimately related, as the discussion of Barthes in Chapter 2 bears out, or that what is consciously or unconsciously 'expressed' by clothes is worth investigation, as evidenced by the consideration of psychoanalysis in Chapter 1, but rather to affirm that the material existence of clothing beyond, or aside from, its relation to its wearer pushes the linguistic comparison past the equation of dress and conversation in a more universal tongue. Foucault marks the assumptions upon which archaeological analysis rests in his commentary on authorship:

> . . . writing has freed itself from the dimension of expression. Referring only to itself, but without being restricted to the confines of its interiority, writing is identified with its own unfolded exteriority . . . In writing, the point is not to manifest or exalt the act of writing, nor is it to pin a subject within language; it is, rather, a question of creating a space into which the writing subject constantly disappears.[17]

If we substitute clothing for writing in this passage, we can see how it is possible to retain the language/dress relation without assuming the primacy of the author/wearer in the attribution of 'meaning'; in a useful co-incidence of terms, clothes do not 'pin' a subject, but create just such a space as he suggests, into which the wearing subject is always disappearing. Foucault's use of the phrase 'things said', and subsequently the 'statement', to denote the contents of the archive is premised on this assumption of the nature of language, and language is the model through which he goes on to expand his method.

His insistence on the material nature of the statement is clear: 'Could one speak of a statement if a voice had not articulated it, if a surface did not bear its signs, if it had not become embodied in a sense-perceptible element, and if it had not left some trace – if only for an instant – in someone's memory or in some space?';[18] yet for him the statement is an enunciation that is 'neither exclusively linguistic nor entirely material'.[19] This formulation is a neat summary of many of the ideas about dress previously outlined: the actual existence of clothing as physical object is undeniable, it is to be seen and touched everywhere on the planet, in however vestigial a form in some societies. Its materiality is crucial, its functionality equally so; but it also exceeds these qualities by its linguistic scope in ways memorably suggested by Roland Barthes. As we have shown, it is an eminently hybrid item that

---

17. Michel Foucault (1984), 'What is an Author?' in Paul Rabinow (ed.), *The Foucault Reader*, London, p.102.

18. Foucault, *Archaeology of Knowledge*, p.100.

19. Ibid., p.86.

speaks of us, for us and about us, and connects with our physical existence as individual and collective bodies in profound ways. To define a particular garment or set of garments as a statement in this Foucauldian sense is not to limit it either to a place in the history of costume, where it features as an element in a series, with an exclusive focus on the development of its cut, colour and shape; or to the realm of language, where it becomes impossible to appreciate its sensual qualities; but to attempt to take account of all of these modalities.

Foucault delineates certain principles of the statement; exteriority, rarity and accumulation, which relate directly to dress as it has hitherto been considered. He refers to the ambiguous 'visibility' of the statement: 'It is like the over-familiar that constantly eludes one; those familiar transparencies, which, although they conceal nothing in their density, are nevertheless not entirely clear.'[20] This captures something of Freud's notion of the uncanny in its slightly uneasy positioning on the edge of the familiar, and reminds us of the vexed place that dress occupies in the dynamic of the psyche; but it also illuminates the presence of clothing as possibly the most over-familiar aspect of everyday existence. It implies that clothing needs to be de-familiarized in order to be understood more immediately, but that even a radical refocusing will not quite bring it into view. Despite its quotidian reality, dress is not 'entirely clear', as the huge collection of discourses that have continuously embraced it testifies. It has been the subject of every conceivable kind of interpretation, instruction, legal requirement, analysis and depiction, without any final clarity on its purpose or proper deployment ever having been reached. Yet it does not conceal secrets: refusing the boundary between inner and outer, it is wholly *exterior* in character, all possible readings are available on its surface. As such it resists 'the historical description of things said [that] is shot through with the opposition of interior and exterior; and wholly directed by a desire to move from the exterior'.[21] As will be explored further in Chapter 4, the exteriority of clothing is that of 'deep surface', a continuous play of signifiers that has no hidden signified.

This principle of exteriority is linked to that of rarity. By recourse to Saussure's terms *langue* and *parole*, Foucault suggests that statements are always 'in deficit'[22] and therefore rare, because the combinations possible in the *langue* as the totality of the language far exceed those actually enacted in the *parole*, or the individual examples of that language in use. The deficit

20. Ibid., p.111.
21. Ibid., p.120.
22. Ibid., p.119.

is a crucial notion in fashion: as statements exist at the limit point between what is said and what is unsaid, so clothing and combinations of clothes occupy the same realm; the anxiety of the border between the worn and the not-worn is shown in the thousands of pages of fashion advice: what to wear with what, how to make the ingenious combinations of expensive and inexpensive, as well as the frequently articulated individual sense of having chosen the 'wrong' outfit. The deficit haunts the clothing worn, and is exacerbated by the attention focused on it, much in the manner of a Lacanian lack. The arguably false anxiety thus created is flouted and flaunted by designers deriving the 'mismatch' from street styles such as the 'grunge' look of the early 1990s, where delicate skirts are worn with heavy boots and ill-fitting garments deliberately put together in clashing colours. Though this apparently 'uncovers' the deficit, it still speaks of the not-worn, and the deficit remains as large as ever. As this example demonstrates, the principle of exteriority still obtains, 'the enunciative domain is identical with its own surface',[23] the absence of the combinations never made does not constitute a whole field of the hidden or repressed, but 'it is a distribution of gaps, voids, absences, limits, divisions'[24] that produces the statement as it exists; it is not an opposite, but part of the whole.

Just as the gaps and divisions can be accepted as existing in and of themselves, the acknowledgement of discontinuity in temporal terms is vital in archaeological analysis. The third of Foucault's terms, accumulation or additivity, offers a further element in the rejection of the totalizing narrative of the history of ideas or the history of costume: '. . . the discontinuous was both the given and the unthinkable: The raw material of history, which presented itself in the form of dispersed events . . . had to be rearranged, reduced, effaced in order to reveal the continuity of events. Discontinuity was the stigma of temporal dislocation that it was the historian's task to remove from history.'[25] Archaeology endeavours to free itself from the search for origins, or the detection of return to those origins, through its analysis of the relations between statements and of the gaps that represent the 'between'. In a 'history' of fashion freed from insistent linearity and continuity we can accept individual examples of dress as statements, making them capable of legibility without reducing them to isolated and unconnected events. Dress '. . . like every event is unique, yet subject to repetition, transformation and reactivation . . . it is linked not only to the situations that provoke it, and to the consequences that it gives rise to, but at the same

23. Ibid.
24. Ibid.
25. Ibid., p.8.

time, and in accordance with a quite different modality, to the statements that precede and follow it.'[26]

Fashion therefore posits itself as one of the many partial archives or libraries of traces and indirect representations through which the subject may learn something about a past that is simply not graspable outside representations, any more than the body or indeed the relationship between the body and its clothes are. Fashion in the present is peppered with intertextual and paratextual cross-references to past ideas, styles and motifs, which give it the characteristics of collage and, implicitly, are inimical to the myths of seamlessness and continuity treasured by classic realism in all forms of cultural production, no less than by traditional historiography: 'In the spectacular world of fashion, history is frantically and fantastically restaged in any, or in all its moments, all at once, as the now detemporalized past ever immediately and instantaneously present.'[27]

Dress, by analogy with postmodern approaches to history such as Foucault's, may, as a result, both foster and dramatize a 'willingness to confront heroically the dynamic and disruptive forces in contemporary life. The historian serves no-one well by constructing a specious continuity between the present world and that which preceded it.'[28] Given fashion's emphatically theatrical character, the heroic stance referred to by White in the above quotation could be taken to allude not so much to a penchant for stoical resilience as to the subject's disposition to move in and out of a plethora of fictional roles, personas, stage heroes and heroines. The task required of this multifaceted creature is akin to the one outlined by Eco in his assessment of medieval culture, as an 'immense work of bricolage balanced among nostalgia, hope, and despair' and linked to a process of 'constant translation and reuse'.[29] Baudrillard likewise highlights the interminability of history in a register that vividly evokes not only the operations of fashion but the very functionings of the human body: '. . . and all these things will continue to unfold slowly, tediously, recurrently, in that hysteresis of everything which, like nails and hair, continue to grow after death'.[30]

The processes of incessant translation and deferred action, discontinuous reshuffling, mediation and narrativization described by these critics, amongst many others, are central to one of fashion's most prominent traits and no

26. Ibid., p.28.

27. Gail Faurschou (1990), 'Obsolescence and Desire: Fashion and the Commodity Form', in H. J. 28. Silverman (ed.), *Postmodernism – Philosophy and the Arts, Continental Philosophy III*, London, p.235.

28. White, 'The Burden of History', p.25.

29. Umberto Eco (1987), *Travels in Hyperreality*, trans. William Weaver, London, p.84.

30. Jean Baudrillard (1994), *The Illusion of the End*, trans. Chris Turner, Cambridge, p.116.

less striking paradoxes, i.e. its tendency to glorify the cult of radical *innovation*, on the one hand, and that of malleable *renovation*, on the other. An illustration of this incongruity may be found in Devlin's account of developments in fashion photography since the 1920s. The text is pervaded by an uncanny feeling of *déjà vu*, as each new decade is ushered in as the harbinger of unprecedented transformations and shifts of perspective. Yet change is constructed as a constant whose regular recurrence somewhat pre-empts the possibility of authentic novelty; at the same time, its constancy serves to de-historicize the specific contexts within which the new is supposed to manifest itself and to reinforce ideals of continuity and ideological stability. So, for instance, the 1940s are associated with the dramatic changes brought about by the war, to which fashion is expected to respond through its flair for converting the squalid into the fabulous:

> *Vogue's* readership soared during the war. Its photographs of women still managing to look marvelous while making do, the conviction that fashion was an essential part of life, war or not, the refusal of its editors to be disheartened by new restrictions and regulations, supplied not only guidance and glamor but also a reassuring sense of continuity and civilized living... A new American look in fashion was created, totally confident, self-contained, with a spirit of its own.[31]

Fashion's role in the 1940s, then, is equated with the ability to metamorphose a depressing present into glittering memories of a more prosperous and glamorous past. Wilson corroborates this point by reminding us that in spite of the infiltration of female clothing by the traditionally male cult of the uniform, 'frivolous, flowery, veiled hats (hats were never rationed) and precious silk stockings'[32] were retained, very possibly as vestiges of better times, both gone and to come. The 1950s, on the other hand, are said to embody the ideal of change in the guise of a bold leap into future possibilities:

> The 1950s were a time of new beginnings, of recovery and discovery. Years of rationing were over, and a deprived population, on both sides of the Atlantic, set about becoming consumers, reaching out eagerly towards a prodigal future. Many changes that the war had brought had become permanent. Aspirations to self-awareness and self-fulfilment, which were to become real quests in the following decades, were already evident, and traditional standards were being questioned and discarded. .... Fashion taboos were broken with relish.[33]

31. Polly Devlin (1984), *The Vogue Book of Fashion Photography*, pp.72–3.
32. Elizabeth Wilson (1985), *Adorned in Dreams*, London, p.44.
33. Devlin, *Fashion Photography*, pp.92–3.

But the taboo-breaking process does not stop here and, only a few pages later, it is the following decade that is acclaimed as the initiator of unprecedented changes, particularly in its drastic revision of notions of femininity and female beauty. The *New Woman*, it would seem, is an eminently brindled being: 'on the one hand, the glamorous, recherchee, poised lady; on the other, the free, freaky individualist dressing in whatever mood took her. Gradually the two images came together to make one amazing composite creature.'[34] The apparent new freedom achieved by fashion in the 1960s is the theme of Richard Goldstein's ecstatic proclamation that: 'Now Beauty is free. Liberated from hang-ups over form and function, unencumbered by tradition or design. A freaky goddess . . . She is larger than fantasy and loftier than modesty . . .'.[35]

The celebration of the New Woman operates as something of a refrain in the endless performance of fashion's paean to change. Woman, it is repeatedly suggested, keeps changing as fashion changes, and as each new decade pits itself against the preceding one in an effort to erase the past and announce the advent of exclusive novelty, woman, too, is constantly remoulded. Indeed, the New Woman had already been the object of enthusiastic acclaim back in the Thirties: 'From dolls, the women of fashion have become individual works of art. The creed of modern beauty is personality.'[36] The fabrication by the clothing industry of this protean figure as a recurring motif automatically entails the continual resurgence of the notion of self-construction. For example, Devlin identifies the hard work of self-beautification as the distinctive feature of fashionable women in the 1930s: 'to be a well-dressed woman . . . was a time-consuming business involving serious dedication, endless fittings, and infinite changes of hat and costume'.[37] However, a description of *Nouvelle Couture* in the Nineties to be found in *Harpers and Queen* closely and somewhat eerily echoes the characteristics attributed by Devlin to the pre-war period:

> *Nouvelle Couture* is the catch-phrase of the Nineties. What does it mean? It means that the whole business of designing clothes which private customers will then have made to measure has not only revived, it is thriving. Why? Not only have the margins between luxe ready-to-wear and couture become narrower and narrower, but there are more rich women who are prepared not only to pay for something made expressly for them, but are also willing to spend time on the six or seven fittings a complicated suit may take.[38]

34. Ibid., p.149.
35. (*Vogue*, 1968), Ibid., p.142.
36. (*Vogue*, 1934), Ibid., p.120.
37. Ibid., p.46.
38. *Harpers & Queen*, March 1990.

Changing characterizations of the New Woman ideal are often associated by historians of costume with the individual contributions made by particular designers, arguably in an attempt, as suggested earlier, to give shape to fashion's amorphousness by recourse to notions of authorship and origin. So Bond, for example, attributes the creation of the New Woman of the early 1900s to the genius of Paul Poiret, with his claim to have liberated women from the tyranny of the corset through the introduction of dresses with high and loosely marked waists, allowing the shapes of thighs and legs to show clearly, and his popularization of vivid colours and accessories such as scarves and turbans.[39] No less importantly, the cult of the New Woman is closely bound up with an equally recurrent topos, i.e. the alternation of trends intent on highlighting their emancipating, even transgressive, thrust and of imminently ensuing backlashes. Bradfield, for example, notes that the early nineteenth century signals a liberating move away from the constraints of the tight-fitting corset, the dome-shaped hooped petticoat and materials such as stiff brocades and heavy silks, marked by the triumph of white muslin gowns across all social classes, the discarding of stays and petticoats and the reduction of underwear to a minimum. The momentous impact of this trend is amply documented by magazines of the period: *The Lady's Monthly Museum* of June 1802, for instance, gives a contemporary opinion of 'female demi-nudity . . . the close, all white, shroud looking, ghostly chemise undress of the ladies, who seem to glide like spectres, with their shrouds wrapped tight about their forms' and again, in March 1803, it states that: 'it really was as much of hazard of health, as it was trespass against modesty, to come into public en chemise'. In June of the same year, the same publication humorously points out that: 'a dress may now be made so exceedingly fine and thin, that it may be carried in a pocket-book or conveyed by the two-penny post to any part of the town'.[40]

However, as Bradfield goes on to point out, by 1820 tight lacing is already making its way back into fashion, and between 1835 and 1870 we witness an ostentatious and flagrant return to dresses with tiny waists and billowing skirts extended over hooped foundations, compounded with the use of stiff horsehair skirts worn below an ever-increasing number of petticoats or, at a later stage, of underskirts held on whalebone hoops. Between 1870 and 1900, moreover, developments in technology, such as the advent of the sewing machine, encourage an abundance of frills, flounces, pleating and ruching motifs, which once again lead to a veritable obsession with the width of the female waist, to be emphasized by the juxtaposition of plain tight-fitting

39. David Bond (1981), *The Guinness Guide to 20th Century Fashion*, London.
40. Nancy Bradfield (1975), *Costume in Detail 1730–1930*, London, p.86.

bodices and an explosion of trimmings and draperies from the waist down; in 1897, the tailor T. H. Holding emphatically states that: 'You cannot pay a woman a greater compliment than to make her so tight in the waist that she is miserable.'[41]

The examples offered above, though necessarily selective and perhaps arbitrarily so, have hopefully succeeded in illustrating fashion's paradoxical cultivation of apparently incompatible models, which inevitably revolve around its schizophrenic attitude to time: restless change/novelty and infinite recycling; specificity/innovation and timeless perfection/genius; freedom/ autonomy and uniformity. In contemporary, postmodern societies, these paradoxes are further problematized by the simultaneous encouragement of a notion of the clothed self as an unrepeatable work of art and the subjection of both the body and its clothes to the logic of potentially ceaseless mechanical reproduction. The section that follows will concentrate on the present culturescape in an attempt to evaluate some of the repercussions of these and other related inconsistencies.

Production and Reproduction

Today, of all commodities, the fashion object initially appears the most superfluous, transitory, and especially trivial – infinitely distanced from its historical origins in the magic and mystic of ceremonial costume and bodily adornment.[42]

The volatile nature of fashion would seem to make it an ideal tool for the exploration of the transience and decentredness of postmodernity as a whole. Dress incarnates, perhaps more pointedly than any other contemporary mode of production and consumption, an ethos of endless and vertiginous permuta-tion and recombination; reappropriation, repetition and recycling; imitation, simulation and dissimulation. But if, in this way, fashion underscores the commodifying thrust of late capitalism by magnifying the orbit of its reproductive modalities in what could be deemed a totalizing and reactionary move, it also, as was indicated in the preceding section, retains subversive potentialities by challenging the concept of history as an evolutionary trajectory. It would be quite misleading, of course, to assume that fashion's blatantly theatrical metamorphosis of all objects into beautified simulacra, which respect no historical boundaries and mock any attempt to ground meaning in anything deeper than the ephemerality of exchange value, is an utterly new phenomenon. Arguably, there has never been a time or place

41. Ibid., p.288.

in which the discourse of dress has adhered exclusively to the logic of use value. This idea may be investigated further with reference to the intriguing hypothesis that clothing may have found its inception in the practices of ritual and magic.

Many fashion historians seem to subscribe to Laver's tripartite mapping out of the possible motivations lying behind the wearing of garments, based on the Utility Principle, the Hierarchical Principle and the Seduction Principle. In this perspective, human beings are supposed to don clothes which either make them feel comfortable, or help them assert or disguise their identities, or aim at attracting erotic attention. This influential theory does not preclude, however, the supposition still popular amongst scores of anthropologists that the original aim of dress was magical and that clothing was accordingly utilized as a means of magnetizing positive animistic energies and warding off negative ones. There are instances, as Lurie emphasizes, of both contagious magic, as in the wearing of a 'necklace of shark's teeth' meant to endow the wearer with strength, and of sympathetic magic, as in the wearing of 'a girdle of cowrie shells', which 'resemble the female sexual parts' and are thus believed 'to increase or preserve fertility'.[43] Magical garments survive today in several forms: advertisements tell us that certain items of clothing will make us capable of performing successfully in a variety of contexts, ranging from sports activities, through business, to sexuality; many ornaments retain talismanic qualities; and even ordinary garments 'may be treated as if they had *mana*', as in the notion of the 'lucky' dress.[44]

Of particular relevance to the present discussion is the idea that the possible association between dress and magic serves to blur the margin between use value and exchange value: although ceremonial garments endowed with spiritual and mystical attributes may not have been primarily or exclusively subjugated to economic imperatives, they surely must have accrued meaning from something other than sheer functionality, and hence participated in symbolic circuits of exchange. What dress highlights is precisely the human proclivity and ability to extricate objects from the confines of practical instrumentality and consequently invest them with figurative connotations. A garment is, in this sense, more or at least other than an object: it operates as a metonym for an exchange, a dialogue or contract between the individual and the collective.

However, argues Faurschou, the type of exchange entailed by traditional ritual and its vestimentary codes is clearly not coterminous with the type of

42. Faurschou in Silverman, *Postmodernism*, p.234.
43. Lurie, *The Language of Clothes*, p.29.
44. Ibid., p.30.

exchange involved in commodity capitalism, since in the latter scenario, 'the exchange relation, which is a strictly quantitative one (usually taking place at the checkout counter), hardly allows for symbolic investment or the generation of meaning'.[45] The issue would seem to revolve, at this point, around the question of whether or not the discourse of dress in contemporary culture may still hold scope for creative intervention or whether, in fact, it is completely subsumed to the reifying logic of the post-industrial apparatus. The former position is sustainable by recourse to the ambivalent concept of *fetishism*. In keeping with the ethos of capitalism, and tuned to its fluttering pulse of alterations and alternations, clothes are fetishized according to their material value, their marginal differences, or the *frisson* of planned extinction, as though fetishization could engender stability out of a heady vortex of change. But they are also fetishes of a different order, capable of facilitating what, in Freudian terms, could be termed a *disavowal*, i.e. the splitting between knowledge and what the subject wants to believe or perform, as a means of narcissistically protecting the self from the non-self ('I know, but . . .'). This process does not merely amount to a more or less willed act of misrecognition, such as would be encapsulated in the self-deluding statement: 'I know I am not buying, consuming or embodying uniqueness and related ideals, but I can live as if I didn't know it.' In fact, in so far as the disavowing subject's fetishistic narcissism splits the self into conflicting personas, it also enables it to embrace an eminently liminal role and outlook, based on the self-conscious appropriation of a condition of displacement and forever deferred satisfaction, akin to the 'heroic' confrontation of instability described by White. In Burgin's words: 'The "postmodernist" subject must live with the fact that not only are its languages "arbitrary" but it is itself an "effect of language", a precipitate of the very symbolic order of which the humanist subject supposed itself to be the master. "Must live with", but nevertheless may live "as if" condition were other than it is.'[46]

At its most productive, the disclaiming move promulgated by fashion fetishism could lead to a contemplation of the mutual interdependence of things as they are and of alternative scenarios, to be inaugurated not by the fulfilment of utopian dreams projected on to an indeterminate future, but rather by forms of resistance to common sense and by a denaturalization of the *doxa* in the here-and-now. The ability of clothes to function as alternative, ambiguous fetishes that ultimately resist classification would seem to be corroborated by their radical departure from the concept of the fetish as originally defined by Freud, i.e. something 'irreducibly and irreplaceably

45. Faurschou in Silverman, *Postmodernism*, p.237.
46. Victor Burgin (1986), *The End of Art Theory*, London, p.49.

unique; moreover, it has a punctual quality, it is not in any way diffused or extended in space and time, it is as if framed'.[47] This character portrait is evidently inapplicable to the fashion fetish, given the latter's aversion to any totalizing strategy: in fact, it is never 'unique', is patently 'diffused' both temporally and spatially and is, above all, unamenable to 'framing'.

It could be argued, of course, that fashion is still implicated in a unifying programme, as evinced, for example, by today's imperative to co-ordinate one's environment to the point that clothes will mirror and be mirrored by the rest of the world one inhabits, in a manner reminiscent of Leibniz's monadic universe. Paradoxically, however, this total-look ethos is forged out of atomized entities, derived from a stridently discontinuous phantas-magoria of contexts and styles, which patently subvert the possibility of systematic harmonization. There are no pure, self-contained and hermetically sealed objects, as everything is always contaminated, infiltrated and thus redefined by something else. In this respect, the manoeuvre towards cultural deterritorialization that characterizes contemporary fashion, perhaps more blatantly than was the case in the past, could be associated with post-modernism's interdisciplinary import, by contrast with the modernist desire for self-referential autonomy, as formulated, for example, by Greenberg:

> What had to be exhibited and made explicit was that which was unique and irreducible not only in art in general, but also in each particular art. Each art had to determine, through the operations peculiar to itself, the effects peculiar and exclusive to itself. . . . It quickly emerged that the unique and proper area of competence of each art coincided with all that was unique to the nature of its medium. The task of self-criticism became to eliminate from the effects of each art any and every effect that might conceivably be borrowed from or by the medium of any other art. Thereby each art would be rendered 'pure', and in its 'purity' find the guarantee of its standards of quality as well as of its independence.[48]

In undermining the logocentric devotion to the belief in the existence of singular motivating presences behind representation – author, tradition, structure, genius, *Zeitgeist* – the language of dress underscores the diffusion of meaning as an effect rather than the origin of interpretation. Creativity is not a question of producing isolated objects in an isolated medium, but rather consists of a series of interlocking, yet divergent, operations, performed within a network of signifying practices that cannot be limited to or by a specific medium.

47. Ibid., p.44.
48. Clement Greenberg (1982), 'Modernist Painting', in Francis Frascina and Charles Harrison (eds), *Modern Art and Modernism: A Critical Anthology*, London, pp.5–6.

The intertextual unspecificity of fashion, intensified by postmodern approaches to both history and (re)production, implicitly affects the relationship between the public and the private, in so far as its cross-fertilizing tendencies involve transactions and negotiations not only amongst different media, techniques and methodologies, but also amongst individual and collective facets of experience: for example, it is arduous, if at all possible, to ascertain to what extent the ego images promoted by fashion are supposed to fulfil personal aspirations – at an imaginary level – and to what – on the plane of the symbolic – they incarnate culture-wide epistemic dominants. Ryle relates the relationship between the private and the public spheres to the mind versus body binary opposition, as one of the pivotal dichotomies cherished by Western thought, particularly in its role as the staple of a dualistic (Cartesian) world-view: 'A person . . . lives through two collateral histories, one consisting of what happens in and to his body, the other consisting of what happens in and to his mind. The first is public, the second private. The events in the first history are events in the physical world, those in the second are events in the mental world.'[49]

Moreover, 'the transactions between the episodes of the private history and the public history remain mysterious'.[50] Although in the discourse of clothing, too, the relationship between the private and the public may appear 'mysterious', this is not so much due to the two dimensions' ultimate incommensurability, as to their inextricable interconnection: no knowledge may be gleaned from or about the one independently of the other. In its function as a nebulous margin, dress precludes any neat differentiations, not least owing to its proclivity to hide the individual body's lack by playing the role of a collectively intelligible appendage, yet, at the same time, to reveal that lack by foregrounding its own all-pervasiveness and the flimsiness of the physical frame it cloaks. The structure to which dress appends itself may fancy itself as replete and securely bounded, but this structure's daily dependence on multifarious ancillaries and accessories unmasks a fundamental absence. Therefore, clothing is neither merely decorative nor indispensable in purely logical terms, but – paradoxically, perhaps – exhibits some of the features ascribed by Eagleton to the character of 'high culture' in postmodern society: it represents 'a properly marginal presence, marking the border where that society both encounters and exiles its own disabling absences'.[51]

As an omnipresent highlighter of the coexistence of presence and absence, plenitude and lack, concealment and revelation, dress contributes in vital

49. Gilbert Ryle (1963), *The Concept of Mind*, London, p.13.
50. Ibid., p.14.
51. Terry Eagleton (1984), *The Function of Criticism*, London, pp.91–2.

ways to the collective conceptualization of corporeal existence. Three main models seem worthy of investigation, in this context. Firstly, it is necessary to address the question of desire as a phenomenon *vis-à-vis* which the body is construed as lacking and incomplete, its yearnings being proverbially insatiable. Yet desire cannot be totally demonized, as this is what is conventionally held to trigger the body's potential as a useful reproductive machine. These two apparently incompatible perspectives are ideologically reconciled by a system that emphasizes the mutual interdependence of the body's longings and the imperatives of reproduction, by compelling the former to replicate the latter. In this scenario, the individual body must learn how to channel its drives, fantasies and impulses into collective structures of production and reproduction. This first model of conceptualization is therefore based on the principle of *reflection*. The function of dress is to mediate between private desires and public expectations by means of collective objects that can be assimilated to the individual body's desires, to the point that although that body is not truly autonomous in selecting what it desires, it may still come to regard those objects as mirror images of itself. In the first movement, external objects elicit subjective desires; in the second, the subject narcissistically misrecognizes its desires as stemming from the resemblance that the objects bear to its own fantasized self ('I desire you because you mirror *me*').

This self-delusion may fuel the subject's dream of the sealed body: threatened, albeit unconsciously, by the intimation that dress might be more tangible and enduring, in collective/symbolic terms, than the body itself, the subject, like the Lacanian child, identifies with dress as the source of plenitude and permanence, yet disavows its own subordination to dress by choosing to see it as an incarnation of personal desires.

The second model of bodily structuring is related to disciplinary mechanisms that encompass elements of both self-control and external management and that spring, fundamentally, from the body's tormented sense of its own ephemerality and uncertainty as to the scope of its powers and the degree to which its performance may be reliably predicted. The individual subject's alliance to collective fashions may neutralize the body's anxieties about the precariousness of its boundaries and ontological transitoriness by providing an illusion of predictability. By linking the private to the public, clothes frame the body as a putatively foreseeable component of a predictable whole. Paradoxically, however, this socializing action does not truly harmonize the private and the public: in so far as dress delimits the body by appealing to the ideal of individuality, it effects a separation, whereby the clothed body performs amongst others but not *with* them. Moreover, the body may become disassociated from itself, too, if it is the case that the coherent and continuous status to which it aspires may only result from its participation in communal games. In this scenario, dress collectivizes the individual, yet simultaneously detaches it from others and from itself. The *community* forged by the fashion industry is thus a Janus-faced phenomenon, which mirrors adroitly the double-bind mentalities of postmodern culture at large. As Faurschou observes: 'the power and seduction of consumption lies in the degree to which it establishes itself as the only form of collective activity in which the atomized individual of bourgeois society can participate. . . . The collection of objects thus dissimulates the disappearance of the collectivity of subjects.'[52] The intermittent appearance and disappearance of notions of both individuality and communality may be related to the fact that the translation of the *contingent* (individual, unclothed) body into a *predictable* (collective, clothed) body via framing strategies opens up not one unequivocal vista, but rather a scene of indeterminacy and undecidability. Indeed, it both separates the individual from others by promoting the cult of distinctiveness, for example through the glorification of personal practices of choice, self-adornment, image-maintenance, and so on, and detaches the body from itself: for how can the subject come to know itself once it has been severed from the collective discourses that alone would endow it with signifying stature?

The third model to be considered is based on the idea of the subject's *relationality* to others and to itself. This entails two fundamental questions: do we have a sense of our private bodies as self-contained entities or do we only exist by virtue of a reciprocality of definitions? Do we identify with or disengage ourselves from our own carnality? If, with regard to reflection, dress nourishes the illusion of individual autonomy and, with regard to discipline, it both compels communality and isolates the body through dividing practices, where relationality is concerned its primary function is to highlight the body's very dependence upon the clothes it wears, without this dependence's necessarily amounting to reification. If, in the instances of both reflection and discipline, dress is itself a body of sorts, owing to the incidence of either narcissistic identification or disassociating alienation, in the case of relationality, the body itself is conceived of as dress, as a decorporealized structure fully reliant on its external casing for the purposes of relating to both itself and others. The sartorialization of physicality is, after all, quite an ancient trope: 'The body as "garment" was a widely used metaphor in Antiquity. Gnostic writers [for example] often made use of the image, to underscore the disassociation of the person from the physical form.'[53] To adopt a nihilistic stance and assume that dress cannibalizes the

52. Faurschou in Silverman, *Postmodernism*, p.242
53. M.A. Williams (1989), 'Divine Image – Prison of Flesh: Perceptions of the Body in Ancient Gnosticism', in M. Feher, R. Naddaff and N. Tazi (eds), *Fragments For a History of the Human Body, Part One*, New York, p.136.

body, or indeed reduces it to an inert package, complete with best-before and sell-by dates, would, however, be quite inappropriate, as these metaphors could conceivably apply in the realm of the imaginary, but not in that of the symbolic, where dematerialization has always already occurred. Dress does not deprive the body of its corporeality, therefore, but rather emphasizes the processes of symbolic mediation through which the body is translated into a culturally significant, i.e. signifying, apparatus. The present argument is willing to support Benthall's assertion that: 'Until we become aware of the body's power and resourcefulness, we will not feel a sufficiently educated outrage against its manipulation and exploitation. Rather than campaigns for literacy and numeracy, we may need a campaign for corporacy.'[54] However, it must be stressed that without an understanding of the inevitably mediated and hence rhetorically displaced character of the body in society, any image of 'corporacy' would amount to yet one more mirage, yet one more collective hallucination.

Unlike less ambiguous forms of organization of subjective desires, dress may, at its most theatrically productive, capitalize on the reality of the body's contingency rather than perpetuate or merely anaesthetize the fear of the unpredictable. Fashion's instability, or, as suggested earlier, its ironical marriage of impermanence and recurrence by means of its concurrent valorization of eternal standards of taste and decorum and immanent admixtures of styles, eclectic citations and parodies, may ultimately facilitate the ascendancy of what Frank evocatively describes as the 'communicative body': its 'essential quality is that it is a body *in process* of creating itself . . . The body's contingency is no longer its problem but its possibility.'[55]

It is precisely such a grasp of the body's contingency and unquantifiable potentialities that suggests an analogy between fashion and the phenomenon of *contagion*. Clothes, of course, may seem to militate against contamination and infection, as metaphors for the infiltration of the self by the other, in so far as they visibly contain the body as material barriers. Whilst the naked body would appear to dissolve all boundaries, its many orifices suggesting both the relentless oozing out of corporeal elements and the body's equally unstoppable absorption of extraneous matter, clothes may be deemed capable of insulating the body from its surroundings. The mutual transmission of affects that characterizes, in various forms, the phenomenon of contagion would appear to be kept at bay by fashion's many-shaped armours. On

54. J. Benthall (1976), *The Body Electric: Patterns of Western Industrial Culture*, London, p.79.

55. A. W. Frank (1991), 'For a Sociology of the Body: An Analytical Review', in M. Featherstone, M. Hepworth and B. Turner (eds), *The Body: Social Process and Cultural Theory*, London, p.79.

another level, however, clothes are deeply implicated in the dynamics of allegorical infection. Indeed, they play a prominent role in processes of personality formation by transmitting to the body that wears them certain stylistic traits and, concomitantly, a particular identity. In its relationship with dress, the body is an eminently osmotic shell: when we adopt certain garments, we do not confine ourselves to *knowing* their qualities and attributes, since, through direct physical contact, we also *assimilate* them, we make them our *flesh*.

It is widely recognized that whole cultures have defined themselves allegorically through vestimentary practices, based on principles of inclusion, exclusion and symbolic exchange, as ritual dramatizations of spiritual and mythical concepts akin to sacrificial and redemptive ceremonies. It could be argued that in the simultaneously fully saturated and hollow hypersociality of contemporary culture, there is no room for such grandiose allegorizations of dress. Yet fashion still harks back to those religious or magical practices by underscoring the body's penchant for ceaseless transformation, by allowing it to disappear whilst apparently defining its form and sphere of action, and by erasing the dividing line between the body and its environment, as though the body were no longer opposed to the outside world but could absorb it, by *infection*, into its own shifting appearances. This fizzling out of carnality into a gallery of depthless portraits is not necessarily a form of alienation, if this term is meant to describe the loss of an essential nature, since dress, by encouraging us to make and remake ourselves over and again, renders the very idea of essence quite absurd. Fashion's detractors accuse it of being instrumental to the emplacement of a nihilistic postmodern world view; however, its relativizing discourses may help us realize that what we lack is not the experience of plenitude – which was probably a utopian illusion in the first place – but rather the ability to face to our own inner diversity and plurality, our foreignness in and from ourselves.

The prospect that dress may acquire the status of flesh as the body's deputy also intimates the possibility that if dress, as an artificial addition to the body, could be seen as the body's other, the body itself, as a symbolic category inconceivable outside representation, could be regarded as the other of dress, as a supplementary entity that, having been banned from discourse, still lingers on the edges of visibility, haunting the space from which it has been ostracized. Dress may then be said both to compete with the body's decarnalized frame, by asserting its own materiality as an alternative to the body's own, and yet also to operate as a kind of guardian angel, by filling the vacant space left behind by the elimination or filleting of the corporeal. In both its private and public functions, dress polices the body's interior no less than it guards its frontiers, but also replenishes it by conferring a surrogate density

Figure 9. Mme YEVONDE, *Machine Worker in Summer*, 1937. © Yevonde Portrait Archive.

to its depleted shell. What the socialized body, reduced to a nameless and residual other, a detritus compulsively dependent on simulacra, encounters in dress is an equivocal partner. On the one hand, dress operates as a repressive disciplinary structure intent on shaping the illegitimate configuration of the private body as an unorganized and sprawling membrane of drives and thus eliding the stigmata of carnality, in the service of public requirements designed to place an official seal on the body's absence: in this respect, dress contributes to the production of a discourse wherein individual bodies do not inhabit the collective formation but are actually inhabited by it. On the other hand, however, dress does not totally consign the desiring body to quiescence, in so far as it supplies it with means of tangibly staging its desires and thus gaining novel palpability. In this respect, the container may turn out to encourage the contagious spilling over of its contents, by releasing the body to fresh forms of productivity and promoting the exploration of the creative potentialities of lack and absence themselves. Dress helps the body resist solidification into a stultifyingly discrete object by dispersing it across multiple surfaces that ultimately taunt the feasibility of any rigid separation of the private from the public, the individual from the collective, the personal from the social.

As in the phenomenon of contagion, in the process of transmission of affects between dress and the body, what is at stake is never a singular entity but rather a collectivity. Transmission inevitably occurs on a communal scale, since the individual body, beside being exposed to the direct material influence of the clothes it literally wears, is also open to contamination by other individuals' clothed bodies, either as physical presences or *in absentia*, through the rhetoric of the image, as embodiments of what it, too, might become. Dress produces and reproduces subjectivity through a spurious appeal to individuality that however does not aim at constructing distinct bodies but multiplicities – classes, bands, packs, waves. Deleuze and Guattari posit the case of contagion, as opposed to so-called natural reproduction, as a main form of mediation between the individual and the group, and highlight its subversive potential as a challenge to the myth of organic development. Associated with the process of 'becoming-animal', contagion throws into relief the body's most blatantly monstrous, unbounded and bestial connotations: traits of corporeality that are varyingly embodied, throughout time, by figures as disparate as multi-limbed or many-nippled deities, both diabolical and angelic hybrids, metamorphic bodies, robots, *et al*. Dress, in this context, could be seen as a secular or semi-mystical variation on the theme of the composite body; as will be suggested at a later stage in greater detail, dress in this function is tantalizingly akin, to resort to a contemporary popular image, to the figure of the cyborg.

Deleuze and Guattari's theorizing on the process of 'becoming-animal' could be regarded as a parable about the operations of fashion, in its capitalizing on the notion of the pack, on contagion and on borderline states, to the point that although dress is supposed to exemplify dominant symbolic dicta, it may turn out, ironically, to flout their sustaining principles, which are, indeed, those of natural reproduction, naturalism, naturalization, mimesis and discrete identities ensuing from the systematic distribution of the One into the Many – where the many are both countable and accountable for. In the discourse of fashion, nothing is anomalous, yet everything is: dress both cares and it doesn't, for it neither respects nor despises, and therefore leaves little room for humanist versions of morality.

> A becoming-animal always involves a pack, a band, a population, a peopling, in short, a multiplicity . . . Society and the State need animal characteristics to use for classifying people . . . Animal characteristics can be mythic or scientific. But we are not interested in characteristics; what interests us are modes of expansion, propagation, occupation, contagion, peopling. I am legion . . . What we are saying is that every animal is fundamentally a band, a pack. That it has pack modes, rather than characteristics . . . It is at this point that the human being encounters the animal. We do not become animal without a fascination for the pack, for multiplicity. A fascination for the outside? Or is the multiplicity that fascinates us already related to a multiplicity dwelling within us?[56]

Dress may be in a position to alert us precisely to our internal plurality and thus to the fact that participation in external forms of communality is inextricable from a basic condition of self-dividedness and fragmentation. More importantly, in terms of the argument put forward in *A Thousand Plateaus*, dress invites us to wonder how affects and ideas may be propagated within a multiplicity which simply cannot appeal to 'the unity of an ancestor'[57] and must therefore rely on anti-mimetic reproductive mechanisms. According to Deleuze and Guattari, contagious growth is inevitably associated with a discarding of 'filiation', which fittingly echoes fashion's rejection of mono-lithic parental authority.

> We oppose epidemic to filiation, contagion to heredity, peopling by contagion to sexual reproduction, sexual production. Bands, human or animal, proliferate by contagion, epidemics, battlefields, and catastrophes. Like hybrids, which are in themselves sterile, born of a sexual union which will not reproduce itself, but which *begins over again every time*, gaining that much more ground.[58]

As Thom points out, boundaries, however vital they may be to the fabrica-tion of discrete identities, cannot be traced by a desocialized individual, in that they require collective action: 'each individual moves randomly unless it sees the rest . . . in the same half-space; then it hurries to re-enter the group.

56. Gilles Deleuze and Felix Guattari (1988), *A Thousand Plateaus – Capitalism and Schizophrenia*, trans. Brian Massumi, London, pp.239–40.

57. Ibid., p.241.

58. Ibid., pp.241–2 (emphasis added).

Thus stability is assured . . . by a barrier'.[59] And the barrier itself is a movable feast, since 'a multiplicity is continually transforming itself into a string of other multiplicities, according to its thresholds and doors . . . there is a string of borderlines, a continuous line of borderlines (*fiber*) following which the multiplicity changes'.[60] Multiplicity is a dimension external to the subject, either as the shimmeringly kaleidoscopic collectivity of fashionable people with whom it may yearn to be associated, or as the ill-assorted mass from which it longs to separate itself. But multiplicity is also an inner experience, as a tangle of fantasies, drives, desires and only partially registered intro-jections. The multiplicities engendered by fashion stem from reproductive techniques that are in sharp contrast with, indeed almost a parody of, natural processes of filiation. For one thing, the deliberate and self-conscious way in which designers appropriate references and themes from disparate historical contexts and amalgamate them with present terms and concerns suggests that, though dress is everywhere, it comes from nowhere in particular: it has no singular author or progenitor. Within the discourse of contagion, the obliteration of origins promoted by dress runs parallel to its dissolution of the shielding boundaries held capable of separating the physical and the literal from the symbolic and the rhetorical. The erasure of frontiers engineered by dress is an eminently narrative phenomenon: whilst endowing itself with the power of acting as the body's substitute carnality, its central plot device is the conversion of flesh into metaphor. Helman documents this process with reference to the discourse of 'germism', as a narrativization of physical experience which impudently confuses private and public orbits of signification: 'the germistic way of thinking places the blame for our misfor-tunes on powerful, capricious "forces" that are said to rule over our lives – just as they were once ruled by devils, or by Divine grace or punishment. . . . [It] implies a sense of passivity, and of helplessness.'[61] Just as germs are the present-day substitutes for the old demons of myth and magic, so 'vaccines' stand in for spells and talismans. But germism, like fashion, is also a paradoxical phenomenon, requiring simultaneously the acceptance of an individualistic ethos (as when we talk of *my* germ, or *my* bug) and participa-tion in a social event of infection, based on the apprehension of the body as a porous entity.

The splitting of the body and its attributes into personal possessions, on the one hand, and objects for public consumption, on the other, arguably

59. Rene Thom (1975), *Structural Ability and Morphogenesis*, trans. D. H. Fowler, Reading, Mass., p319.

60. Deleuze and Guattari, *Thousand Plateaus*, p.249.

61. Cecil Helman (1992), *The Body of Frankenstein's Monster: Essays in Myth and Medicine*, London and New York, pp.34–6.

originates in the moulding of the *modern* apprehension of physicality. According to Barker, the modern body is both a marginalized entity, resulting from the purging of its supposedly unwieldy impulses as 'dead flesh, a *mere* residue' and a systematized, 'structured, organized object of investigation' whose drives are methodically and clinically harnessed to societal norms.[62] Where dress is concerned, this ambivalence manifests itself in the twofold role played by clothing, as a system simultaneously able to operate as a sanitizing agency that may turn the physical body into an incorporeal persona, by effecting an elision of concreteness in the service of the sign, and as a problematizing vehicle, intent on asserting the inescapability of physicality by foregrounding its own stubborn and unyielding materiality.

In its quest to either assert or deny its materiality, the modern body conceptualized by Barker – as a suitably tremulous entity – is sooner or later confronted by its 'artificial' counterparts, by the possibility of 'replicated or mimicked animate bodies, whether mechanical or pseudo-organic'.[63] The compound of body and dress could be read as possibly the most enduring and widespread manifestation of an artificial ensemble, potentially capable of challenging the cult of subjectivity as a sacrosanct whole. The challenge posed by the body's technological *alter ego* draws attention to the fact that the hybridization of subjectivity engineered by dress ought to be located in the broader context of a generalized and profound preoccupation with the simultaneously riveting and menacing character of part-objects, aggregates and simulated compounds. As was hinted earlier, an illustration of this ongoing concern that bears stimulating, if indirect, affinities to the discourse of clothes, is supplied by the culturally pervasive figure of the cyborg. It is to a selective case study of this particular conglomerate, seen as a metaphor for the hybrid character of the discourse of dress in contemporary culture, that the following section will be devoted.

Cyborg Clothing

The cyborg self can be understood as combining an omnipotence fantasy of self-control with fear and aggression directed against the emotional and bodily limitations of mere mortals. Through this fantasy we deny our dependence upon nature, upon our own nature, and upon the 'bloody mess of organic nature'.[64]

---

62. Francis Barker (1995), *The Tremulous Private Body*, Michigan, p.vii.
63. Ibid., p.viii.
64. Les Levidow (1995), The Cyborg Self: Clean in Mind and Body', abstract of paper given at the conference *Bodily Fictions*, Brunel University College, London, September 1995.

The meltdown of the discrete body and its replacement by circuited body images, as well as an increasing awareness of the complex aesthetic and ethical reverberations of notions of proximity and promiscuity, make the concern with the breach of physical boundaries one of the most prominent traits of contemporary culture. The boundaries in question, as has been the case for time immemorial, may be those between human and animal; special urgency, however, has recently been gained by the interpenetration of human and machine. In both instances, the interfacing of the human body by the non-human problematizes the relationship between subjectivity and sexuality. Whilst animalization could be seen as a rehabilitation of the subject's sexual nature (as in Bacchic cults or in the phenomenon of vampirism), mechanization could be associated with its repression. In the domain of dress, the analogy between the wearing of clothes and the adoption of alternative skins would, accordingly, suggest a move towards animalization and the magnifying of the carnal, whereas the parallel between clothes and the artificial ensemble would seem conducive to mechanization and hence a policing of the erotic. This is not necessarily the case: rather than repressing sexuality, dress, even at its most blatantly artificial, allegorizes and translates it into a multiplicity of roles and masks, by disseminating teleologically intended activity into more polymorphous possibilities. It is this dissolution of the body's limits, promoted not only by the proverbially demonic beast but also, perhaps more disturbingly, by the putatively sanitizing machine, that propels the desire to bound physicality, render it discrete and thus guard it against contamination. The sealed body is not a natural substratum to be protected from external infractions, but rather a reaction to the troubling recognition of its violated boundaries. It is indiscretion that produced discretion, not the other way round.

The hybrid of machine and organism is very possibly the most recent chapter in the long history of the West's relationship with technological development, a problematic nexus that simultaneously involves fascination with and dread of the mechanical, the artificial, the reproduced. This ambiguity of attitudes and responses may be traced back to the advent of industrialization, with its mixed feelings of excitement at the prospect of unlimited progress and of fear of the machine, often resulting in escapist retreats into myth and legend. Today, anxieties about the technological domain frequently take the guise of troubled responses to the very notion of birth:

> Take Ridley Scott's *Alien*, for instance, where the little monster is born right out of the chest of a man, a squealing fetus who then retains its curious shape, even as it grows large, gorging itself upon human victims . . . There was *The Kindred* and

Ghoulies and *Leviathan* and those writhing clones being born like fetuses out of pods in *Invasion of the Body Snatchers* . . . Take the remake of *The Fly*. Didn't the hero wind up looking like a fetus? And what about *Fly 2*, with its images of birth and rebirth? . . . Horror movies are our troubled dreams . . . and we are obsessed now with birth, and birth gone wrong, and birth turned against us.[65]

In a postmodern scenario, the preoccupation with 'birth gone wrong' is complicated by the spreading of cybercultures and cyberspaces, the increasing emphasis on the highly mediated character of all cultural practices and the collapse of traditional barriers between subject and object, the producer and the produced. According to Haraway: 'It is not clear who makes and who is made in the relation between human and machine. It is not clear what is mind and what body in machines.'[66] Fashion's problematization of concepts of creation and reproduction, which are foregrounded, as indicated in the preceding section, by the anti-parental phenomenon of contagion, could be situated in this broader atmosphere of anxiety about the question of origin. This anxiety is obviously intensified by our increasing awareness of the inevitably encoded status of postmodern bodies and machines alike, and of their constitution according to principles of substitution and permutation that are indeed redolent of fashion's governing mechanisms:

communication sciences and modern biologies are constructed by a common move – the translation of the world into a problem of coding, a search for a common language in which . . . all heterogeneity can be submitted to disassembly, reassembly, investment and exchange . . . The organism has been translated into problems of genetic coding . . . No objects, spaces or bodies are sacred in themselves; any component can be interfaced with any other if the proper standard, the proper code, can be constructed for processing signals in a common language.[67]

The muddling of physiological and technological bodies, in particular, undermines any conventional tendency to posit the body as the last refuge for a natural and organic, as opposed to an artificial and synthetic, identity. Simulacra, replicants, electronic bodies and cyborgs may be read precisely as incarnations of deep-seated concerns about the demise of unimpaired corporeality. The feeling of uneasiness surrounding the figure of the cyborg has largely to do with its ability to intimate that if the machine can assume the semblance of humanity despite its mechanical, non-human core, the humanness of the biological ensemble may, in turn, be penetrated by the

65. Anne Rice (1991), *The Witching Hour*, London, p.83.
66. Donna Haraway (1985), 'A Manifesto for Cyborgs: Science, Technology and Socialist Feminism in the 1980s', in *Socialist Review*, No.80. p.201.
67. Ibid., p.188.

artificial. But, equally importantly, that feeling also stems from a recognition of the human subject's dependence on the machine, both as an embodiment of its own deep-seated fears and apocalyptic projections, and as a vehicle through which to assert its otherwise questionable and precarious humanity.

According to Pyle, 'the technological other is nothing less than our own quite "human" images and fears'.[68] Cameron's classic dramatizations of this topos suggest, moreover, that the human organism needs the mechanical cyborg in order to consolidate its own humanity, no less than the machine is supposed to be defined in relation to the human. *Terminator 2: Judgement Day* humanizes the cyborg, by making him able to learn, act as an ideal father figure, supply his audience with a redemptive, Walt Disney type of ending and, last but not least, put on human clothes with an uncanny naturalness. Arguably, however, what is really uncanny is our reluctance to accept, by the standards of narrative realism, that a cyborg knows exactly how to attire itself, although we seem to have virtually no difficulties conceding that it *is* a cyborg and that, moreover, it has just come back from the future. Yet, the humanizing of the cyborg is not a triumph for the humanist ethos, in that it does not demonstrate the superiority of human beings over machines, but rather the fact that both humanness and humaneness may only be preserved through artificial constructs. 'The opposition between human and machine is placed at the mercy of the cyborg... However much the film may want to extricate itself from the logic of machines, the knotting of human and cyborg is inextricable: in *Terminator 2*, the triumph of humans and humanism is made dependent on the humanizing of cyborgs.'[69] Humans may only be humanized via the agency of the non-human, just as in the discourse of dress as outlined earlier the disembodied subject relies on dress as the provider of a surrogate flesh. By analogy with the discourse of the cyborg, it could be argued that the humanization of the body requires the humanization of its apparently artificial and inanimate envelope.

This idea is thrown into relief by Cameron's rendition of the concerns and aims of artificial intelligence, as the strand of cybernetics specifically devoted to exploring the issue of whether machines only appear to be intelligent or may develop partly autonomous processes, eventually able to shed light on the processes of human cognition itself. In *Terminator 2*, this is issue is handled by the opposition of two different types of cyborgs: unlike the hypersophisticated T-1000, the older Cyberdine Systems Model 101 is

68. Forest Pyle (1993), 'Making Cyborgs, Making Humans: Of Terminators and Blade Runners', in Jim Collins, Hilary Radner and Ava Preacher Collins (eds), *Film Theory Goes to the Movies*, London, p.233.
69. Ibid., pp.239–40.

not tied exclusively to technological criteria, but is actually able to acquire knowledge through its increasing contact with humans ('no problema, baby'). Although the humanizing of the machine depends on its being pre-programmed according to the logic of total obedience, which necessarily places its autonomy within boundaries, this apparent restriction of cyborg faculties simultaneously reminds us of our dependence on machines of a humanizable kind, in so far as we may only legitimize our powers to the extent that these come to be embodied by non-human structures. Relatedly, when we define our clothes as inactive products of human creativity, we must automatically grapple with their productive influence upon our bodies and psyches, their ability to endow us with attributes and energies that the material body, figuratively eviscerated by its admission to the symbolic, could only ever fantasize about but never tangibly incarnate. If, like the T-1000 – a cyborg made entirely of liquid metal – the compound of body and dress presents itself as capable of endless permutations that utterly ignore the surface/depth dichotomy, concurrently, like the 101 model, it displays self-enhancing competences that preclude the possibility of clearly establishing which of the two parties is the active inculcator of knowledge and which its receiver. 'The presumed superiority of "organic" over "mechanical" ... is upset at a moment in the text which reveals that the "organic" needs the "mechanical" or proves them to be inextricable ... The hybrid figure of the cyborg ... "plays" on a borderline that we come to see as shifting and porous.'[70] By analogy, the hybrid figure of the clothed body exposes the non-autonomous nature of physicality, as well as its infinitely permeable character, by underscoring the body's liminality.

As a possible metaphor for postmodern culture, the figure of the cyborg does not ineluctably prelude a scenario wherein hideous and life-devouring machines storm heedlessly across a blasted landscape, any more than the parallel trope of the networked and viral fusion of body and dress necessarily alludes to an unredeemably commodified version of carnality, its drives, emotions and affects. Although Levidow may be correct in associating the cult of the cyborg with an impulse to transcend the 'messiness' of organic matter, what should also be considered is the possibility that any quest for transcendence may end up laying bare an unexpected profusion of physical forms that no monolithic system may ever accommodate in a single move-ment. Pursuing the comparison between the idea of the human–machine conglomerate and that of the body–dress nexus, it could be argued that clothing's bounding aspirations tend to produce analogously fragmenting effects. In what reads as an apt account not only of cyberculture but, more

70. Ibid., pp.227–9.

generally, of the ultimate consequences of a critical outlook that is willing to accept the inevitable interfacing of the human and the non-human, the natural and the manufactured, Haraway observes:

> from one perspective, a cyborg world is about the final imposition of a grid of control on the planet, about the final abstraction embodied in a star war apocalypse waged in the name of defense. From another perspective, a cyborg world might be about lived social and bodily realities in which people are not afraid of their joint kinship with animals and machines, not afraid of permanently partial identities and contradictory standpoints.[71]

Following the latter perspective, the fracturing of identity implied by the ambiguous figures of the cyborg and of the clothed body could be read as symptomatic of postmodernism's challenge to the Western obsession with unity, self-contained subjectivities and holistic metanarratives: both symbolize 'a kind of disassembled and reassembled postmodern collective and personal self'[72] that harks back to the fluid personas of shamanism and contagious magic.

As such a 'disassembled and reassembled' apparatus, the body/dress composite renders void the question as to whether the body is a constant in a world of flux or whether the body's multi-accentuality actually epitomizes instability. In fact, it suggests that these two possibilities are not necessarily mutually exclusive, since a constant does not have to be an unchanging substance or essence, retaining fixed qualities throughout time and space, but may actually be a function that, whilst featuring repeatedly and regularly, does so in ways that also involve an irreducible element of difference. Dress both reinforces and destabilizes the notion of the body as a constant, in so far as the clothed body is, at one and the same time, an enduring cultural image ceaselessly produced and consumed and a contingent mask. The only form of constancy that may be realistically associated with the body/dress relationship is that of a spectacle: a recurring phenomenon whose repetition exhibits not permanence but divergence and displacement, not the continuity of identity-as-sameness but rather decentred and disguised subjectivities. It would be misleading, however, to regard theatricality as a peculiarity of the body/dress relationship, divorced from the rest of the symbolic forum. Indeed, as Debord points out: 'The spectacle in its totality, is both the result and the project of the existing mode of production. It is not a supplement to the real world, an additional decoration.'[73]

71. Haraway, 'Manifesto for Cyborgs', p.179.
72. Ibid., p.187.
73. Guy Debord (1983), *The Society of the Spectacle*, Detroit, p.6.

Deleuze emphasizes the theatrical character of all cultural and philo-sophical situations that interrogate metaphysical concepts of universality and permanence through the principle of repetition. Repetition, as opposed to generality, flouts universal rules, its transgressive thrust deriving from its inextricability from the category of difference and the latter's dislocating proclivities. The paradoxical status of the clothed body as an inconstant constant – or constant inconstant, perhaps – exemplifies the trespassing impulse inherent in ways of thinking and acting that acknowledge precisely the interdependence of repetition and difference, recurrence and discontinuity, to the point that 'philosophy' itself 'becomes theatre'.[74] This, argues Deleuze, is:

> a theatre of multiplicities opposed in every respect to the theatre of representation, which leaves intact neither the identity of the thing represented, nor author, nor spectator, nor character... Instead, a theatre of problems and always open questions which draws spectator, setting and characters into the real movement of an apprenticeship of the entire unconscious.[75]

Far from promoting ideals of stability, the concept of repetition that is so pervasive throughout the discourse of dress and its discontinuous history, turns out to be inseparable from the phenomenon of difference, as an eminently and playfully impertinent and flippant occurrence: 'Repetition belongs to humour and irony; it is by nature transgression or exception, always revealing a singularity opposed to the particulars subsumed under laws, a universal opposed to the generalities which give rise to laws.'[76] The spectacle of fashion is a paradigmatic illustration of precisely this type of irreverent repetition, thriving, as it does, on rhythms of unrelieved transi-toriness, paradoxically sustained by the return of the old and on patterns of apparent stability, no less paradoxically backed up by a thirst for novelty.

---

74. Scott Lash (1991), 'Genealogy and the Body: Foucault/Deleuze/Nietzsche', in Featherstone, Hepworth and Turner (eds), *The Body: Social Process and Cultural Theory*, London, p.265.
75. Gilles Deleuze (1994), *Difference and Repetition*, trans. Paul Patton, London, p.192.
76. Ibid., p.5.

4

Surface/Depth — Dress and the Mask

This chapter will explore the relationship between surface and depth in the discourse of clothing, with a focus on the image of the mask as both a material object and a trope for the complementary dynamics of concealment and revelation that, arguably, characterize all forms of dress. The symbolic connotations of the mask and of related garments, such as the veil, will be briefly investigated in the opening section, as a means of introducing the broader historical, psychological and ideological significance of the surface/depth binary and hopefully highlighting the latter's deconstructive traits. A close reading of John Donne's poem *Elegy XIX* will provide a detailed illustration of the complex interactions of concealment and revelation in representations of the dressed and undressed body.

Masks and veils intensify the enigmatic character of clothes as structures that are simultaneously capable of both hiding and disclosing bodily attributes and desires, thus underscoring the baffling quality of the relationship between the clothed and the naked bodies. Fontana voices a popular opinion in asserting that: 'While nakedness symbolizes innocence and freedom from worldly taint, clothes are more ambivalent. The cloak stands for secrecy and magic powers, while fine robes connote authority and privilege, as well as foolishness and pride.'[1] However, even the association of nudity with purity and the garbed body with earthly knowledge or vanity is not unproblematic, as evinced, for instance, by contrasting interpretations of images such as Titian's pictorial rendering of *Sacred and Profane Love*, where both the naked and the clothed female figures could, in turn, be seen to exemplify the former or the latter. Masks and veils further complicate the indeterminate nature of dress, by appearing to secrete the body, yet concurrently holding figurative implications that allude to their illuminating and hence revealing powers. Related to this central uncertainty is the mask's ability to both separate and connect individual bodies, and thus to amplify the function of clothing in general as both a boundary and a margin. In

1. David Fontana (1993), *The Secret Language of Symbols*, London, p.126.

the language of symbolism, the coexistence of concealment and exposure, insulation and mediation, is one of the principal features of all screening garments and is conveyed by their explicit incarnation of the imperative of secrecy and the attendant invitation to unmask the secret. The mask also magnifies the notion of dress as a structure endowed with autonomous powers, based on the ability either to sustain or shatter the wearer's identity, as dramatically evoked by the ancient belief that if an uninitiated subject were to behold a ritual mask, it would instantly die.

In the history of symbols, the wearing of a mask is usually related to the summoning of supernatural agencies, in order to ward off enemies or dangers, invoke one's ancestors, commune with the instinctual wisdom of animals, transform oneself or mark alliances in the course of rituals and ceremonies. But the mask is also a means of erasing personal identity. The Shaman mask, for example, is central to ecstatic experiences wherein spirit powers, normally associated with animals, take possession of the shaman and endow him or her with knowing and healing powers, as well as the authority to maintain order within the community. Both the Shaman mask and Aboriginal 'bush-soul' masks are supposed to enhance their wearers' faculties in a state of trance; the zigzag shape of lightning flash typical of the Shaman mask symbolizes the ability to cross the bridges separating different worlds. The notion of dress as a hybrid discourse finds an appropriate parallel in the threshold personality fostered by shamanism, no less, as suggested in the previous chapter, than in the analogously borderline figures of the vampire or the cyborg. Moreover, the shaman's process of initiation may include the dismemberment of the subject's body, the removal and substitution of flesh: a ritual that could be read as metaphorically redolent of the phenomenon of decorporealization triggered by the entry into the symbolic, which dress both ratifies, by positing itself as a substitute skin or flesh, and challenges, by foregrounding its own irreducible materiality. Both dress and the body could be said to play a shamanistic role: if it is the case that the body is figuratively decarnalized by its subjection to linguistic codes and conventions, of which sartorial and vestimentary ones are no negligible part, it also seems to be the case that this dismemberment ushers in new powers, specifically connected with the assumption of an enunciative position. The body, in this respect, is a shaman of sorts, emptied of individuality and stripped of carnality to make room for the acquisition of alternative faculties. At the same time, it is dress that enacts the part of the shaman, by allowing itself to be possessed by a body, whose animal energies may give both literal shape and rhetorical means of expression to an otherwise limp casing.

In Eastern philosophy, the world itself is the mask of god, *maya*, and hence a web of illusions imperfectly representing divine truth. In symbolic/

theological terms, the mask also occupies a liminal position between the halo, as the emblem of divine radiance, a glorified wig emanating from the head as a life force, and the shadow, as a token of the density of form and of material nature, in that the mask may be seen to conceal one's true self by fashioning an artificial public persona, but, as in shamanism and Tibetan Buddhism, is also supposed to help individuals transcend their limited roles and relinquish their egos. Bakhtin talks of the mask as an involvement shield, whereby individuals protect their privacy at the same time as they commune with others, for example in the eminently social contexts of carnivals and masquerades, and hence manage to isolate themselves, yet simultaneously project intended identities on to the external world. Brilliant underscores the function of the mask as an exhibitionist disguise, an insulating mechanism that, paradoxically, emphasizes and occludes visibility in one single movement:

> masks seem to be self-imposed disguises allowing the wearer to impersonate someone, even himself, in a favourable guise; that is, to manifest some aspect of the wearer not otherwise visible, whether or not that representation is wholly imaginary, delusional, self-serving, or meets the expectations of others. Real masks are hollow, but the masks that civilized people put on have no physical existence separate from their own flesh, their 'own' face, although what lies behind them may be impossible to know. They are both transparent and opaque, because such masks conceal the being within from others, blocking their access to it, while simultaneously making a social commitment to these same others by presenting some visible, comprehensible form of the self that might be recognized.[2]

The mask is a garment that advertises that it has something to hide; but the nature of what is hidden is not fixed, depending upon the context in which it is worn. Henry Porter notes that where the balaclava mask was once the device that protected the anonymity of the terrorist or criminal, it is now more likely for the 'good guys' to appear with their faces concealed, as in the recent emergence of serving and ex-SAS soldiers, 'once almost exclusively associated with acts of illegal violence . . . [the mask] has moved swiftly to become a protective headress and more significantly, the badge of a glamorous covert operative'.[3] It could be argued that these examples are not different – the acts of violence that the masks speak of could both be defined as legitimate or illegitimate; but both do refer to a context in which having no face, but having a present and active body is desirable. Removal of the face releases the body, but also suggests that the person covered is not negligibly anonymous but on the contrary is important enough to require

2. Richard Brilliant (1991), *Portraiture*, London, p.113.
3. Henry Porter (1996), *The Guardian*, June 10, p.2.

protection. It is implied that ordinary people do not need the safety it offers, because they are simply not interesting enough. This can also be seen in the adoption of mask-like covering by other people in the public eye: Jackie Onassis and Marilyn Monroe, for example, wearing large sunglasses and head scarves speak not of anonymity but of fame, a double message of look-at-me-I don't-want-to-be-looked-at. Dark glasses are a particularly tantalizing instance of protective clothing. Whilst purporting to hide one of the most significant parts of the anatomy, through which emotions are supposed to pass in a peculiarly immediate fashion, and hence facilitate self-effacement, they are also a vehicle for self-exposure, and might prove more telling than the unmasked eyes would ever be. Indeed, Barthes describes dark glasses as 'a double discourse'.[4]

> The hiding must be seen: *I want you to know that I am hiding something from you* . . . I want you to know that I don't want to show my feelings: that is the message I address to the other. *Larvatus prodeo*: I advance pointing to my mask: I set a mask upon my passion, but with a discreet (and wily) finger I designate this mask.[5]

The double discourse is further doubled in the wearing variants of the mask of fame by those who simply aspire to notoriety: they have nothing to hide except the very fact that they have nothing to hide; instead of advertising them as well known it reveals them as nobodies. The signification of the mask is beyond individual control, as suggested in a recent film, *The Mask*, where the mask apparently releases the ordinary Jim Carrey into the world of the superhero, but blurs the nature of the desires enacted: whose desires are they, those of the man whose mask enables him to act, or those of the mask, the wearing of which allows its desires to be actualized? One of the most striking uses of the mask by a contemporary figure is Michael Jackson's wearing of a black silk surgical mask. It operates as the 'veil of fame' in the manner of Jackie O's sunglasses, separating him from the public body; but it also makes overt the underlying suggestion of this separation, that he occupies a different, more superior and *cleaner* space; the masses are dirty and a possible source of infection, of physical illness, but also of ordinariness. He attempts to contain himself, in erecting a barrier that prevents both ingress and egress, recalling Kristeva's notion of abjection, and the effort to shore up the boundaries of the body that both leaks and is leaked into. As an attribute of public identity his mask participates in the construction of the self, a task made more significant by his well-known reconstructions of his

4. Roland Barthes (1990), *A Lover's Discourse*, trans. Richard Howard, London, p.41.
5. Ibid., p.43.

physical body through plastic surgery. What Jackson's mask covers is not his face, but another mask, one made of flesh to his own design. The choice of the surgical veil suggests that the face is unfinished, it is still 'in surgery', a grotesque recollection of Lacan's notion of the ongoing drama of identity. The mask signifies another signifier, the face-in-process: there is no 'real' face to be covered. The mask of flesh again appears, in another gruesome contemporary version, in Jonathan Demme's film *The Silence of the Lambs*, where Hannibal Lecter removes the face of his guard and puts it over his own in order to escape. It is an ironic undermining of the common-sense notion that the face can be read and trusted when uncovered, precisely because we do not know when a face is masked or not, even when it appears to be flesh. Lecter's fashioning of a temporary identity mirrors that of the other murderer in the film, Buffalo Bill, who is making himself a woman's dress, literally a dress made of women, to fulfil his fantasy of identity. Bill's dress is the most stark of examples of the Lacanian rim: the unfinished subject, perceiving his whole body as a raw cut, attempts to incorporate the detachable object of clothing, and in this case it is organic clothing, in the hope that the transplant will 'take' and his identity will finally be completed as the woman whose 'clothes' he has stolen. It is his attempt to fashion a newly tailored self that reveals him and leads to his identification. The mask, therefore, both protects and exposes its wearer, conceals and reveals its attributes, metamorphoses and crystallizes identity, separates and mediates the self and the other, promulgates being and collapses it into non-being.

Closely related to the mask is the veil, as a garment that, like Freud's *unheimlich*, operates both as a distorting mechanism that conceals truth by giving familiar realities an unfamiliar turn and as a means to enlightenment, to the extent that defamiliarization enforces discovery. Traditionally, the veil is associated with darkness, a pre-dawn or unenlightened state, either cosmic or spiritual, as well inscrutability and esoteric knowledge. Passing the veil, incidentally, is part of an initiation rite on the way towards the gaining of hermetic knowledge. Yet, once again, what conceals may also reveal: direct or naked truth, many beliefs maintain, can be dangerous, and the ceremonial role of the veil lies in its ability to operate as a protective shield. It too, like the mask, is contingent: the wearing of the *hijab*, the Muslim woman's head scarf, is a political act. In pre-revolution Iran women were not allowed in public wearing the veil, so that its adoption became an act of defiance; after the Shah's deposition and the institution of strict Islamic law going without the *hijab* became a similar act. It is seen by both Muslim and non-Muslim women variously as a token of oppression and of liberation. The veil signifies submission to authority, as well as the renunciation of the flesh, chastity, modesty and constancy – as in the nun's and the bride's veils – and sacrifice

– the heads of victims to be immolated in many a culture are frequently veiled and garlanded. Covers are worn on the head by both executioners and victims: for the executioner it is to present him as an impersonal force of justice, to make him safe from retribution but also to allow him to distance himself from the task, like an actor in classical tragedy. For the victim it also depersonalizes, making it easier to kill someone with no face, no identity already marking him off from society. Though an apparent kindness, in not allowing him to know the exact moment of his death, it serves also to increase the fear by intensifying the anticipation, a further stroke of sadistic humiliation. Both participants are re-identified, concealing their selves, yet revealing them differently. Like the mask, the veil obscures personality whilst facilitating collective integration, as in ancient priesthood. The Egyptian veil of Isis vividly encapsulates the coexistence of illumination and deception, revelation and concealment: 'I am all that has been, and shall be, and my veil no mortal man has yet lifted. The veil is the universe which the goddess weaves.'[6]

Surface/Depth

The equivocal characteristics of masks, veils and other similarly screening garments throw into relief the problematic nature of the relationship between surface and depth, by intimating that truth cannot be explicitly associated with a deep dimension, hidden beyond or beneath an illusory surface, and indeed that the surface cannot be unambiguously equated with deceptive appearances. In fact, the realization that the mask may reveal by concealing, that the subject's identity may constitute not so much a secret, inner core of meaning as a play of contingently superficial and external manifestations, interrogates at once the validity of both the depth-versus-surface and the truth-versus-deception binaries. Whatever is understood by the category of truth, as the regimes of signification to which a culture is prepared to accord value, may lie precisely on the surface; this surface, moreover, may turn out to conceal not a presence but an absence, not a depth but a vacuum. Accordingly, truth may be so notoriously hard to grasp because we look for it in the wrong places, i.e. in the spectral regions that are presumed to stretch indefinitely beyond a specious façade, rather than in superficial phenomena themselves.

Barthes corroborates the idea that we are most desperately blind in the face of the obvious, perhaps because its very clarity seems to discourage

---

6. Proclus, quoted in J.C.Cooper (1982), *An Illustrated Encyclopaedia of Traditional Symbols*, London, p.185.

further scrutiny: 'The darkest place, according to a Chinese proverb, is always under the lamp.'[7] Barthes also speculates, however, about the possibility of doing away altogether with the stale opposition between surface and depth: '[what] if . . . some day . . . consciousness were finally to become this: the abolition of the manifest and the latent, of the appearance and the hidden?'[8] Poe, along similar lines, maintains: 'There is such a thing as being too profound. Truth is not always in a well. In fact, as regards the most important knowledge, I do believe she is invariably superficial.'[9] Lacan embraces these insights into the relationship between surface and depth, by suggesting that the unconscious itself, though traditionally conceived of as a hidden or submerged dimension, is, in fact, superficial, since it manifests itself through language and rhetorical displacements, i.e. eminently superficial phenomena. This position is of crucial relevance to the discourse of dress, since it invites an understanding of clothes, which are themselves emphatically exposed rhetorical structures capitalizing on repeated dislocations of identity, as capable of incarnating unconscious drives and desires in their staging of superficial language games. Lacan's rejection of traditional psychoanalytical approaches devoted to the search for concealed meanings inaugurates what Felman aptly describes as a shift towards 'an analysis of the signifier as opposed to an analysis of the signified'.[10] Where dress is concerned, the adoption of this type of methodology would serve to discourage any attempt to penetrate the surface of clothes as unreliable signifiers, in order to access an underlying signified or content and to foster, instead, an investigation of the signifiers themselves that is not committed to the discovery of meaning: 'what can be read (or perhaps what should be read) is not just meaning but the lack of meaning; . . . the signifier can be analyzed in its effects without its signified being known'.[11]

Of course, it is inherent in the operations of truth as a culturally legitimated construct to efface its own superficiality, since admitting to this feature of its being would automatically lead to an acknowledgement of its very constructedness and immanence. Dress, quite obviously, capitalizes on surfaces: whatever value it may be ascribed, whatever truths it may be deemed capable of conveying, guarding or indeed erecting, are continually dispersed and reinscribed, contained and spawned, across prismatic exterior facets of

7. Barthes, *Lover's Discourse*, p.59.

8. Ibid., p.61.

9. Edgar Allan Poe (1967), 'The Murders in the Rue Morgue', in David Galloway (ed.), *Edgar Allan Poe: Selected Writings*, New York, p.204.

10. Shoshana Felman (1987), *Jacques Lacan and the Adventure of Insight – Psychoanalysis in Contemporary Culture*, Cambridge, Mass. & London, p.44.

11. Ibid., p.45.

cultural and personal experience. This is not tantamount to saying, however, that the shallowness of clothes consigns them finally to a world of unrelieved triviality, to the hollow space of non-meaning or to the category of a fleeting hallucination. In fact, by analogy with Lacan's positions, it could be argued that the surfaces relentlessly woven by the discourse of dress offer *profoundly* important allusions to the broad cultural mechanisms through which subjectivity is structured and rendered both signifying and signifiable. Dress does not simply operate as a camouflaging strategy, since its ever-proliferating masks speak volumes about the sunken remnants of our drifting subjectivities.

Dress, then, could be described as a *deep surface*, a system of signs that fundamentally relies on superficial modes of signification for the purposes of expressing the underlying beliefs of a given culture and the character of the subjects fostered therein. This function of dress can easily be traced back to the late Middle Ages. Although it is not within the scope or ambitions of this project to present a detailed historical survey of clothing's implication in the surface/dress nexus, it seems appropriate to provide a few selective illustrations of ways in which clothes may have developed their knack of deepening the surface by literally appropriating the bodies of their wearers. In late medieval culture, the accumulation of increasing layers of clothing on the naked body makes the surface more and more important as the conveyor of cultural meanings and, concomitantly, minimizes the value of the physical apparatus itself. It would be misleading, however, to view this valorization of the surface as a surrender to the lure of the ephemeral, since the incremental proliferation of surfaces enacted by dress in proto-modern Western cultures is symptomatic of profoundly important changes in society's perception of the body and its physiological and biological functions and of the urgency with which the desire to domesticate the more overtly animalistic of those functions is addressed. According to Mennel, these shifts signal 'a long-term trend . . . towards greater demands on emotional management and more differentiated codes of behaviour'.[12] In commenting on changing apprehensions of the body and dress after 1350, Vigarello highlights the rampant growth of the surface:

> The body as a whole was hardly involved, hidden away inside clothes which were all that people really saw. The nature of the clothes, therefore, became all-important to an understanding of what constituted propriety. Their precise role in a strategy of good manners reveals the extent to which attention never went beyond the visible . . . The focus of attention in clothes was their surface. It was this which not only caught the eye, but held it. The existence of the skin and the concrete

12. Stephen Mennell (1989), *Norbert Elias – Civilization and the Human Self-Image*, Oxford, p.36.

conception of the body were largely forgotten . . . It was as if everything should relate to the visible, as if material and form exhausted the potential qualities. The envelope assumed the role of the body.[13]

The social and ideological significance of superficial visibility intensifies, throughout the Renaissance, to reach its peak in the late sixteenth century, when the cult of the body as an object for public display firmly asserts its dominance: politics, aesthetics and sexuality equally thrive on principles of theatricalization[14] and, argues Breward, 'transformation, elaboration, and the cultivation of artifice begin to describe the nature of elite modes of dress'.[15] Writers and commentators of the period are keen on emphasizing the explosion of decorative elements with a taxonomic compulsiveness that vividly evokes the disappearance of the corporeal beneath ever-increasing superficial masks:

> Five hours ago I set a dozen maids to attire a boy like a nice gentlewoman, but there is such doing with their looking glasses, pinning, unpinning, setting, unsetting, formings and conformings, painting blew veins and cheeks; such stir with sticks and combs, cascanets, dressings, purls, falls, squares, busks, bodies, scarfs, necklaces, carcanets, rebatoes, borders, tires, fans, palisades, puffs, ruffs, cuffs, muffs, pusles, fusles, partlets, frislets, bandlets, fillets, crosslets, pendulets, amulets, annulets, bracelets, and so many lets that yet she is scarce dressed to the girdle; and now there's such a calling for fardingales, kirtles, busk-points, shoe ties, etc. that seven peddlers' shops – nay all Stourbridge Fair – will scarce furnish her: a ship is sooner rigged by far, than a gentlewoman made ready.[16]

The above account partly alludes to the metamorphosing powers of dress as a form of playful masquerade, no doubt; but also to a means of translating the material body into a symbolic system, carnality into a social metaphor, fashionable deception into a metonym of political and diplomatic discourse. Breward remarks on the especially prolific spawning of surfaces in the tradition of Renaissance portraiture, as a genre based on the aesthetic and ideological imperative to incorporate a phenomenal range of elements into the dress of the sitter: 'The communication of reputation relied not so much on individual choice as it did on the recognition and comprehension of a complex set of formal visual codes that included references to colour, shape,

13. G.Vigarello (1988), *Concepts of Cleanliness: Changing Attitudes in France Since the Middle Ages*, Cambridge, pp.48–53.
14. Stephen Greenblatt (1980), *Renaissance Self-Fashioning*, Chicago, p.162.
15. Christopher Breward (1995), *The Culture of Fashion*, Manchester, p.42.
16. T.Tomkis (1607), ' Lingua or the Combat of the Tongues', in J. Arnold (1988), *Queen Elizabeth's Wardrobe Unlock'd*, Leeds, p.110.

texture, and specific recourse to figures taken from mythology, history and the natural world.'[17] Strong espouses this view by noting how, in the portrait, 'the face becomes an element in an arrangement of fabric and jewels . . . the sitter [is] transmuted into a jewel-encrusted icon.'[18] Portraits of Queen Elizabeth I are particularly conspicuous manifestations of the appropriation of the corporeal by a profusion of ornamental surfaces. In the Armada portrait (1588), for example, pearls, rubies and emeralds, silk bows, gold thread and edgings, to mention but a few instances of majestic adornment, enclose the body so completely that 'only the face and the hands are visible. The exaggerated sleeves and the gigantic skirt efface between them all other indications of a human body.'[19] Brilliant points out, along similar lines, the allegorical thrust of royal portraits, with special emphasis on their masking properties, the mask alluding not so much to the concept of concealment, as to the process of translation of individual identity or personhood into an iconic encapsulation of collective, political and theological values:

> For Queen Elizabeth, the masque (or mask) is all. No other access to her exists, not just because majesty keeps its distance but as if to suggest that in her the ruler's two bodies – one temporary, the other temporal – have joined together in this image of the untouchable Virgin Queen. Recognition of her comes through externals, while her face, almost insignificant in the visual field, appears as a reductive, nearly impersonal sign . . .[20]

There is a central question that the problematization of the surface/depth relationship by both literally and figuratively masking garments and accessories throws into relief: what is more real, ultimately, the face or the mask that covers it? Although recent studies on the ascendancy of the simulacrum – to which this discussion will return – have foregrounded the pervasiveness of simulating strategies in contemporary culture, this puzzling issue is certainly not new. In the late European Renaissance, for example, it was mystifyingly common for revellers to wear a double mask, so that when the first layer came off, others would think they were beholding the true face. That masks, and perhaps clothes generally, have the power of revealing rather than occulting their wearers' actual or imaginary identities is overtly conveyed by items whose role is to function as signifiers of authority. In this instance, more emphatically than in others, the mask obviously does not

17. Breward, *Culture of Fashion*, p.65.

18. Roy Strong (1965), *Hans Eworth: A Tudor Artist and His Circle*, Leicester, p.x.

19. Andrew Belsey and Catherine Belsey (1990), 'Icons of Divinity: Portraits of Elizabeth I', in Lucy Gent and Nigel Llewellyn (eds), *Renaissance Bodies*, London, p.11.

20. Brilliant, *Portraiture*, p.103.

hide but actually gives official shape to its wearer's powers: the priest wears a figurative mask when he listens to the penitent through the screen of the confessional, which symbolically invests him with divine authority; the surgeon dons a protective but also dauntingly deindividualizing shield that may well have the effect of awing the patient into submission; the robber derives authority from the wearing of masks, be it in the form of rather unglamorous stockings or explicitly carnivalesque props such as the ones employed in the film *Killing Zoe*.

These authoritative masks also draw attention to the function of the false face as a kind of shelter. In this respect, the mask is a token of the desire for self-protection, which is varyingly exemplified by the growing of beards, the elaboration of hairdos or the artful reshaping of eyebrows, the wearing of wigs, jewellery, or make-up, the practices of dyeing, plastic surgery, cranial moulding, foot-binding, circumcision and countless other forms of physical editing. These may be seen as instances of violation of and interference with the putatively natural body, but also offer insights into the ways in which dress itself operates, in its apparently gentler but no less momentous manipulations of the body: after all, many clothing contraptions, such as pads, heels and bras, simulate deformation quite deliberately.

Masking, of course, is also a way of confronting a deep-seated uneasiness about nudity that is pivotal to Western constructions of sexuality. Paradoxically, however, at the same time as the unclothed body is declared indecent and dress is invested with the ethical function of policing its frontiers, clothing itself has been frequently branded as immoral: perhaps because, whilst it regulates corporeality, dress cannot claim to transcend the body but is ineluctably attached to it, carries the taint of an alliance with the material and is indeed literally soiled by the body's leaky surfaces. As Ribeiro observes: 'Dress, as an art so closely linked to the body, so revelatory of conscious or unconscious sexuality, is constantly liable to hostile interpretation.'[21] The medieval belief that 'too great a concentration on worldly things [such as dress] demeans human spirituality'[22] is still observable in much more recent times: Rousseau and many a Romantic after him, for their part, viewed fashion as a form of corruption of the natural state to which so-called civilized societies ought to seek to return; and Wollstonecraft, for example, asserts that 'an air of fashion is but a badge of slavery',[23] marking a diminution of intellectual faculties in the service of frivolity.

21. Aileen Ribeiro (1985), *The Art of Dress: Fashion in England and France, 1750–1820*, New Haven and London, p.3.

22. Ibid.

23. Mary Wollstonecraft (1792), *A Vindication of the Rights of Woman*, quoted in Ribeiro, *The Art of Dress*, p.3.

If clothes are unreliable partners, the fact remains, however, that in the West, nakedness has been construed as proverbially disturbing, primarily because it acts as a particularly unsettling reminder of the body's boundlessness and diffusion. Western societies seem to have dealt with this problem in two main ways, and both hinge on the principle of sublimation. On the one hand, the sprawling body has been translated into art: in his seminal study *The Nude*, Clark maintains that the aesthetic transmutation of the body into an artefact succeeds in metamorphosing the unsatisfactory physical organism into a harmoniously balanced and therefore satisfying entity. Whilst nakedness signifies, for him, the absence of clothes as a source of embarrassment, nudity stands for a successfully sanitized, refined and legitimately displayable material structure, safely emptied of all troubling vestiges of carnality. Nakedness, in Clark's discourse, is a demeaning memento of animality; nudity, by contrast, indicates the ability to transcend corporeality and its flickering frontiers through the hypostatizing of the body and its transformation into an icon of shimmering impregnability.[24] Berger opposes Clark by arguing that to be naked and to want to be naked is a means of accepting one's bodily status and of hopefully relishing it, whereas the transposition of anatomical nakedness into artistic nudity amounts to a colonization of the body's most instinctual drives.[25] Nead, in the wake of Kristeva, observes that it is quite pointless either to prioritize the nude as an aesthetically pleasing and ideologically stabilizing whole over the naked as a disturbingly disorganized jumble of fleshly fragments and mental affects, or indeed to idealize the naked as an uncorrupted corporeal dimension in contrast with the nude as a policed adaptation of the physical being, because the translation of the body into art is not an option, but rather a reminder of the fact that the body only exists through representations of the body.[26]

If the body is not transposed into art, the alternative possibility is its translation into dress. The body is actually translated into dress rather than merely covered by it because the clothed body is not the binary opposite of the unclothed body, as a site of eroticism and desire, but a variation on or version of it: dress can be invested with the power to evoke sexual fantasies analogous to the ones that the subject may aim at eliciting by parading an ungarbed form. These fantasies, moreover, are not only stimulated in the observer of a clothed body, but also, sometimes more importantly, in the wearer: dress, in this regard, may be equated with an experience of intoxication that involves simultaneously the psychological and physiological

---

24. Kenneth Clark (1956), *The Nude: A Study of Ideal Art*, London.
25. John Berger (1972), *Ways of Seeing*, London and Harmondsworth.
26. Lynda Nead (1992), *The Female Nude: Art, Obscenity and Sexuality*, London.

dimensions of the subject's being. Clothes fit, or fail to fit for that matter, their wearers mentally no less vitally than physically. In the masking of the body and of its nakedness, what is concurrently at stake is the obliteration of its precarious boundaries, of the intimation that its hypothetical depths may turn out to be wholly fictitious, indeed of the prospect that the body may only exist in and through representations. Such representations are always, to some degree, sartorial, since even the nude figure immortalized by high art is an artfully tailored construct, designed to frame the body's potential seamlessness.

Covering and Uncovering: Donne's *Elegy XIX*

John Donne's attention to the body in his poetry has received a good deal of critical comment, but his poem *Elegy XIX: On His Mistress Going to Bed* is unusual in his work in that it explores in some detail the relationship of clothing to the body and illustrates a number of different perspectives on dressed and undressed bodies and the processes that accompany them. It turns on the process of revelation and its paradoxes, writing and rewriting the surface/depth relation so frequently that the oblique dividing line is rendered obsolete. On first reading the poem would appear to have a fairly simple and predictable trajectory: at the outset a woman is fully clothed, and she removes each item of her clothing in a slow-motion striptease until she is naked. A male speaker commentates on her actions, rhapsodizing at each new revelation. The poem is constructed of multiple layers, and its unfolding is anchored to the stages of clothing: in a neat reversal of placing clothes on hangers each garment and accessory is a peg upon which hangs a new speculation. On looking more closely however, clothing proves to be a far from unified or unifying trope: through it the poem lays bare the heterogeneous premises of its own construction, undressing itself and undermining any easy notions about relationships within the poem, whether between subject and object, male and female or dress and the body. Borders and frames are set up, but simultaneously dissolved into a ragbag of disparate scraps, unconvincing in their finality.

The first question that arises is who, or what, is being undressed here, and as a supplementary, is there actually any undressing at all? Curiously, the effect is not of becoming naked, of uncovering, but the opposite, an accumulation of detail, visual, textual and material, that covers and indeed over-dresses. At the most obvious level, the bare page is clothed, Donne uses long lines and continuous text with no breaks for stanzas; it is a substantial block decorated with punctuation and capital letters. In textual terms too it is by no means a stripped-down piece of writing: it is swagged and festooned with conceits and diverting frills of reference to a range of different discourses. This immediately questions the simple division between dressed and undressed, between a 'true' unadorned essence and a falsifying superficial layer, because the two cannot be separated, the poem cannot exist in a pure form outside the dressing of language, and the conceits and diversions are not extra embellishments but the substance, the fabric of the writing itself. Just as a garment is a collection of surfaces, and would collapse without its seams and trimmings, so the poem is dependent on its surfaces; despite its outward protestations of the distinction between such surfaces and the depth that is 'true', it demonstrates that no such distinction is possible.

This is admitted tacitly in the failure to deliver the naked female body that is promised. Despite the enticing suggestion that we as readers will see the unnamed woman undressed, no part of her body ever appears, no limb or organ is named. Instead we are given a strangely surreal experience in which the taking off of a piece of clothing reveals not the expected body inside the material casing, but the outside, the external world. The girdle when removed shows 'a far fairer world', the gown a sunny landscape with hills and flowers, and these open into an even more dizzying perspective of America and the new Empire. Removed objects are even replaced by themselves, as with the coronet, which when taken off shows a 'diadem', an exactly synonymous decoration, as if there is nothing to reveal but an endlessly receding succession of almost identical items: like the mask, it only conceals another mask. The woman has no body within the text, only the most textual of bodies, being made up entirely of sliding metaphorical and metonymical signifiers that have no corporeal signified.

The poem is *not* without a body, however: flesh does appear and is named, but it is not hers but that of the male speaker. From the beginning we are provided with a running commentary on the condition of his own body, starting with the veiled reference to his erection, and moving through direct naming of other parts. The specifically named physical axes around which the scene revolves are his eyes, his hands and his penis, three of the most significant items in the panoply of masculine power. The coincidence of these organs and limbs suggests a voyeuristic masturbatory fantasy, organized around the speaker's solitary pleasure, exclusive of any participation by the object-woman, and appealing to the equally solitary pleasure of the reader. The elusive quality of the woman is a function of the narrative technique of the poem: she has no name other than 'madam', she does not speak and she has no body, only the onion-like wrapping of metaphorical layers that have no centre. If we exclude for the moment the closing couplet, it is easy to believe that the speaker is in fact alone and the scene entirely imaginary. In this series of absences, of shifting signifiers, the necessary guarantee of the poem's meaning and the legitimacy of the sexual enterprise (and by train of association the colonial project that serves him as metaphor) is the phallus, his rising 'flesh' that by being contrasted with rising hair enables him to distinguish between the impulse of angels and the prompting of evil sprites.

To return to the final couplet, these lines produce a new sequence of interpretation, which while not nullifying the possibilities already outlined, introduces a further range of reference. The lines are a typically dense conceit, 'To teach thee, I am naked first; why then/ What needst thou have more covering than a man?' The staged striptease, real or fantasized, is reassigned in this sentence, in which the speaker shows that it is fact *he* who has been undressing during the course of the poem: he is 'naked first', suggesting that she has remained clothed, and the elaborate descriptions of her disrobing are an incitement to her to comply with them and not an account of her actions. The poem becomes, through the transformation of the last lines, an exhortation to an unwilling partner that resembles more closely others of Donne's poems, such as *The Flea* or works like his contemporary Andrew Marvell's *To His Coy Mistress* than the elaboration of a private sexual display. This shift alters the character of the woman from an immodest exhibitionist to someone rather more reticent. It is he who is made naked by speaking, literally revealing himself through words, and the words that he casts off reassemble themselves as clothing for the woman who, as we have seen, is densely covered in text by the end. In doing this he gathers to himself the erotic effects of undressing previously attributed to the woman; as it is now he who is stripping he becomes both the source and the destination of eroticism, underlining the solitariness of the pleasures suggested by the earlier conjunction of eyes, hands and penis.

Apart from this surprising shift of subjectivity, there are at least two other significant ideas in the couplet, teaching and covering, that summarize much of what has gone before. The first, teaching, is crucial to the poem's manipulation of the body/dress/nakedness triad. In her book *Seeing Through Clothes* Anne Hollander contests the common-sense notion that nakedness remains the same regardless of time and place and that only clothing changes:

But art proves that nakedness is not universally experienced and perceived any more than clothes are. At any time, the unadorned self has more kinship with its own usual *dressed* aspect than it has with any undressed human selves in other times and places, who have learned a different visual sense of the clothed body. It can be shown that the rendering of the nude in art usually derives from the current form in which the clothed figure is conceived. This correlation in turn demonstrates that both the perception and self-perception of nudity are dependent on a sense of clothing – and of clothing understood through the medium of a visual convention.[27]

This argument has a number of implications for the analysis of Donne's lines. Hollander suggests that the perception of nakedness is learned according to the visual conventions that attach to the clothed body in any period. What the speaker in the poem seems to be doing is engaging directly in the process of producing nakedness in accordance with visual conventions. The process of learning nakedness is evident: the woman is being instructed by the tutoring male voice, who finally admits that he is teaching, ostensibly by his own actions, but also through a series of comparisons, metaphors and references to other discourses such as geography, theology and warfare.

He is not referring simply to these discourses, however, but to the pictorial representation of them. Although the poem seems to be in constant movement, it is actually a series of tableaux, briefly held poses of bodies with careful disposition of accessories, a succession of diachronic moments rather than a continuous film. He states explicitly that 'like pictures . . . are all women thus arrayed', clearly drawing her, and our, attention to a visual frame of reference. The 'spangled breastplate' is an allusion to armour that derives from the extended metaphor of battle that opens the poem, but it also carries a strong association with paintings of warlike goddesses and amazons who have removed their armour for dalliance. It echoes the cast-off jewelled bodice of Tintoretto's *Susannah and the Elders*, a painting in which several clearly identifiable discarded garments litter the visual space, and one that constructs neatly the kind of titillating revelation the speaker is endeavouring to encourage. By reference to this type of painting he offers a way in which the woman can see herself, and be at ease with an image of herself undressed. This recalls John Berger's assertion that a woman is always accompanied by the image of herself, she can only 'be' by reference to her visual double.[28] The speaker evokes another genre in the landscape envisaged when the gown is taken off: this time one that speaks of the natural world and offers the possibility of seeing herself, again in terms of a classical context, as a pastoral nude. The comparison drawn in this kind of painting is between the naturalness of the landscape and that of the naked body, so that the latter's being 'natural' is nothing to be ashamed of. As well as instructing the woman in the visual etiquette of nakedness, the speaker is also eroticizing the scene for himself. As Hollander asserts, awareness of the absence of clothes is a necessary predicate to the erotic experience of the undressed body:

---

27. Anne Hollander (1975), *Seeing through Clothes*, Berkeley, p.xiii.
28. Berger, *Ways of Seeing.*

Since the erotic awareness of the body always contains an awareness of clothing, images of bodies that aim to emphasize their sexual nature will make use of this link. They will tend to display the emphatic outline, posture and general proportions of a body customarily clothed in fashionable dress, so as to make it seem denuded.[29]

The descriptions in the poem conform to this statement: the focus in terms of clothing is on the upper body, the girdle, the breastplate, the busk, the coronet, which are the elements emphasized in contemporary female portraiture; legs and buttocks are the sartorial and erotic focus of the masculine form, as we can see in the close-fitting hose and exaggeratedly padded shorts worn by gentlemen in life and on canvas. The naked woman that Donne and the speaker wish to create has the overstated breasts and belly common to both painted nudes of the period and current fashion. Kenneth Clark's observations on the distinction between nakedness and nudity are also of relevance, Donne has no desire to create an awkwardly naked woman, but a polished and refined object of beauty, an improvement on the disorderly female flesh. It is an inversion of Clark's notion in which he sees the shabby real body translated into the pleasing order of art: Donne adds an extra stage to the process, in which the translation is applied backwards to create an ordered real body. It also nicely illustrates Nead's contention of Clark's idea, that the body does not exist outside representation of it.

Awareness of the flesh prompts a consideration of its relation to matters unearthly within the frame of reference of religious painting, and here he casts his net widely to include both Christian and non-Christian iconography. The removing of shoes is linked to entering a temple, a practice that does not correspond to Western Christian rituals, but is picked up in the next lines as related to 'Mahomet's Paradise'. Through this link the shoes are confounded with the 'white robes' of Christian angels, and he clearly wishes to suggest that no sin is being committed, that her actions are both natural like the landscape and supernaturally sanctioned; and he hedges his bets by invoking the gods of Christianity and Islam alongside the pagan deities of his earlier examples. His theology at this point is weak, however: Mahomet's paradise contains virgins as a reward for the faithful, and angels, as Donne demonstrates elsewhere in *Air and Angels*, were the subject of considerable learned consternation on the issue of their corporeality, and were finally decided to possess a body that enabled them to carry out their function as visible messengers of God, but that was composed of a substance entirely unique, and bearing no similarity to human flesh.

29. Hollander, *Seeing Through Clothes*, p.88.

The invocation of Christian theology seems doomed to run counter to the speaker's purpose, as it raises the constantly troubled relation of body to soul, particularly acute in this immediately post-Reformation period, where the body is increasingly being settled at the edge of the visual field, yet always returning to disrupt the cleared spiritual space. The simplicity of the equation he makes 'As souls unbodied, bodies uncloth'd must be/ To taste whole joys' is a deception that the complexity of the relation between the three elements underscores. His swift elision of spiritual and sexual pleasure attempts to banish both the corrupt body and obstructive clothing; but the central pivot of the lines 'unbodied, bodies' proves the necessity of flesh and garments – their apparent absence means that any pleasure taken in this absence is predicated on the importance of their existence. Expelled, they return insistently to occupy the pure vacuum that cannot be sustained: there is no dichotomy of clothes and body.

As if aware of the weakening force of his analogies from religion, he launches into another discourse, no less graphic than the others – cartography. This too is a metaphor he uses in other poems, most notably in *Hymn to God my God, in my Sickness*, 'Whilst my Physicians by their love are grown/ Cosmographers, and I their Map, who lie/Flat on this bed . . .'. Here he acknowledges the passivity of the person as map: he is the love-object of the doctors, situated as a woman by their activity relative to his lack of it. The map is flat on the bed as he wishes the woman to be in *Elegy XIX*; but there is another persuasive comparison to be drawn from the specific map in this case, that of America. The colonial metaphor is an obvious one, and commentators have drawn attention to the gendered implications of colonial language, with its reference to virgin territories and the kind of mastery that Donne speaks of in the poem. This refers directly to the kind of scopic regime elaborated by Foucault, in which the gaze secures power over the object gazed upon. But a slightly different interpretation is also possible in this instance, by drawing on the tradition of Renaissance portraiture, and in particular of representations of Elizabeth I. In many of the portraits of Elizabeth she appears in relation to a map, and in a number of them actually becomes the map itself. The Ditchley portrait is probably the best-known example; but there are others, including ones in which she transcends the earth and becomes a map of the whole universe.[30] It is a strategy for bracketing her powerless female body and assuming a god-like power of control of more than the land itself; she is the force that moves it. She cannot be secured by the gaze because she is located outside any possible

---

30. See: Belsey and Belsey, 'Icons of Divinity'.

viewing position, looking down from the heavens. In the period of Elizabeth's reign the portrait of the aristocratic woman carried with it some of this charge of power: to possess or to violate such a woman was to aspire dangerously to an assault on power itself. Leonard Tennenhouse observes the double drive in Jacobean dramatic practice, to represent and to destroy the female, and particularly the aristocratic female, body: '. . . such violence is never simply violence done to them as women. It is always violence done to one occupying a particular position in the social body as it was conceived at the time.'[31] The pleasure in looking on a portrait like this is coloured by such transgressive urges: Donne's desire for mastery is greater than that of the colonist, it reaches to the highest level.

What is clear from the descriptions that the speaker gives is that the woman is of some status: her clothes are rich and ornate, and part of his pleasure is in the clothes themselves; they carry an autonomous erotic charge. The comparison is made with Atlanta's balls and the 'coveting' experienced in relation to them, which distracts attention from the female body. Here the ornaments are not erotic because metonymic, but independently so: they are objects of desire for the viewer just as much as for the wearer. As metonym, though, the clothes indicate wealth, and the speaker's desire is for the wealthy woman, not the ordinary female flesh. The sexual *frisson* of possession is heightened by the costliness of the prize, 'the mine of precious stones'. The aristocratic position of the woman immediately summons the destructive desires suggested by Tennenhouse. As well as a wardrobe inventory in which the clothes are examined and strewn about, the body that wears them is also inventoried, its parts considered and thrown aside. The convoluted syntax of the lines '. . . show/ Thy self: cast all, yea, this white linen hence' suggests that it is parts of herself, rather than the linen, that is being cast. The undertone of violence and dismemberment that is inaugurated in the metaphor of warfare with which the poem opens persists, and recalls Lacan's 'imagos of the fragmented body', the aggressive intentions that he immediately goes on to relate, among other things, to fashion.[32] There is a confusion of agency, in that the woman is being encouraged to dismember herself through the removal of her clothes, yet the activity, as we have noted, is all on the part of the male speaker. It is an invitation to participate in the reduction of her body to fragments. Laid flat on the bed, she is not only a map of the world, but an anatomical diagram of herself, subject to the dissecting and investigative hands of the 'licenced'

31. Leonard Tennenhouse (1989), 'Violence Done to Women on the Renaissance Stage', in Nancy Armstrong and Leonard Tennenhouse (eds), *The Violence of Representation: Literature and the History of Violence*, London, p.77.

32. Jacques Lacan (1977), *Ecrits: A Selection*, trans. Alan Sheridan, London, p.11.

lover–surgeon. The medical image has a faint echo in the 'midwife' of later lines; the only possible model for the representation of female genitals is from the veiled aggression of the depiction of the dissection of a corpse or the often brutal practice of seventeenth-century gynaecology.

The public justification for anatomical scrutiny, as well as for map-making, was the expansion of knowledge. The idea of knowledge has a correlation with the thread of teaching and instruction that is woven into the poem, and this tie is exploited in its final section. The speaker sets up the opposition across the scene between the eyes of fools, that are unknowing because they cannot see beneath the woman's clothing, and his own knowing eyes. He compounds the link between seeing and knowing in the image of women as books; and here their clothing is compared to the book's cover and the women themselves to the volume within. Again, the body is text, and he wishes to be able to read it in order to 'know' her. It is private knowledge, not be revealed to 'fools', and its privacy hinges on the punning double sense of knowledge where to know a woman is to have sexual intercourse with her. He is declaring, in effect, that clothes obstruct both sexual and intellectual knowledge, that they are an unbreachable boundary that armours it (as he has already implied) against his penetration. Despite this declaration, he has demonstrated that garments are no such thing, and are in fact instrumental to his display of knowledge, eminently permeable to his mastering gaze and crucial to his erotic experience. The common synonym for a book's cover is its 'binding', but his pretended belief that the woman's self is integrated and contained neatly within her fabric casing is a fallacy: her clothes do not bind her into a smoothly boundaried whole, but enable her to be severed and divided, making her complicit in her own fragmentation. All of the layered and multiple meanings are triumphantly gathered in almost the last word of the flourish of the final couplet – covering. This one word releases in a flood, a textual *jouissance*, all the previously compartmentalized notions: it is the covering of clothing, the 'discovering' of bodies and countries, the unbinding/binding of the book/body, and another euphemism for sex. Such is the impact of this cacophony of meanings that it is difficult to distinguish them, they cross and re-cross, echoing and resonating so that no final closure is possible, despite the formal device of the rhymed lines. The woman has apparently been undressed in order to be covered, he has undressed to become a covering: yet the neat exchange of clothing for nakedness collapses, pulled apart by the multivalency of the meaning of dress. The boundaries between the clothed body and the naked one, the male and female bodies, the represented body and the real dissolve, and the final effect is of a whirling world of paint and text, of fabric and flesh.

Simulation and Repetition

These instances of effacement of physicality revamp the need to address the surface/depth relationship. As suggested earlier, this necessity, which is both epistemological and ontological, has gained special urgency as a result of, or at any rate in conjunction with, recent evaluations of contemporary culture, such as Deleuze's, Baudrillard's and Eco's, as a culture of simulacra. The following section will focus on the relationship between dress as a discourse of simulating representations and phenomena of reproduction and repetition.

According to Deleuze, the ascendancy of the simulacrum in contemporary culture entails that identity, deprived of substance, is itself simulated, 'produced as an optical "effect"'.[33] Any object or idea is endlessly repeatable, recyclable and reproducible: fashion, superfluous to say perhaps, epitomizes this pervasive condition, thus challenging conventional myths of origin and originality, as well as the humanist association of identity with sameness, by positing a subject that is always more than one, as an alternation of masks, costumes and disguises. Nothing ever begins; everything is always already a reiteration, for the very concept of the original presupposes the possibility of its being imitated:

> If repetition requires something that is already fixed and finished, already consti-
> tuted as an essence, then it is equally true that originality or essence can never be
> apprehended as such unless the possibility exists for it to be copied or reiterated.
> The question 'how can you have repetition without an original?' brings with it the
> less obvious question 'how can you have an original which it would be impossible
> to represent or duplicate? . . . origin and repetition are to be understood as moments
> in an unending process of mutual definition and redefinition.[34]

However, repetition inevitably holds scope for an element of difference, however minute or imperceptible: indeed, repetition could not be identified, were it not for this degree of divergence from the source, for how could we say that it was replicating anything at all, if we were not in a position to relate it differentially to something else? Because of the incidence of difference, repetition cannot be exploited as a guarantee of stability, permanence or constancy. Moreover, the interplay of repetition and difference posits itself as an eminently theatrical phenomenon, without which there would be no movement, no narrative, no intercourse, since signs would amount to one-use-only units unamenable to recognition if used again in different contexts.

33. Gilles Deleuze (1994), *Difference and Repetition*, trans. Paul Patton, London, p.xix.
34. Steven Connor (1988), *Samuel Beckett: Repetition, Theory and Text*, Oxford, pp.3–5.

The notion of difference plays a central part in the discourse of fashion, in so far as it is precisely through crafty variations on a given theme, however minimal, marginal, indeed inessential these may be, that the clothing industry pays homage to the myths of novelty and uniqueness. As Baudrillard points out: 'no object presents itself as a mass-produced object but rather as a model. Every object distinguishes itself from others through a difference, whether of colour, accessory or detail.'[35] On the one hand, although the domain of clothes is one of serial commodification, the idea of difference allows the fashion trade to personalize its objects as unprecedented creations. On the other, in so far as any new object is only a reinterpretation of previous objects, a slightly altered replica of anterior models, the concept of difference serves to underscore the untenable character of the ideal of originality. As a corollary, fashion's insistence on difference may yield two quite opposite readings of the original's significance. On one level, the diversification of the original's meaning creates scope for experiment and playful relocations of both its denotational and connotational messages. On another level, reproduction may invest the original with fresh authority and restore its uniqueness, its value now lying, in Berger's words, 'in it being *the original of a reproduction*'.[36] Though deprived of its literal uniqueness and uncontested prerogative to communicate a particular message, the original may again become the focus of worship, of a nostalgic 'bogus religiosity',[37] designed to compensate for what it has lost by being made endlessly reproducible. A fashion photograph based on the 'popularization' of a canonical painting, provides a good example of the ambiguous relationship between originals and their copies, reproductions or parodies. The contemporary image is decidedly polyphonic in its use of the techniques of visual quotation and stylistic pastiche. Whether or not we recognize its artistic antecedent, there can be little doubt as to its derivation from iconographic sources steeped in tradition. But the photograph also raises somedifficult and perhaps unanswerable questions. Does the present-day image gain authority from its explicit reference to High Art? Or is the illustrious predecessor's own charisma reinforced by its contemporary reworking? Is the original's power diminished by its transformation into a fashion plate? Or is it enhanced by such an overt reminder of its ongoing hold on the visual imagination?

Arguably, cultural status lies neither with the original nor with its recreation, for past and present, the old and the new, the work of art and its mass-produced replica are constantly mapped by citation on each other. The

35. Jean Baudrillard (1988), 'The System of Objects', in John Thackara (ed.), *Design After Modernism – Beyond the Object*, London, p.174.
36. Berger, *Ways of Seeing*, p.21.
37. Ibid., p.23.

Figure 10. Michael SANDERS, *Virgin*, 1997, photograph. © Michael Sanders, 1997.

creations of internationally renowned designers have attained to the position of works of art, amenable to the idolizing strategies described by Berger in relation to painting, no less than traditional art objects have increasingly come to be defined on the basis of their market value. However, fashion's relentless and ineluctable involvement in dynamics of mass-production, serialization and reassemblage in accordance with the logic of 'organized flimsiness'[38] as its defining traits, has no viable competitors in its exposure of the mythical nature of the original and the spuriousness of the concepts of wholeness, harmony and homogeneity that are presumed to distinguish it. This is precisely a consequence of the fact that even though, as Baudrillard stresses, '*The object must not escape death*',[39] this demise never amounts to the object's total obliteration, but rather to prospects of resurgence, replication and mutation, of translation of the fragile and perishable into the enduring and self-perpetuating, in an unarrestable process of semiotic vampirism guaranteed by the interaction of repetition and difference.

It is difference that produces activity, meaning and stories, by spotlighting the inconstant rhythms through which repetition manifests itself: 'Repetition is no more the permanence of the One than the resemblance of the many. The subject of the eternal return is not the same but the different, not the similar but the dissimilar, not the one but the many, not necessity but chance.'[40] Furthermore: 'It is because nothing is equal, because everything bathes in its difference, its dissimilarity and its inequality, even with itself, that everything returns.'[41] Recurrence, then, does not certify the enduring validity of a stable self but actually underlines the inconsistencies and continuous modifications of any form of subjectivity. Things return not because of the inherent stability of their essences, but rather because, lacking any fixed substance, they need to reformulate themselves ceaselessly. Identity, accordingly, emerges as a series of fictional roles, briefly entertained and casually discarded, as that which gets repeated is not a stable personhood but the action of substituting one persona for another, one costume for another.

Concomitantly, recurrence cannot be conceived of as a deep structure, capable of perpetuating the correctness of a crystallized set of personal or collective characteristics, despite the changing appearances of all cultural configurations, since its import is purely *superficial*: '[Repetition] is not underneath the masks, but is formed from one mask to another ... The masks do not hide anything except other masks. There is no first term which

38. Baudrillard, 'System of Objects', p.177.
39. Ibid.
40. Deleuze, *Difference and Repetition*, p.126.
41. Ibid., p.243.

is repeated . . . There is therefore nothing repeated which may be isolated or abstracted from the repetition in which it was formed . . .'.[42] The thrust of Deleuze's argument is evidently anti-Platonic. It is quite ironical, in this respect, that Plato should have endeavoured to legitimize his distinction between 'things and their simulacra' by recourse to a myth, i.e. the parable of the cave, which is itself a kind of 'play'.[43] 'Overturning Platonism', therefore, does not only amount to 'denying the primacy of original over copy, of model over image; glorifying the reign of simulacra and reflections',[44] but also to an exposure of the fact that theatricality inexorably intrudes upon even the most illustrious manifestations of Western metaphysics in action.

Traditionally, repetition has been varyingly associated with either a sense of reassuring regularity – the movements of the planets, the recurrence of the seasons, the constancy of the heart beat – and with mechanical rhythms that carry dehumanizing and automatizing connotations. Recurrence may thus be deemed capable of stabilizing experience; yet it evinces instability and uncertainty. This incongruity is amply documented by the discourse of fashion, founded as this is on the subject's desire to flee habit and its parallel enslavement to it: any new identity is merely a variation on previous ones; all roles are interchangeable, their power to signify resting with differential and relational criteria rather than essences. The self is simply not inviolable. However, whilst the notion of ceaseless return – indeed, the return of the imperative to make, unmake and remake ourselves endlessly – frustrates all claims to novelty, the constant recirculation of already known motifs estranges and alienates the subject by questioning the very grounds on which familiar knowledge is based. It then becomes impossible to differentiate between originality or innovation as self-contained and autonomous categories, on the one hand, and plagiarism or imitation as parasitic on anterior texts, on the other, for all new forms carry traces of the old – in the Derridean sense of signs entailing evidence of what is absent from them – and all simulations displace the import of their sources:

Whether in the order of spoken or written discourse, no element can function as a sign without referring to another element which itself is not simply present. This interweaving results in each 'element' . . . being constituted on the basis of the trace within it of the other elements of the chain or system. This interweaving, this textile, is the *text* produced only in the transformation of another text. Nothing,

42. Ibid., p.17.
43. Ibid., p.60.
44. Ibid., p.66.

neither among the elements nor within the system, is anywhere ever simply present or absent. There are only, everywhere, differences and traces of traces.[45]

Fashion capitalizes at all times on this interaction of presence and absence, by grafting each of its novel texts upon prior narratives, in such a way that none of these is either left unadulterated or utterly cancelled. Fashion's text, then, is essentially a palimpsest, a 'manuscript, the original writing on which has been effaced to make room for a second'.[46] It is vital to observe that the palimpsest entails an effacement of the anterior text, not its erasure: the coalescence of the old and the new thus delivers a pattern 'through which the traces – tenuous but not indecipherable – . . . of previous writing should be translucently visible'.[47] Deleuze also draws attention, no less importantly, to certain crucial qualitative differences between copies and simulacra. The copy, though second-rate, is still supposed to be related to the worthy original, whereas the simulacrum is a free-floating entity: 'The copy . . . is far from a simple appearance, since it stands in an internal, spiritual, noological and ontological relation with the Idea or model . . . What is condemned in the figure of simulacra is the state of free, oceanic differences, of nomadic distributions and crowned anarchy . . .'.[48]

The copy aims at operating as a transparent envelope, enclosing the original it is supposed to replicate as its own supreme icon, ancestor, source of meaning and being; and in so doing, it paradoxically admits both to the independent existence of an original behind the replica and to its own desire to eliminate any reminders of difference between the original and the replica. Hence the logic of the copy exposes the instability of the concept of boundary: it frames something, the independent ontological status of which it is prepared to acknowledge, yet implicitly denies that autonomy, by deleting all indices of divergence and displacement, as though to suggest that the original and the replica were One. Simulacra, on the other hand, thrive on dislocation and uncontainable difference, on multiplicity and errantry. It is precisely in response to these subversive proclivities that they are demonized as inimical to the highest ethical principles. Primarily, they upset traditional oppositions, particularly the one between depth and surface, by refusing to embody any pre-existing values: their significance is deliberately and solely contingent and founded upon difference – not simply difference from something, but difference within:

45. Jacques Derrida (1982), *Positions*, trans. Alan Bass, Chicago, p.26.
46. *Concise Oxford Dictionary* (1964), Fifth Edition.
47. Jorge Luis Borges (1970), 'Pierre Meynard, Author of the *Quixote*', in *Labyrinths*, Donald A. Yates and James E. Irby eds, trans. James E. Irby, Harmondsworth, p.70.
48. Deleuze, *Difference and Repetition*, pp.264–5.

The power of simulacra is such that they essentially implicate at once the object = x in the unconscious, the word = x in language, and the action = x in history. Simulacra are those systems in which different relates to different by means of difference itself. What is essential is that we find in these systems no prior identity, no internal resemblance.[49]

The discourse of dress, like the simulacrum, blatantly flouts rigid compart-mentalizations and hierarchies, by fusing together psychological, linguistic and historical dimensions of experience, to the point that these become inextricable from one another: its manifestations cannot be traced back to the authority of a privileged point of origin or to a pure transcendent Form of the Platonic sort. As a result, dress treats everybody in the same way, i.e. with neither respect nor contempt, through the abolition of depth and the cultivation of repetition as the primary symbol not of stability but rather of discontinuity.

Fundamentally, then, the simulacrum challenges the doctrine of 'an Essential Copy [which] proposes that at a utopian extreme the image will transcend the limitations imposed by history, and will reproduce in perfect form the reality of the natural world'.[50] Indeed, the simulacrum does not merely call into question the existence of an original behind the copy – let alone the former's privileged status – but also problematizes the copy's meaning by deriding its claims, if not to authenticity, at least to its ability to encapsulate something of the original's excellence and hence to communicate didactically both the original's truth and its truthfulness. Relatedly, it would be quite self-deceiving to treasure an item of dress as a microcosmic incarnation, albeit conditional and imperfect, of an original conceived by the designer's genius, since, as was argued at length in the section on fashion and history, no such item could be unproblematically referred back to a single spatial or temporal source.

However, not all forms of reproduction and simulation transgress with equal vigour the ethos of mimesis. In fact, Deleuze draws a distinction between two main types of repetition and their respective effects: 'One is a "bare" repetition, the other a covered repetition, which forms itself in covering itself, in masking and disguising itself . . . it is the masked, the disguised or the costumed which turns out to be the truth of the uncovered'.[51] 'Bare', or, as the French term could also be translated, 'naked' repetition is only a crude form of reproduction, whilst 'covered', or, alternatively, 'clothed' repetition modifies its sources through the superimposition of metaphorical

49. Ibid., p.299.
50. Norman Bryson (1983), *Vision and Painting: The Logic of the Gaze*, London, p.13.
51. Deleuze, *Difference and Repetition*, p.24.

masks, shields and veils. The clothed variety displays a greater degree of truthfulness, in so far as it dismantles both the myth of originality and the illusion of depth. Not only is clothed repetition more authentic than its naked counterpart: it is actually its precondition, for it mirrors more faithfully the dislocating effects of all signification, the fact that depth is an effect of surfaces and that we could never conceive of depth were it not for our continual confrontation of surfaces and their unsettling insinuations that there may not be any reality beyond the facade.

In the frame of reference proposed by Baudrillard, the simulacrum – with, implicitly, the vestimentary masks that repeatedly underscore the theatrical/ simulating operations of the language of clothes – marks the most recent of four phases in the development of the relationship between representation and reality. Baudrillard thus attempts to answer the question 'what is representation?' in terms of the following modalities:

– it is a reflection of a basic reality
– it masks and perverts a basic reality
– it masks the *absence* of a basic reality
– it bears no relation to any reality whatever: it is its own pure simulacrum.[52]

The first stage corresponds to the quasi-metaphysical notion that fashion incarnates the Spirit of the Age, the underlying concerns, aspirations and beliefs of a whole society. The second alludes to the conviction that dress as a surface conceals a deep self, to be uncovered through the implementation of harsh iconoclastic measures. But it also echoes the tendency to ridicule fashion as a peripheral occurrence, a trivial aberration in an otherwise profoundly meaningful culture, so as to expunge all traces of that culture's own economic and ideological promulgation of principles of deferred satisfaction and planned obsolescence. The third case could be said to refer to the symbolic disembodiment whereby carnality is transmuted into dress as a substitute flesh: here, artificial clothes do not shroud the supposedly natural body, but rather its absence. In the fourth scenario, the obligation to relate dress to an essential reality is lifted: dress is no longer a superficial signifier, elusively yet incontrovertibly connoting a deep signified – be the latter a presence or an absence – since the very notion of the signified has been removed from the agenda. If stage three required us to confront the possibility of the body's absence beneath the sartorial envelope, it still retained, however, an implicit faith in the depth/surface binary: the deep meaning lurking under

---

52. Jean Baudrillard (1983), *Simulations*, trans. Paul Foss, Paul Patton and Philip Beitchman, New York, p.11.

the surface was not, of course, a plenitude, a potentially fulfilling presence, but could nonetheless be envisaged as a separate category, a secret to be protected and guarded. Stage four invalidates the distinction between surface and depth much more drastically by suggesting that dress does not hide anything at all: it is itself a surface, or rather an interplay of surfaces, which neither occults a corporeal entity endowed with solidity and three-dimensionality nor obscures the lack of concreteness that attaches to this putatively deep substance. In fact, in referring only to itself and its superficiality, it simultaneously throws into relief the body's own depthlessness; dress neither reflects nor masks the body's reality; nor does it merely secrete the hollowness of that reality: though permanently connected to the body, it has no links with any reality whatsoever, because the body is simply not a reality of the kind promoted by mimetic regimes of signification but a Barthesian text that, onion-like, is enfolded circularly around an emptiness.

5

Clothes in Art – Painting In and Out of the Frame

It is pictorial art that dress most resembles, and to which it is inescapably bound, in its changing vision.[1]

The visual arts abound with examples of all the functions appropriated and dramatized by clothes presented in the preceding discussion: dress as an insulating frame or boundary and dress as a margin or connecting tissue; dress as a decarnalizing mechanism, operating in the service of the symbolic order, and dress as a material and materializing agency; dress as an ambiguous rim alluding to the return of the abject; as a sprawling body-without-organs propagating itself through contagion; as a fickle partner in an amorous relationship; or as a mask simultaneously impeding and facilitating disclosure. The multi-layered and polysemous character of even the simplest visual representation would seem to discourage any final categorization of the image, based on its articulation of any one single function, and foster, instead, an evaluation of its ability to combine disparate, indeed conflicting, functions. As a result, whilst assessing the status of the representation as an iconic boundary, say, or as a margin, rim, mask, and so forth, it would also seem appropriate to consider the extent to which different modalities criss-cross and interact within its discursive field.

Of course, the image's propensity to amalgamate divergent apprehensions of the role played by clothing in its structuring and displaying of the human body will depend, to a considerable degree, on the socio-historical circumstances under which it comes into being, the flexibility of their creative schemata and the scope for experimental challenge they may afford. So, for example, royal portraiture in the Western Renaissance could be said to emphasize the bounding and disembodying attributes of clothing far more explicitly than modernist art; or, as a further example, it could be argued that Surrealist painting offers more prominent illustrations of the liminal

---

1. Anne Hollander (1978), *Seeing Through Clothes*, New York, p.452.

nature of dress than styles less overtly concerned with the symbolic expression of submerged psychological events. What is hardly deniable, however, is the fact that the artistic presentation of the clothed body is a crucial index of codes of both self-discipline and self-display, behavioural and ritual conventions, structures of production and consumption and, last but not least, culturally sanctioned regimes of vision and visuality. The next section will be devoted to a survey of a few of the uses to which dress may be put in the visual arts, in the understanding that the range of both their actualized and their potential manifestations is virtually limitless.

Marc Chagall's *The Green Violinist* (1923–24) provides an interesting illustration of the proclivity, frequently exhibited by painted clothing in non-mimetic art, to act as a defining frame and as a blending agent at one and the same time. The central character's garments, with their vibrant colours set against a neutral background and their eminently geometric, quasi-Cubistic shapes, serve to isolate him from the surrounding world and thus clearly demarcate the boundaries of his body. Indeed, the physical form is not merely bounded by the clothes in question, but also somewhat decorporealized, by means of an irreverent distortion of both anatomy and perspective. As the fiddler's body is transmuted into a symbolic peg for its clothing, the garments themselves, primarily the exuberantly purple coat, acquire the status of a substitute flesh, as suggested by the juxtaposition of separate areas, in a fashion that is reminiscent of the rendering of muscular structures in anatomy textbooks. Compositional and iconographic analogies between the violin and bow and whatever may be glimpsed of the musician's body beneath the coat's schematic folds further reinforce the overall impression of disembodiment. However, if, on one level, the picture may be seen to dramatize the bounding and decarnalizing power of the symbolic, on another, Chagall's blatant defying of laws of time, space and gravity and his peopling of the canvas with floating forms and logically unconnected figures hints at a carnivalesque celebration of semiotic pulsions. The violinist's identity itself is fractured and dispersed into multiple personas, culminating in that of the hovering body, lifted to the rooftops by musical passion and Dionysian rapture. Accordingly, his clothes, far from operating unproblematically as a vehicle for self-differentiation or a guarantee of self-containedness, become so many joining filaments, connecting the central figure to the environment and its semi-spectral buildings, animals and humans. Whilst the upper part of the painting reflects, or is reflected by, the fiddler's clothed body by means of chromatic parallelisms, in the lower part of the canvas, the specular effect is conveyed through a formal and structural resemblance between the musician's trousers and the ladder and the windows of the houses over which he is suspended. The establishment of compelling connections between the

Figure 11. Marc CHAGALL, *The Green Violinist*, 1923–24, oil on canvas. Solomon
R. Guggenheim Museum, New York. Gift, Solomon R. Guggenheim, 1937.
Photograph by Robert E. Mates, The Solomon R. Guggenheim Foundation,
New York (FN 37.446).

central figure and its surroundings through the subtle manipulation of the visual effects of clothing suggests a painterly semiotization of the symbolic, the ultimate result of which is an unlimiting of the frame of the picture itself.

A striking example of clothing's ability to drain the body of any autonomous energy is supplied by Frederic Leighton's *Winding the Skein* (1878). The dominant mood evoked by this picture is ostensibly soporific, static, indeed stagnant. The sky and mountains in the background are overly stylized; the water is so excessively becalmed as to appear almost solid; the plant emerging behind the parapet, to the left of the figure of the little girl, is as rigid and motionless as it would be if it had been literally painted over the landscape; all the objects that populate the terrace are frozen and stubbornly resistant to change, including the shadows, which, like the plant, look as though they had been superimposed on the floor as compact objects intended to remain in the same place for ever. The two bodies themselves, in their harmoniously balanced immobility, exhibit sculptural traits that make even the most minutely rendered indices of physical activity, such as the curling of the toes, appear frozen and unamenable to further motility. Leighton's bodies, here as in many others among his most famous paintings, are purged of all vestiges of dynamic carnality, systematized, structured and methodically organized. It is in the clothes, by contrast, that all of the picture's loving vitality is instilled. Each pleat, fold or crease oozes vibrancy and energy, as though cloth and fabric were the only substances affected by a Mediterranean breeze to which the rest of the image is otherwise conspicuously oblivious. The vestimentary function dramatized by Leighton in *Winding the Skein* would seem to allude to the power of dress to recarnalize metaphorically the socialized body, by challenging the symbolic through its own unsuppressible, dynamic materiality.

Frida Kahlo's *The Two Fridas* (1939) depicts dress as a rim. The relationship between inner and outer dimensions is problematized by the simultaneous presentation of containing and bounding garments, which allow limited visual access to the flesh, and of an eminently graphic mapping of the body's inside on its outside. This subversion of conventional barriers exposes the precariousness of the rim and harks back to the mechanisms of expulsion typical of the phenomenon of abjection. The picture's pre-symbolic connotations are most obviously carried by the splitting of the subject into two complementary personas, connected by a concurrently umbilical and specular bond. The garments here depicted relate this fracture to a decentred cultural identity, forged out of both Latin American and European affiliations. The anatomical/surgical tropes bring out into the open concealed aspects of bodily existence with an explicitness that borders on audacity, thus provocatively

Figure 12. Frederic, Lord LEIGHTON, *Winding the Skein*, 1878, oil on canvas. © The Art Gallery of New South Wales, Sydney.

Figure 13. Frida KAHLO, *The Two Fridas*, 1939, oil on canvas. Courtesy of Museo de Arte Moderno, Mexico. Photo: AKG London.

infringing the divide between the private and the public. At the same time, the picture mocks the laws of traditional anatomical illustrations, by harnessing their hyper-mimetic ethos, here exemplified by the naturalistic rendering of the cardiac muscle and its ventricular structure, to a patently anti-mimetic project. The hidden body, methodically and clinically sanitized through abjection, as a necessary precondition of the subject's entry into the symbolic order, resurfaces in the guise of an excess over precise meaning. What is arguably most disturbing about the superimposition of the two halves of the heart over the chests of the two Fridas is that at the same time as it suggests an explosive breaking out of the submerged body, it also transmutes the organ into something of an accessory, an adjunct to clothing. This sartorialization of physicality is reinforced by Kahlo's inclusion 'into the lace bodice of her European self' of 'a stylized image of the female genitals'.[2] Thus, whilst the painting articulates a return of suppressed carnality, it simultaneously subsumes organic reality to a superficial system of symbolic codes and conventions, the vestimentary, whose effect is to seal the body's status as a decorporealized signifier. What we witness, therefore, is a hybrid register that nakedly enshrines an unresolved conflict between the forces of the imaginary and those of the symbolic, waged over the territory of the body and its clothes, the latter functioning at once as an insulating wrapper and as a permeable margin. It is in this unsettled tension that the abject manifests itself, as a tangled skein of affects dominated by a dread of the unbounded body as a breathing detritus, a palpitating carcass, an Undead.

An instance of the function of dress as an equivocal wrapper, drawn from the realm of dance, is supplied by a still of one of the opening scenes of the Royal Ballet's production of *Apollo* (1995). The body's gradual emergence from its chrysalis-like white bindings alludes to processes of birth and rebirth, which underscore the association of dress with both pre-symbolic and symbolic scenarios. In hermetically enveloping the body, the wrapper protects and insulates the vulnerable physical apparatus, but also precludes the possibility of interaction between the individual and the collective bodies. In this respect, Apollo's unbinding signals the subject's birth into the symbolic order, as a network of signifiers that enables and indeed requires discursive intercourse between the self and the Other. Yet the unwinding of the bands of cloth also represents a metaphorical rebirth into the semiotic, since the naked body it discloses operates as a potent reminder of the porousness of identity, of the individual subject's continual exposure to phenomena of introjection of the external world and projection of the internal one, of

2. David Lomas (1993), 'Body Languages: Kahlo and Medical Imagery', in Kathleen Adler and Marcia Pointon (eds), *The Body Imaged: The Human Form and Visual Culture Since the Renaissance*, Cambridge, p.18.

Figure 14. Still from The Royal Ballet's, *Apollo*, 1995. Photo Lesley Spatt.
© Lesley Spatt 1995.

expulsion and absorption through the rim of the skin itself. Moreover, the intimations of potential endlessness conveyed by the stretching of the unfurled wrapper beyond the limits of the picture's frame bring to mind the unterritorialized, diffuse and sprawling body that is supposed to characterize the pre-symbolic stages of psychic development.

Marchesa Casati, by Augustus John (1878–1961) is obviously an incarnation of the *femme fatale* type, as a subject whose seductiveness results from iconographic connections with the registers of the occult, the demonic and the vampiric, and that is conventionally associated with a penchant for luring man into the dismal abyss of perversity, owing to her inherent deceptiveness, sphinx-like mysteriousness and capricious duplicity. The *Marchesa's femme fatale* attributes are emphasized by vivid analogies between the colours and texture of her clothes and those of the romantic, almost sublime background against which she is set. Her role as an arch-seductress is further conveyed by the licentious and almost reptilian intensity of the woman's piercing eyes. While the red patches and streaks which interrupt the smooth creaminess of the garments, by evoking images of blood-shed and dismembered flesh hint at the stereotype of feral femininity. The fashionable propriety of the portrait is only a thin disguise, for connotations of potential wildness and ferociousness typical of the pictorial rendering of woman-as-animal. The bestial features of the garments in which the body is encased, their amalgamation of harshness and voluptuousness, attraction and threat, function as a metaphorical reminder of what might be hidden beneath the insulating barrier of dress: the fanglike quality of many a brushstroke would seem to allude to the dreaded phantom of the *vagina dentata*. As the clothing stuck to the woman's body transforms itself into the hide of a predatory animal, her supposedly bestial nature rises to the surface: dress as a façade turns out to be deeper than the depths it covers, just as the veil is ultimately a more authentic embodiment of the character's attributes than the natural body itself. If the association of femininity with brute animality is easy enough to deconstruct in the context of paintings that capitalize on the tempting powers of nudity or partial nudity, the dramatization of the beast–woman topos through the discourse of dress may make the decoding task more arduous: whilst summoning up apparitions of the female as 'a blind force of nature',[3] 'driven . . . by animal desire and animal instincts',[4] the clothed beast problematizes to an unparalleled degree the intricacies and vagaries of processes of cross-fertilization between the natural and the cultural, the private and the public, the human and the non-human.

3. Bram Dijkstra (1986), *Idols of Perversity: Fantasies of Feminine Evil in Fin de Siecle Culture*, New York and Oxford, p.240.

4. Ibid., p.290.

Figure 15. Augustus JOHN, *Marchesa Casati*, 1918–19, oil on canvas. Art Gallery of Ontario, Toronto, Canada. Photo: Bridgeman Art Library, London.

Dress may enhance the legibility of the body as a fundamentally animalistic compound; but it does so by constructing that body as, or through, artifacts. Hence its rhetoric may simultaneously camouflage and assimilate certain uncomfortable premonitions of destabilization where both the individual and the collectivity are concerned. Clothes that concurrently carnalize and disembody, bestialize and purge, both facilitate and hinder interpretation, in that they articulate a language, obstreperous in its silences and mute in its verbosity, that juxtaposes the latent and the manifest and thus interweaves a discourse of exteriority and display with a narrative of restraint and occlusion.

An alternative depiction of the mask as a simultaneously concealing and revealing tool is supplied by Nolan's *Kelly, Spring 1956* (1955). The painting bears witness to Nolan's devotion to the rediscovery and critical reappropriation of Australian mythology and folklore, specifically, in this case, the adventures hinging on the bushranger Ned Kelly, outlaw and folk hero, fighting against the oppressive authority of the colonial government. *Kelly* records the climax of Kelly's ordeal, namely the final shoot-out in which Kelly is injured and captured. The box-like mask around which the representation is orchestrated is an imaginative adaptation of the conspicuous helmet that the bushranger would actually wear in the course of his raids, and evokes, at one and the same time, a sense of protective insulation and an image of self-exposure and self-display by virtue of its very ostentatiousness. The helmet, moreover, could be seen as a reworking of aboriginal ritual apparel, the bush-mask that, like the shaman's mask, is supposed to enable its wearer to attain a close communion with natural and spiritual forces and thus relinquish personal identity. If, as an encasing structure, the mask hints at feelings of painful isolation and defeated loneliness, appropriate to the event documented by the painting, as a ceremonial accessory it simultaneously alludes to an interpenetration of self and other, inside and outside, which the translucent amorphousness of the setting vividly reinforces. The mask's ritual connotations may perhaps justify a reading of the quasi-pyramidal form dominating the painting's background as the awesome figure of a hooded priest presiding over a ceremony. Whilst fulfilling its task as an insulating boundary, therefore, the mask also operates as a mediating device between the internal and the external dimensions: indeed, it closely resembles a house with shuttered windows, through which the inner self may gaze out on to the outside world and through which the outside may, in turn, gain access to the subject's innermost being, as intimated by the partial, wound-like opening placed between the two eyes. The sense of undifferentiation between self and other conveyed by this ambivalent mask is intensified by the blending and criss-crossing of multiple planes within the picture's overall

Figure 16. Sidney NOLAN, *Kelly, Spring 1956*, Pipolin on board. Arts Council Collection, Hayward Gallery, London.

composition, the barren landscape and endless sky moving in and out of the stylized architectural structures that both replicate and amplify the basic design of Kelly's helmet. Further correspondences between inside and outside are implied by means of structural analogies between the central figure and its environment: the harrowing diagonals traced by the staves, for example, mirror the nervous tautness of the tendons in Kelly's neck. The shreds of patterned cloth/wallpaper echo the emotional fragmentation of the beaten outlaw, as well as insinuating the annihilation of living and germinating Nature: there is hardly any inkling of growth, let alone prosperity, in the desolate portion of the natural world visible in the picture's background. Nature, it seems, has been reduced to the socialized, tailored, indeed colonized dimension of interior design.

Closely related to the depiction of dress in art is the representation of activities such as weaving, spinning and embroidering, which highlight the indecisive character of clothing and the multifold symbolic connotations of cloth in general by means of their own hybrid status. Indeed, whilst weaving and other germane operations may evoke the image of a connecting and potentially harmonizing network, they simultaneously suggest the figure of the tangle, a random and rebellious mingling of threads, or even that of the web, as a structure that is both symmetrically contrived – and hence symbolic of order – and intended to entrap – and therefore evocative of a perilous loss of control. Cooper elucidates the ambivalent nature of the activity of weaving and of the image of the web, as signifiers of both hierarchy and system, on the one hand, and confusion and anarchy, on the other:

The primordial Weaver, the Great Weaver, is the creator of the universe, weaving on the loom of life the fate of all. All goddesses of Fate and Time are spinners and weavers. The Weaver is also the Cosmic Spider and the thread of the Great Weaver is the umbilical cord which attaches man to his creator and his own destiny and by which he is woven into the world pattern and fabric . . . The web of life, fate and time is woven by divine powers. The spider's web is a cosmic plan, with the radiation of the spatial components from the centre; the radii are the essential, with the circles as the existential and the analogous. The spider in the centre of the web can represent the sun surrounded by its rays reaching in all directions, but it is also lunar as depicting the life and death cycle of the manifest world and the wheel of existence, with death at the centre. It also shares the symbolism of the labyrinth as the dangerous journey of the soul.[5]

The network, then, suggests a relatively stable pattern of interaction, wherein change itself is predictable, as a manifestation of quantifiable permutational

5. J. C. Cooper (1982), *An Illustrated Encyclopaedia of Traditional Symbols*, London, p.190.

processes. The tangle, by contrast, disturbs and obscures any prospects of lasting stability by either blatantly resisting the regimentation of fluid threads into an orderly structure or turning the structure itself into a subversive weapon. If the network proposes the translation of a potentially pluri-directional skein into a delimited map, of a smooth into a striated space, the tangle transmutes striatedness back into smoothness.

Waterhouse's *Penelope and the Suitors* (1912) provides an example of the pictorial representation of weaving as an ambiguous activity. This ambiguity is largely conveyed through an emphasis on the traditional association of weaving and femininity: a problematic partnership laden with conflicting connotations. On the one hand, woman is conventionally invested with the responsibility of spinning the fabric of the community and sewing threads of connection; on the other, her engagement in the act of weaving is symbolically equated with deceitful plotting. This unresolved tension mirrors, moreover, the simultaneous celebration and demonization of female product-ivity, as both the index of woman's special role in the evolutionary chain and a reminder of her animalistic tendencies and potential for monstrosity. The impossibility of firmly securing the female body's boundaries, exacer-bated by its reproductive faculties, posits woman as a brindled being, lurching uncomfortably between two incompatible models. As well as perpetuating a stereotype of femininity centred on the conspiratorial inclinations of the weaver/deceiver, the association of woman with the production of cloth, fabric and ornament also serves to reinforce the binary opposition that conventionally equates modern male dress with integrity, functionality and simplicity and female clothing with surplus adornment, vanity and excess. As Fer observes, in fashion writing influenced by an aesthetics of purity, 'male dress manifested an advanced state of civilization in its lack of ornament, whereas women's dress marked an earlier state of development; the simplicity of male dress contrasted with the variety of decoration and ornament typified in women's clothes'.[6]

In *Penelope and the Suitors* the making of materials is a metaphorical equivalent for the making of the self. The legend underlying the picture emphasizes that the act of un-making, or undoing, is no less vital to the process of self-construction than the act of creation itself. Penelope will eventually have to yield to one of the many suitors who have occupied her house in Odysseus's absence, once the tapestry she is busy weaving has been completed. By undoing, at night, the work dutifully carried out in the course

6. Briony Fer (1993), 'The Hat, the Hoax, the Body', in Kathleen Adler and Marcia Pointon (eds), *The Body Imaged: The Human Form and Visual Culture Since the Renaissance*, Cambridge, p.167.

Figure 17. John William WATERHOUSE, *Penelope and the Suitors*, 1912, oil on canvas. Courtesy of the City of Aberdeen Art Gallery and Museums Collection.

of the day, she is able to defer that unpalatable decision and hence maintain her relative autonomy. Her identity is dependent on a destructive act that, paradoxically, turns out to be more productive, where self-fashioning is concerned, than the creative process itself. Penelope's duplicity alludes to the metamorphosis of a striated space – the orderly, hierarchical and fundamentally patriarchal power structures of the society she inhabits, which purposeful labour is supposed to epitomize – into a smooth space, a calculated and potentially transgressive purposelessness where making becomes, in Barthes's terms, an intransitive verb: weaving turns out to be not a means to an end but an end in itself.

That the acts of weaving and unravelling are pivotal aspects of Penelope's existence is confirmed by the fact that the gazes of all the figures presented in the painting converge on the thread she is about to sever, as a twofold signifier both of her creative project, in so far as the thread enables her to continue weaving, and of her hidden agenda, in so far as the act of breaking implicitly refers to destructive potentialities. Penelope's own look appears to flutter between the thread positioned below her eyes and the men located behind her. The contrast set up by Waterhouse between the fixedness of the suitors' staring eyes and the intermittent mobility of Penelope's look is reminiscent of the distinction, theorized by Bryson, between the Gaze, as a 'penetrating, piercing, fixing', 'vigilant' and 'masterful'[7] way of seeing, and the Glance, as a 'flickering' and 'ungovernable'[8] scopic mode. Although the situation captured by the painting would seem to offer scope for a classic rendering of the dominating Gaze, with man as its active bearer and woman as its passive object, Penelope's vibrant Glance disrupts the freezing and immobilizing power of the Gaze and, concomitantly, encroaches upon the power structures on which its traditional primacy rests. This transgressive move is aided by the dynamic interplay of diagonal lines, interfering with the compositional order of carefully balanced horizontal and vertical structures. Penelope's arms, the spool and the thread itself articulate a focal area of attention, constructed precisely on the basis of oblique lines, further echoed by more peripheral limbs, items of furniture, props and architectural motifs. Like Penelope's flickering glance, these diagonals introduce a sense of energy, movement, tension, even conflict, which serves to unsettle both the feeling of motionlessness and earthbound solidity associated with the horizontal direction and that of elevation and spiritual transcendence connected with verticality.

7. Norman Bryson (1983), *Vision and Painting:The Logic of the Gaze*, London, p.93.
8. Ibid., p.121.

As a spatial interweaving of the vertical and the horizontal, diagonals metaphorically suggest the operations of weaving itself, as an interplay of conflicting, yet complementary, movements, which carry multiple symbolic implications:

> The warp is the vertical plane, joining all degrees of existence; the qualitative essence of things; the immutable and unchanging; the *forma*; the masculine, active and direct; the light of the sun. The weft, or woof, is the horizontal; nature in time and space; the quantitative, causal and temporal; the variable and contingent; the human state; the *materia*, feminine and passive; the reflected light of the moon. The warp and weft in relationship form a cross at each thread, symbolizing the union of opposites, the male and female principles united.[9]

By deploying the disruptive power of obliqueness, *Penelope* sabotages the adversarial relationship that emplaces the vertical and the horizontal as mutually exclusive dimensions and, by symbolic analogy, polarizes in a totalitarian fashion the masculine and the feminine, quality and quantity, form and matter, the sun and the moon. It thus maps out a borderline region wherein creative and dismantling processes prove inextricably intertwined and the making of cloth/clothes constitutes an intriguing but inevitably provisional means of fashioning the self, which is incessantly open to prospects of reinvention and renegotiation.

As we have seen, one of the most prominent parts played by the representation of clothes in the visual field is to define, limit or unlimit, the body's space, by either framing it or hinting at the possibility of its spilling over and fading into the Other. Pictorial renderings of dress also, however, often serve to elucidate the body's relation to space, the latter signifying both an abstractly geometrical, architectonic or broadly compositional structure and a material embodiment of cultural and ideological modalities. A distinction should be drawn, in this respect, between representations of the clothed body in rural and urban settings. The paintings discussed below articulate the friction between these alternative spaces, as partial records of the transition from pre-industrial to industrial dispensations and hence of the inception of configurations of subjectivity specifically connected with the discourse of modernity.

What the rural typology most frequently yields is images of isolated figures (individuals, couples, small groupings) within a picturesque and idyllic landscape: their idealization of the countryside is primarily a means of empowering these solitary figures by investing them with exemplary status. Dress both facilitates and encapsulates this project of secular deification.

9. Cooper, *Traditional Symbols*, p.190.

Gainsborough's *Mr and Mrs Andrews* (*c*.1748–9) offers a paradigmatic illustration of this artistic trend. Despite the bucolic atmosphere of timelessness conjured up by the charming and mellow rendering of the landscape, the painting's chosen location is very real indeed: it represents the Andrews' estate, the 'Auberies' (outside Sudbury, Suffolk) and thus points directly to their worldly power and wealth; moreover, the realistically depicted rolling farmland is not only symbolic of the sitters' social standing but also of their productive and reproductive abilities, the sheaves of corn traditionally alluding to human fertility. What we are presented with, then, is a potent collusion of pastoral informality and a carefully contrived articulation of economic values and imperatives. The characters' clothes and postures parallel this ambivalence: on the one hand, they suggest a sense of casual repose, as indicated, for instance, by the man's relaxed demeanour – his elbow rests gently on the back of the bench, his stockinged legs are crossed in a decidedly unruffled pose – and by his clothes, particularly the informally unbuttoned jacket. On the other hand, Gainsborough's thoroughly structured arrangement of the figures, their garments and accessories leaves nothing to chance: the gun is there to remind us of the male character's authority, even in the midst of this peaceful and arcadian scenery; the unfinished area around the woman's hands was most probably intended to be filled by a bird shot by her husband, as yet another signifier of male mastery; her clothes, for their part, show remarkable sophistication and exactitude in the rendering of cuts and fabrics and are symmetrically balanced, both structurally and chromatically: even the touch of informality suggested by the visibility of the yellow underskirt beneath the opulent sky-blue folds of the main dress is held in check by the regularity with which the strip of yellow peeks out at the viewer. Furthermore, the female figure's imperturbable expression, whilst conveying a sense of composed calm appropriate to the pastoral matrix of the picture, simultaneously sums up notions of propriety to be automatically expected of a woman of her standing, no matter how informal the circumstances of her display. The characterization of the sitters on the basis of gender-related conventions is corroborated by the contrast between their respective headgear: whilst the man's hat evokes a sense of elevation, the woman's suggests proximity to the earth. (The stereotypical association between woman and Nature will be returned to later in this section.)

The aesthetic editing of Nature by recourse to vestimentary codes is borne out, in a nutshell, by the fact that the dog itself is collared! At the same time, the presence of incontrovertibly human-made objects, such as the bench, the fences, the church tower in the distant background, reminds us that we are not in the presence of sheer uncontaminated Nature: in fact, natural forms themselves serve specific technical purposes, as evinced by

Figure 18. Thomas GAINSBOROUGH, *Mr and Mrs Andrews*, c.1748–9, oil on canvas. National Gallery, London.

the employment of the tree situated behind the sitters as a means of anchoring the overall composition and thus lending it equilibrium in spite of its emphatic asymmetry. Accordingly, the viewer's eye is strategically, albeit gracefully, guided deeper and deeper through the picture's planes, as if to suggest the unfathomable depth of the Auberies and hence of its proprietors' riches. What the painting implies, therefore, is that rural settings and the depiction of clothed bodies within them are artfully organized spheres of discourse and hence hybrid combinations of the cultural and the natural, despite their professed commitment to the glorification of Nature.

For example, representations of dress in urban contexts often encode the relationship between the clothed body and space by evoking simultaneously a healthy atmosphere of dynamism and dizzying excitement and an unwholesome picture of the indiscriminate mixing of sexes, classes and nationalities. In her evaluation of the impact of the modern crowd on both personal and collective psychologies, Wilson describes the ambiguity of teeming city spaces as follows:

[the crowd] glitters, it triumphs, there is a gorgeousness, a rush of energy and a heady sense of freedom . . . In the crowd the individual lives more intensely. The crowd represents vitality and joy. It is this side that tends to be represented in the light-filled paintings of Renoir and his compatriots. Yet there is another and more sinister side to the crowd. Friedrich Engels wrote of its inhuman indifference in the 1840s. For Edgar Allen Poe it was imbued with an uncanny horror. His 'man of the crowd' could exist only so long as he swam in the crowd – the crowd represents a new element which creates its own form of life, a form of life that is both parasitical and trapped. More commonly the crowd was experienced as uncivilized, unclean and dangerous; and often described in feminine terms, as hysterical, carried away by emotion, or in images of feminine instability and sexuality, as a flood or swamp, engulfing and suffocating . . . There is no stillness, but movement; not eternity, but time flashing by.[10]

If images of the swelling and bustling throng, of congestion and disorder, of crushing and overpowering waves of ceaselessly moving bodies, indeed of a potentially unruly mob, can be read as symptoms of a pervasive anxiety about both the present and the future of urban existence, it is women, in particular, who occupy an especially precarious and vulnerable position within such a blatantly antipastoral context. Traditionally associated with Nature and with the private domain, woman is alien to the urban scene and

10. Elizabeth Wilson (1994), 'Bodies in Private and Public', in Jane Brettle and Sally Rice (eds), *Public Bodies, Private States: New Views on Photography, Representation and Gender*, Manchester, pp.8–9.

the emphatically public character of modern city life: 'whereas a feminine body was seemly and appropriate in a rural landscape – since woman was closer to Nature anyway – a woman in the public spaces of the city was a threat and a danger. She should not be there; she polluted public space.'[11]

The connection between woman and Nature, which, in ideally objective terms, is neither intrinsically damning nor an unequivocal indicator of inferiority, becomes, through its appropriation by patriarchal mythology, a means of relegating femininity to a pre-urban and, by analogy, less urbane realm of discourse. As Ortner enquires rhetorically: 'Could women's pan-cultural second-class status be accounted for simply by postulating that women are being identified as symbolically associated with nature, as opposed to men who are identified with culture?'[12] Since it is always culture's project to subsume and transcend nature, culture would find it 'natural' to subordinate, not to say oppress, them.[13] When the female body is translated into art, woman becomes something of a mediator between Nature and Culture. If the fetishistic option is then pursued, this aesthetic metamorphosis is conducive to an idolization of woman: Nature, sanitized by art, is placed on a pedestal. If, alternatively, the sadistic model comes to the fore, the female body is instantly demonized as a contaminating agency, and its presence in public assumes the threatening dimensions of a symbolic virus.

The intimidating, indeed menacing, connotations carried by the public display of the female body are largely based on the assumption that 'the presence of women in . . . streets and cafes, for example, itself contributed to the blurring of the line between public and private'[14] and on the attendant conviction that only prostitutes or, at any rate, loose and wanton women or women of low class would ever presume to belong in the life of the streets. This belief is confirmed by the fact that there is no female equivalent for the male type of the *flâneur*, the rootless, amoral and nonchalant city-dweller, free to circulate amongst the crowd, observing everything yet surprised by nothing, for:

> Cast in the role of the one to be looked at rather than the one who looks, her body, decorated with garments that draw attention to it rather than rendering it uniform, which is to an extent the case with male fashions, is too much on display, and disrupts the flowing, colourless and all-embracing 'promiscuity' through which she moves.[15]

11. Ibid., pp.10–11.
12. Sherry Ortner (1974), 'Is Male to Female as Nature to Culture?', in M. Rosaldo and L. Lamphere (eds), *Woman, Culture and Society*, Stanford, p.73.
13. Ibid., pp.86–7.
14. Wilson, 'Bodies in Private and Public', p.14.
15. Ibid.

If the clothed female body could be read as an aesthetically purged incarnation of femininity, based on the evacuation of the natural, the conspicuousness and proliferation of adornment conventionally expected of female dress, by comparison with the greater simplicity and uniformity of male attire, still acts as a reminder of woman's putatively natural penchant for overindulgent self-advertising – an intriguing paradox, when one considers that in Nature, for the most part it is the male specimens that, in fact, are endowed with the most unrestrainedly theatrical attributes and knack of prodigious extravagance! Clothing, then, bolsters the polarization of gender roles and positions carried out on the populous stage of city life: whereas the male loiterer sees all whilst remaining relatively unseen, the female body in public is inevitably an object of the gaze, disenfranchised from the right to look, since looking would instantly become synonymous with soliciting. If the relative unobtrusiveness of male dress allows the aloof observer to merge with the crowd and swim through it unheeded, the ostentatious theatricality of female costume forces woman into an exposed participation in social dynamics. In a psychoanalytical perspective, the visible prominence of female clothes makes them akin to the 'fetish', i.e. a substitute, according to Freud, for the penis of which woman is deprived; but also, more importantly, the object of desire upon which the male subject may focus in order to protect himself from the threat of his own loss or lack.[16] As Pointon notes: 'Fetishism functions not so much to conceal woman's castration, her lack of the phallus, as to deny man's.'[17] 'The lack that constitutes castration anxiety'[18] is what further enables, according to Lacan, the production of power relations based precisely on the asymmetrical apportioning of scopic mastery.

In his assessment of Eva Gonzales's *A Box at the Théâtre des Italiens* (1874), Denvir alludes to the sense of trepidation that would accompany a woman's appearance in public: 'The couple are obviously respectable, despite the low-cut dress which the woman is wearing, and there is no hint of any tension or of any untoward relationship between the two.'[19] Pointing out the moral legitimacy and social acceptability of the situation portrayed by Gonzales may seem unnecessary; yet Denvir is writing with a specific context in mind, that of a culture inimical to the public display of woman, perhaps covertly willing to condone it if the woman in question were a whore, yet

16. Sigmund Freud (1983), 'Fetishism', in *Sigmund Freud on Sexuality*, Pelican Freud Library, Vol.VII, Harmondsworth, p.352.

17. Marcia Pointon (1990), *Naked Authority – The Body in Western Painting, 1830–1908*, Cambridge, p.51.

18. Jacques Lacan (1977), *The Four Fundamental Concepts of Psychoanalysis*, trans. Alan Sheridan, Harmondsworth, p.73.

19. Bernard Denvir (1991), *Impressionism – The Painters and the Paintings*, London, p.250.

Figure 19. Eva GONZALES, *A Box at the Théâtre des Italiens*, 1874, oil on canvas. Musée D'Orsay, Paris. Photo: Reunion des Musées Nationaux, Paris.

constantly on guard for clues of a so-called respectable woman's potential lasciviousness and immoderate or adulterous plans. A woman artist could likewise raise suspicions of immodest behaviour by presuming to enter the traditionally male domain of public productivity and renown. It may not be coincidental, after all, that Gonzales's painting was rejected when first submitted to the Salon and that when it was eventually accepted, in 1879, the most complimentary remarks meeting her work were comments concerning 'the vigour of her brushwork ... admiringly described as "masculine".[20] Denvir's remarks on the demeanour exhibited by the couple depicted in *Théâtre des Italiens* imply that a female presence in the midst of the modern city crowd, particularly the flourishing world of bourgeois entertainment, could automatically be interpreted as a marker of licentiousness – that the woman would be guilty unless she were proven innocent, a whore unless proven a virgin – and that her clothes would act as a potent index of her sexual intentions.

The presentation of Gonzales's female figure openly demonstrates that a woman in public is an object on display: whilst her partner gazes directly at her, her own look is dreamily lost in space and her exclusion from the prerogative to exercise active vision is symbolically emphasized by her holding the binoculars as far way from her eyes as the length of her outsretched arm would allow. The pictorial characterization of her dress, by contrast with the male figure's clothing, confirms her exhibitionist status, whilst correspondingly validating the man's voyeuristic rights. Although the woman's dress is depicted in an orthodox Impressionist style, capitalizing on the blurring of close-up details to the advantage of the overall 'impression', there is a specificity to her attire that is obviously absent from the rendering of the male character's clothes. Indeed, the dress evinces textural and tactile variety through a mobile interplay of heavier and flimsier materials, and the accessories similarly serve to define a clearly individualized body, particularly the choker, from which a pearl (a traditional symbol of chastity, incidentally) hangs, and the flowers placed over the head and the right breast and mirrored by the bouquet, which opens up towards the viewer in an erotically inviting fashion. The man's clothes, on the other hand, endorse the ideal of austere anonymity associated with contemporary male fashions at large, two relatively small portions of his white shirt being the only glimmers of light breaking an otherwise uninterrupted continuity of dark tones: indeed, the man's jacket merges with the picture's background to the point that his face is the only part of his body that truly stands out. In so far as the face is conventionally held to constitute a natural and immediate vehicle for the

20. Ibid.

expression of inner personality, it could be argued that the male figure's characterization via clothing helps to sustain the symbolic equation of masculinity with truth and that of femininity with duplicity. It thus insinuates that the discreetness of male dress fosters a veracious and unpretentious form of self-projection, whilst the cornucopian lavishness of female fashion points to the construction of subjectivity through dress as a system of acculturation and priming of the self that necessarily relies on distortion, masquerade, falsification.

Renoir's *The Luncheon of the Boating Party* (1880) is a classic example of Impressionist representations of the modern crowd as a shimmering ensemble of male and female figures dramatizing the fashionable encounter of public and private spaces, as well as the modes of visuality entailed by this problematic wedding. In this idealized rendering of a popular weekend outing, the vestimentary asymmetry pointed out by Wilson is foregrounded by the polarization of male and female dress as, respectively, an embodiment of the uniform ideal and an incarnation of the imperative to stand out. The clothes displayed by the male characters point to two complementary types of uniform and, via these, to divergent, if coexisting, socioeconomic modalities: one is encapsulated by the sportsmanlike vests and hats of the boatmen; the other by the suits and top hats, or else 'baggy' garments, worn by the male revellers from the city. The contrast is emphasized by starkly opposed colour schemes, the former evoking country life, light, airiness and sunshine; the latter, city life and either austerity and propriety or else bohemian informality and sartorial *sprezzatura*. Whichever camp they may belong to, the men can be identified on the basis of group traits: they inhabit legitimately a public world and hence have an automatic right to share in its spectacles and rituals. The women's identities, by contrast, rest on each female subject's ability to differentiate herself, however minimally, from the others through a subtle handling of more or less overtly eye-catching elements: lace, floral adornment, colourful headgear. The psychosexual circumstances hinted at here revolve around the traditional association of femininity with an intrinsically isolating private dimension, on the one hand, and, on the other, with a natural penchant for competitiveness: a drive that will manifest itself with varying degrees of explicitness, depending on the extent to which the woman in question cultivates an outgoing and pre-possessing image or a devious and mysterious one. The weaver/deceiver type discussed earlier is reworked, in this context, in the guise of the cheeky/sneaky female.

The sense that Renoir's characters incarnate dominant expectations, rather than individual attributes, is emphasized by the tableau-like nature of the pictorial composition: they are all actors in a carefully contrived scene;

Figure 20. Pierre Auguste RENOIR, *The Luncheon of the Boating Party*, 1880–81, oil on canvas. The Phillips Collection, Washington, DC.

chromatically appealing, yet in no way personally essential, chess pieces on a board, whose cumulative effect would hardly be impaired by the substitution for any of them of an analogous symbolically invested entity. The catalyst through which these figures' implication in an extrapersonal scenario is brought to the fore is, importantly, an artificial, woven object, i.e. the tablecloth, an inanimate, yet mobile, entity, saturated with the vibrant energy of rainbow reflections that appear to move not only to the rhythms of the human figures peopling the canvas but also to changes in the viewer's position. Although the painting epitomizes, in many ways, the gender-based division of labour that animates the functionings of the modern crowd by alluding to the vagaries and incongruities of the vocabulary of self-display, it concurrently draws attention to the difficulty attendant on the task of clearly defining the relationship between the individual agent or patient and the pack on which s/he acts or by which s/he is acted upon. Renoir's exposure of the intricacies of any such enterprise is based on a problematic rendering of the dynamics of the gaze. The image confronts the spectator with a puzzling circuit of visual relations: the male figures are placed in ostensibly dominant, often standing positions, alluding to the potential for movement and action, whereas the female characters are rooted to their appointed locations and more or less intoxicated by the vapours of virile pride emanating from their interlocutors and observers. However, a close investigation of the workings of the look within the picture will show that Renoir's ambiguous handling of the gaze undermines the stability of gender roles and positions: apparently powerful figures turn out to be the unwitting objects of another's look, just as seemingly subordinated characters hold unexpected visual powers, to the point that the painting's focal point could be seen to coincide with a female figure who, paradoxically, gazes at everything and at nothing at once (see Figure 21). *The Boating Party* thus reminds us that in the visual relationship between self and other, no gain is without losses, no projection of mastery devoid of intimations of inadequacy. As Haynes points out:

> Two persons looking at each other do not have the same horizon. Parts of the body (head, face, expression), the world behind the other's back, other objects and relations between objects are only accessible to me. The excess or surplus of seeing is a function of my uniqueness in space and time . . . But this surplus also signals a deficiency, for the other person has the same ability to see more than I can of my own situation.[21]

21. Deborah J. Haynes (1995), *Bakhtin and the Visual Arts*, Cambridge, p.76.

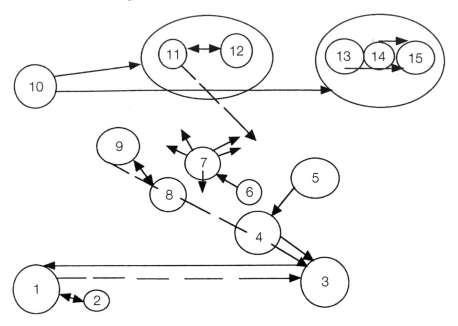

1 (F) & 2 (a dog) reciprocate each other's gaze, yet 1 may also be surreptitiously looking at 3; 3 (M) is staring at 1, whilst being looked at by 4 (F), who, in turn, is the object of 5 (M)'s gaze. 6(M) looks at 7 (F), but 7's look is dispersed in multiple directions; 8(M) and 9 (F) return each other's gaze, yet 9 (like 1) may also be indirectly observing the triangle formed by 3, 4 and 5; 10 (M) dominates the two groups located in the remotest portion of the picture's plane, i.e. the 11 (M) and 12 (M) pair and the 13 (M), 14 (M) and 15 (F) triad. In the former, the two figures look at each other, yet 12 ostentatiously relinquishes any voyeuristic powers by turning his back on the scene, whereas 11's eyes open out towards it. In the latter, 13 and 14 appear to be in full control over 15, yet are unaware of being in turn the object of 10's gaze. If 15 is the weakest of the female figures here portrayed, being the passive object of the gaze of two men and unable to exercise, given her debilitated state, her own scopic powers, the most powerful of the male figures, appropriately situated in a diametrically opposed portion of the canvas, is 10, his gaze encompassing the periphery of the scene, as his physical body dominates the portion of the tableau closer to the foreground. 1 and 9 embody stereotypes of feminine 'modesty' and 'duplicity', in directing their looks ambiguously and obliquely in two possible directions at once; however, their unstable glances also challenge the masterful power of the gaze. Paradoxically, the focal point in the picture's asymmetrical perspective is 7, a figure whose eyes are directed towards nothing in particular and who, accordingly, seems oblivious of being the object of anybody else's gaze. Her state of advanced inebriation may discourage, however, the interpretation of this character's function as a genuinely liberating move.

Figure 21. *The Luncheon of the Boating Party* and the Dynamics of the Gaze.

Though the subject may indulge in the illusion that other people exist primarily as objects of and for its gaze, it is not, however, in a position to perceive itself as a finite object, for it has no means of seeing the boundary that separates it from the world: 'in order to experience my boundaries, I need the other'.[22]

In Renoir's painting, the manipulation of structures of visuality, conducted by recourse to an ironic sabotaging of conventional gender positions, then also acts as a reminder of the viewing self's precarious status. Indeed, the *Boating Party* could be read as a popularization of Sartre's account of the uncanny transformation of the viewing subject from an unchallenged and masterful spectator into a passive spectacle. The owner and bearer of the gaze may at any point become its dispossessed object, her/his vulnerability residing in a lack of awareness of the fact that whilst confidently looking at others, s/he may be also looked at by them. The fantasy of autonomy and self-determination nourished by the myth of the seeing subject as an unquestioned observer is redolent of the commitment to decarnalized monocularity that has governed Western approaches to vision since at least the advent of perspectivalism and the Cartesian codification of a desensualized Eye/I. Interrogating the observer's freedom by emphasizing her/his simultaneous subjection to another's gaze and to culturally ratified scopic conventions potentially amounts to a radical assault upon the cult of unitary vision and creates scope for a multiplicity of viewing positions that are not mutually exclusive but continually interact with one another.

Of course, endowing the female subject (as Renoir's painting does, to some extent) with independent gazing powers, or depriving the male subject (as the representation also obliquely suggests) of an unquestioned right to own the gaze does not automatically entail a rectification of the imbalance that mars scopic relations between the sexes. These reversals may invite us to reassess the psychosexual implications of phenomena such as scopophilia, voyeurism, exhibitionism and narcissistic identification and indeed promote a deconstructive redefinition of the fetishism/sadism binary; however, they cannot guarantee a fundamental restructuring of gender positions so long as they go on relying on adversarial relations that revolve around crystallized notions of visual strength and visual weakness. Hence, it matters little whether the object and subject of the gaze are presented as literally female or male: investing a female figure with a viewing authority traditionally regarded as the province of maleness may simply place her in a conventional position of control and relegate the male to a correspondingly stereotypical

22. Ibid., p.84.

state of passivity. Although the characters' biological gender may suggest a repeal of dominant power structures, officially endorsed roles are left unchallenged: the asymmetrical premisses on which they are predicated remain intact. It is therefore vital to consider the extent to which representations apparently committed to revisionary rereadings of the visual canon genuinely dislodge their governing principles or merely indulge in a reversal of parts that, though tantalizing, contributes to the perpetuation of tenaciously prevailing mythologies. Intimately related to this question is the issue concerning the status of the sexually titillating image: are there inherently erotic images or are erotic images only ever functions, corollaries or precipitates of the logic of the gaze?

This conundrum is thrown into special relief by representations of the body in relation to clothes/cloth that exploit the unsettling effects of liminality, for example images capitalizing on semi-nudity as a signifier of intermediate states of being, which serve to remind the viewer of the disturbing potentialities of conditions of incompleteness, transition and transitoriness. As was argued in the preceding chapters, dress is an extension of the body, yet not part of it and, depending on the context wherein the body/dress relationship is acted out, clothes can be seen as integral to the subject's identity or as dispensable appendages. This coexistence of contradictory viewpoints is generated by clothing's ability to both link and separate biological and social entities, both accommodate and hide the body's ambiguous borders (particularly its open orifices). As a rhetorical and ideological construct, the classical nude likewise regiments the body, by investing in concepts of timelessness and permanent beauty and truth. What happens, however, when the represented body is neither clothed nor naked, but rather an admixture of both states? If the fully clothed body sanitizes leaky nature by bounding physicality through materials, and if the aestheticized nude body translates nature into art by fabricating seamless structure, representations of only partially clothed bodies or of naked bodies interacting with cloth undermine these policing acts, by foregrounding the uncertainty of corporeal and sartorial boundaries. The feelings elicited by such representations are comparable to those engendered by abandoned garments: the presence of clothes/ cloth as items detachable from the body underscores their role as social masks to be donned and discarded at will, rather than intrinsic properties of identity; it suggests that discarded items may be adopted again and that the garments presently worn may be cast off and deserted, equally arbitrarily. Dress holds a baleful power to bestow life; but this is a life inevitably devoid of the promise of infinity. Images that propose an interaction between the body and cloth, without bounding the physical apparatus by recourse to either literal clothing or the symbolic armour of the hermetically sealed nude, point up, like 'cast-off clothing', 'the instability of the body as sign'.[23]

François Boucher's *Girl Resting* (1752) and Egon Schiele's *Reclining Woman* (1914) supply two complementary, if vastly different, illustrations of the interaction between the body and cloth, which serve to highlight the borderline character of physicality by capitalizing on ambiguous and shifting boundaries. In the former, carnality is patently heightened by the partial concealment of the body, in ways that clearly distinguish this representation from Boucher's best known 'mythological paintings, where his female nudes conform to a generalized type, which, like all types, has much less power to arouse the erotic imagination than something absolutely specific': in *Mademoiselle O'Murphy*, by contrast, the female figure 'retains sufficient traces of individual identity to make one wonder what it would be like to go to bed with her'.[24] The picture oozes heady sensuality, emphasized by an atmosphere of dream-like laziness and 'pampered lassitude'[25] and by a compositional arrangement favours the employment of gentle diagonals. The luxurious, voluptuous and opalescent feel of the woman's flesh is mirrored by the tactile and luminous texture of the materials by which she is surrounded, just as the curves of her body are echoed by those of the couch, the panelling and, of course, the cloth. Boucher offers us a nude so frankly sexual as to make the painting a 'forerunner of the modern pin-up photograph'.[26] However, the explicitness of the representation's erotic message relies, paradoxically, not on the outright exposure of specifically sexual bodily attributes but rather on an intertwining of flesh and fabric that problematizes the boundaries of both. The inextricability of the two elements is underscored by the depiction of the female body as a landscape, over which the spectator's eye may roam unchallenged, which maintains the topos of woman's alliance to nature and yet firmly inscribes the natural in a culturally contrived milieu: the materials with which the female body is associated act as intermediaries between the natural and cultural dimensions, in so far as they both create the outline of the body-as-landscape and territorialize the flesh as an encultured signifier. Indeed, if those materials have the power to evoke natural images – hills and rocks, sandy shores and foamy waves, picturesque settings bathed in twilight – they also define a fashionable Rococo space. This ambivalence is replicated by the duplicitous qualities of the woman's countenance: the innocence suggested by her cherubic features is obviously at odds

23. Pointon, *Naked Authority*, p.121.
24. Edward Lucie-Smith (1991), *Sexuality in Western Art*, London, pp.98–9.
25. *Great Artists Collection* (1994), London, p.1773.
26. Ibid., p.1779.

Figure 22. François BOUCHER, *Girl Resting*, 1752, oil on canvas. Alte Pinakothek, Munich.

Figure 23. Egon SCHIELE, *Reclining Woman* with Blonde Hair, 1914, watercolour, gouache and pencil. The Baltimore Museum of Art: Fanny B. Thalheimer Memorial and Friends of Art Fund (BMA 1966.38).

with the sexually inviting connotations of her abandoned, reclining posture. Her association with potentially hazardous sexual proclivities is subtly corroborated by the inclusion of the diminutive dragon placed on the lid of the incense burner and turning towards Mademoiselle O'Murphy, as if hypnotized by her beauty. The gaping jaws of dragons feature in many paintings based on the articulation of a 'fantasy' that 'concerns the plight of the bound and helpless victim'.[27] (See, for example, Titian's *Perseus and Andromeda* [c.1554] and Ingrès's *Ruggiero and Angelica* [1819].) In this respect, the symbol of the dragon traditionally constitutes a variation on the theme of the *vagina dentata*, already touched upon earlier in this chapter. In Boucher's painting, however, though open-mouthed, the dragon is lilliputian, pet-like and inanimate, and is obviously not presented as directing any aggressiveness against the female character. Hence, it operates as a symbolic reminder not of the danger woman may be in, but rather of the harm she may inflict on those who succumb to her devouring seductiveness. Mademoiselle O'Murphy is confined by her material surroundings; yet she proffers her body so explicitly as to suggest that her bonds are actually a deceitful prop designed to ensnare the beholder into her lavishly adorned cage. The fabrics that play such a prominent role in her surroundings reinforce this ambiguity: they function at once as both binding/bounding structures and as fluid frames hinting at the possibility of the body's release from its confines.

Schiele's *Reclining Woman* proposes quite a different articulation of the interplay between the body and partially screening materials: these do not secure the preservation of modesty, as they so often do in classical and neoclassical art, for the parts of the body they conceal are, arguably, the least private. In fact, the rumpled sheet over which the female figure reposes flagrantly throws into relief the breasts and the genitalia: the portion of cloth that engirdles the middle section of her body defines both areas in a geometric fashion through the employment of semi-circular and triangular forms. Like Mademoiselle O'Murphy, the woman here portrayed gazes out of the picture's plane; yet her visual powerlessness is counteracted by her ability to challenge the viewer through the image of her rapacious hand, reminiscent of an animal mouth and hence reverberating with the familiar topos of the vampiric female. The angularity of the folds of cloth that the technical rendering of the sheet is so clearly intent on foregrounding evokes the image of a shredded fabric, as if to intimate what that menacing hand may inflict on a living body. The red patches that emerge from an otherwise virtually uninterrupted chromatic continuum of white, grey and pale ochre tones ominously reinforce the pervading sense of danger and pain. In both

27. Lucie-Smith, *Sexuality in Western Art*, p.121.

paintings of reclining female figures, the function of materials is definitely of greater moment than that conventionally accorded to props. Materials supply a means of fluidly framing the body, whilst simultaneously expanding its limits, highlighting its attributes, replicating figuratively its potentialities and hence unlimiting it by creating a dialogue between the physical self and the woven other.

The present survey of representations of clothes and cloth in art is inevitably selective and arguably limited. Hopefully it has succeeded in drawing, however tentatively, a map wherein some of the principal theoretical positions explored in the preceding sections criss-cross over the territory of the visual, and particular artifacts can be read as incarnations of specific facets of the debate on the relationship between dress and the body:

- clothing as an ambiguously bounding structure (for example *The Green Violinist*);
- clothing as a material entity compensating for the symbolic decarnalization of the body (for example *Winding the Skein*);
- clothing as the return of the abject (for example *The Two Fridas*);
- clothing as an ironic celebration of the sprawling, potentially animal, body (for example *Apollo*);
- clothing as a deep surface that reveals by means of veiling (for example *Marchesa Casati* and *After Glenrowan Siege*);
- clothing as a participant in the production of selfhood via the making (and unmaking) of cloth (for example *Penelope and the Suitors*);
- clothing as a means of dramatizing the relationship between the gendered body and its environment, be it rural or urban (for example *Mr and Mrs Andrews*; *A Box at the Théâtre des Italiens*; *The Luncheon of the Boating Party*);
- clothing, metonymically represented by materials and fabrics, as a fluid frame that at once delimits and enhances the body's sphere of emotional action (for example *Mademoiselle O'Murphy* and *Reclining Woman*).

This catalogue sketches out the aptitudes of dress as a discourse capable of metamorphosing the body; of supplying it with opportunities for specular identification and self-definition; of condemning it to a limbo of estrangement from both itself and others, while paradoxically valorizing its corporeal calibre; and ultimately, when the interplay of all these factors is taken into account, of highlighting its kaleidoscopic fragmentation, its standing as an optical toy in which one sees an ever-changing variety of patterns and colours, produced by the wedding of a limited number of elements and a limitless range of plausible combinations.

Dress may transform the body by camouflaging its particularities under the disguise of a homogeneous texture that, by challenging the laws of logic, physiology, anatomy, propriety, common sense and even gravity, can nourish the dream of a temporary release from the constraints of material nature. As a magical mask, operating as a secular version of the tutelar spirits presumed to shape and guard our innermost personalities, dress reminds us that character is not an innate endowment but rather a destiny that is both acquired and performed in fantasy. One of its central functions, therefore, is to assist the enactment of a sensual and intellectual drama where the internal and the external realms are of equal stature and where form and matter are not at war: 'Only a puritan would disagree, seeing in the body only gross matter and a despicable magma of viscera, rather than a mysterious theater which provides a stage for all exchange – whether of matter, mind, or the sense – between inner and outer worlds.'[28]

These theatrical fabrications are not, of course, the product of spontaneously erupting individual desires, since their public display of identity is always ideologically situated: dress, in this respect, serves to underscore the body's status as 'a highly contested site – its flesh is both the recipient and the source of desire, lust and hatred . . . it is sacred and sacrificial, bearing the politics of society and state'.[29] Hence, whilst dress capitalizes on the concept of the body as a common bond, or generalized structure, it simultaneously intensifies our awareness of the personal and idiosyncratic dynamics of the particular body with which we are individually associated, by continually requiring us to assess the extent to which such a body conforms to the dominant attitudes and values of the political systems we inhabit and accordingly to confront our corporeal reality as a potential source of both gratification and alienation. As Bakhtin observes, by linking directly the issue of bodily acculturation to the body's representational significance: 'I cannot react to my own outward body in an unmediated way', for this corporeal dimension 'is unified and shaped by cognitive, ethical and aesthetic categories, and by the sum total of external, visual, and tangible features that make up the plastic and pictorial values in it'.[30]

These plural potentialities of dress are illustrated by Jenkins by means of a helpful diagram, of which a simplified version is offered in Figure 24.[31]

28. Michael Leiris, quoted in Peter Webb (1975), *The Erotic Arts*, London, p.369.

29. Daina Augaitis, quoted in William A. Ewing (1994), *The Body: Photoworks of the Human Form*, London, p.324.

30. Mikhail Bakhtin (1990), 'Author and Hero in Aesthetic Activity', in *Art and Answerability: Early Philosophical Essays by Mikhail Bakhtin*, trans. Vadim Liapunov and Kenneth Brostrom, Austin, p.51.

31. Genny Jenkins (1990), *The Clothes in Question*, London, p.3.

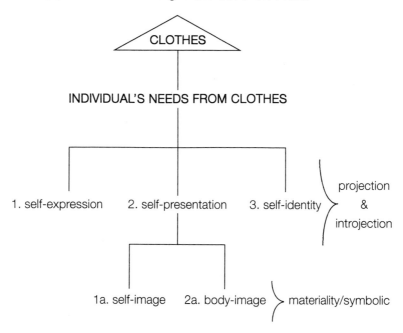

Figure 24. *The Clothes in Question.*

We are here invited to distinguish amongst three forms of relationality between dress and the body, which result, in turn, in two types of image. Self-expression alludes to clothing's role as a means of intersubjective communication, based primarily on projection; self-presentation to the imperative to conform to a proper, encultured version of corporeality, enforced through introjection; self-identity to the socialized compound created by the interaction of projective and introjective processes. The complementary figures yielded by these practices, self-image and body-image, refer, respectively, to the representation of the self as an accultured/encultured, i.e. symbolic, body and to the representation of the self as a material ensemble. Taken in tandem, the two images encapsulate the procedures and the methodologies that enable the fashioning and display of a corporeal identity, indeed the inseparability of material existence from strategies of cultural editing of carnality: 'the "life" of the body is played out through the technical arrangement of clothes, adornment and gesture',[32] through the simultaneous constitution of the self via clothing and translation of the self into clothing: 'From a simple masquerade to the mask, from a "role"

32. Jennifer Craik (1994), *The Face of Fashion*, London, p.1.

(*personnage*) to a "*person*" (*personne*), to a name, to an individual; from the latter to a being possessing metaphysical and moral value; from a moral consciousness to a sacred being; from the latter to a fundamental form of thought and action – the course is complete.'[33]

Whether it frames the body as an ideally inviolable dominion or maps it out as an unbounded landscape; whether it releases corporeality to the free play of fantasy and masquerade or harnesses it to political imperatives; whether it valorizes the physical as an aesthetically autonomous entity or reifies it by foregrounding its commodity status – in all cases, dress outlines a discourse of the body as a scene of competition, an ensemble of part objects, a vulnerable and incomplete apparatus wherein recurring dreams and obsessions coalesce and, of course, a schizophrenic entity that is oppressed and glorified, victimized and fetishized, devalued and overvalued, at one and the same time. All representations of the body engineered by and through dress contribute to both establish or consolidate and erode or destabilize, rhetorically and methodically, belief systems and cultural practices. In visual representation, the role of clothing as a fetish that metonymically stands for the body, yet is not a body, that belongs to the body, yet is detachable from it, manifests itself overtly. Whilst operating as a crucial means of maintaining the social order that the fashionable body is presumed to epitomize, the prosthetic ambivalence of dress as a shifting rim simultaneously throws into relief the socialized body's precariousness and hence the contingency of any naturalized cultural fabrication. Identities obtained through symbolic mediation are inexorably split, deriving, as they do, from phenomena of misrecognition that may only fuel the myth of autonomous selfhood by means of halluci-natory spectacles, effecting a division between the Eye that sees and the Eye that is seen, the I that speaks and the I that is spoken by language. Relatedly, the subject fashioned by dress as a socializing tool is a fractured creature, predicated not upon plenitude and the guarantee of an impregnable cultural order, but rather upon disjuncture, rupture and diremption.

If clothing contributes to the framing of this flimsy being, it cannot – and, perhaps, will not – secure the containment of its divergent impulses, and may therefore alert us to the fact that whilst namelessness is an intrinsic attribute of the pre-symbolic body, the names imposed upon the culturally groomed body are only transient labels. It is therefore not enough to acknowledge the degree to which clothes invested with symbolic and mythical qualities serve to determine and safeguard a particular ideological

33. M.Mauss (1985), 'A Category of the Human Mind: The Notion of Person, the Notion of Self', in M. Carrithers, S. Collins and S. Lukes (eds), *The Category of Person*, Cambridge p.22.

setup, as a critical evaluation of the discourse of dress concurrently requires us to assess clothing's resistance to the traditional binaries on which such a system relies for the purposes of self-emplacement and self-perpetuation. Dress, like the body itself in Barkan's formulation, is 'simultaneously abstract and concrete, general and specific'.[34] The questioning power of dress ultimately lies with its tendency to foster the interpretation not of facts but of interpretations themselves, since what dress exhibits is not the body but rather versions of it, variations on a theme that very possibly does not exist: perhaps all we have is superficial variations, the idea of an underlying theme being only a way of securing the nominal survival of a mythical essence. The term 'variation' itself may simply be a rusty vestige of an ethos intent on differentiating the contingent from the immutable, as though to suggest that, as long as we can speak of 'variations', it must also be possible to retain faith in the existence of a basic theme by which those variations are supposed to be inspired. The mutations and combinations themselves are potentially limitless: a body steeped in pain and jeopardy, a body bathed in glamour, an enduring body, a magnified body, a diminished body . . . – what they all share, however, is the ability to convey the equivocal and mercurial character of vestimentary codes and conventions.

Dress, then, is both a body and not a body; it is of the body, yet separable from it; it maximizes so-called natural properties, whilst parading itself as an eminently artificial construct. In its visual depictions, it represents at once an abstract concept and a tangible possession, a versatile ideal and a material object that, not unlike the flesh-and-blood organism, is subject to deterioration and corruption, but may also expose and mock, by virtue of its materiality, the disembodying agency of the symbolic and its laws. Though branded as marginal and inconsequential, dress, with its fickleness and capriciousness, ultimately typifies the erratic and volatile mentalities on which the economy of desire with which we are familiar today relies for its subsistence: the ostensibly trivial thus becomes significant, as the periphery spotlights the centre.

In summary, a close reading of a contemporary painting is offered in oreder to explore some the issues outlined in the preceding section.

34. L. Barkan (1975), *Nature's Work of Art: The Human Body as Image of the World*, New Haven and London, p.3.

The Ambiguity of Clothed Identities: A Reading of Michael Parkes's *Deva* (1988)

The propagation in dress of problematic meanings that is ambiguity is . . . inextricably intertwined with the subjective states of ambivalence that tear at the identities we mean to convey to others . . . Of the infinity of social objects about which persons can feel ambivalence, that which looms over all else, both in terms of prevalence and salience, is, I would hazard, the *self*.[35]

Deva proposes a vivid pictorial dramatization of clothing's ambiguity, as a visual metaphor for identity that relies on character ambivalences as its basic premiss and is thus capable of documenting the ideologically anchored fluctuations that resonate within and amongst different versions of subjectivity. The painting underscores the equivocal and provisional status of vestimentary discourses and, concomitantly, of the self-images that these are supposed to impart and divulge, by bracketing together disparate and incongruous meanings and hence highlighting the hybrid character of selfhood on both the physical and the symbolic planes. If it is the case, as the preceding chapters have endeavoured to record, that identity is always a package assembled through the amalgamation of contradictory ideas, impulses, affects, desires and body ideals, this type of image compels recognition of this fact by juxtaposing, rather than attempting to harmonize or synthesize, conflicting messages: it does not attempt to tame contrasting viewpoints, but rather capitalizes on dissonance. It does not encourage the relinquishing of one set of virtual identities in favour of another, but rather throws into relief their coexistence.

This penchant for strategies of contiguous association indifferent to principles of unification and integration is explicitly conveyed by the characterization of the female figure as a composite rhetorical structure. On the one hand, she exhibits some of the most prominent traits of the stereotypically alluring woman; on the other, her association with natural forces and dominant position over an invisible – and hence potentially limitless – realm invest her with an authority from which the conventional *femme fatale* is normally excluded. Her latent strength is magnified by a slightly intimidating, if not overtly sinister, beauty: she stands out, in short, as somebody whom it would be quite unwise to cross or offend. Her connection with powerful animals, sustained by analogies in clothing and accessories, and the ceremonial atmosphere of the overall tableau may even bring to mind ritual situations connected with the figure of the shaman: the jaguar

---

35. Fred Davis (1992), *Fashion, Culture and Identity*, London and Chicago, pp.23–4.

Figure 25. Michael PARKES, *Deva*, 1988, oil on wood. © Steltman Galleries, Amsterdam–New York.

Fashioning the Frame: Boundaries, Dress and the Body

is, after all, an especially authoritative symbol of natural and supernatural energies in the shaman's domain, since its eyes are presumed to be a conduit to the world of the spirits and the future may be read through them. Although the symbolic association of feline forms and habits with lunar symbolism has traditionally placed them on the side of femininity as the receptacle of duplicity, mystery, lust, darkness and, of course, satanic witchcraft, non-Western mythologies have ascribed far more positive faculties to the majestic form of the great cat, credited it with the ability to banish evil forces and to symbolize both freedom and protectiveness, independence and watchfulness over human and animal doings alike. Freedom, as the transcendence of corporeal restrictions, is also traditionally evoked by flight and flying creatures, here embodied by the dragon-fly, in whose contemplation the woman appears engrossed and into which her own breath may be instilling life. As a shaman-like guardian of an indeterminate realm wherein naturalism and fantasy meet and merge in mutual suffusion, the female figure depicted in *Deva*, whilst retaining the sphinx-like appeal of the seductress, also hints at an alternative region of imaginative experimentation, thus articulating a tantalizing drama of identity ambivalence.

If we turn to the specific representation of clothes and their symbolic significance, the image's ambiguity becomes all the more apparent. First of all, it is worth noting that although the painting caters to erotic interests via dress, this is by no means clothing's sole function. It does not depict the kind of nude or semi-nude that replicates the shape ideally bestowed on the body by fashionable dress. In mainstream Western painting, the nude female form is time and again conceived on the basis of the dominant sartorial aesthetics of the age, so that the shape imparted to her body by the artist is really dictated not by anatomical considerations but rather by the mould supplied by the clothes she would be wearing, were she not naked. In *Deva*, by contrast, there is no clear notion of a prevailing style by which the woman's form might have been inspired: the painting fosters a deliberately ahistorical, or perhaps eclectic, approach to fashion, which ultimately suggests the ironical marriage of an Apollonian, neo-classical, encultured self and a Dionysian, exotic, animal self. Accordingly, the idea of what should constitute the most overtly alluring zone of the body keeps shifting, as the eye roams over the woman's form: the image proposes a rejection of biological determinism as to what ought to constitute a legitimate trigger for sexual excitement, by refusing to orchestrate the physical components in a hierarchical fashion and relying instead on their interplay. The sinuous back, the prosperous, draped buttocks, the veiled left shoulder, the partly concealed left breast, the fetish-like gloved hand, the face, and indeed individual features thereof, are all presented as virtual candidates to the status of galvanizing sites of erotic charm. No one single part of the body is so clearly and unproblem-atically accentuated as to become a universally recognizable centre of sexual magnetism. At the same time, neither the body nor the clothing is stressed at the expense of the other, the emphasis falling instead on a humorous interaction of reverberating and reciprocally mirroring surfaces. Just as practically any visible portion of the woman's body, clothed or unclothed, could aspire to the condition of a sexual bait, so could the inanimate objects with which she is associated, for example the furs, the ribbons, the jewels and hair bands, the patterned fabric.

The ambivalences pointed out above are heightened by the relationship between the physical structure and its garments. On the one hand, the latter define the woman's body by creating a frame around its contours that replicates the most intriguing traits of the corporeal being itself: thus, the fold of fur to the left of the partially visible breast echoes the curves of the breast itself, of the shoulder and of the chin; the layers of fur around the neck and stretching down to the right mirror both the structure of the hairdo and that of the back and parallel the curve of the right hip; the strip of silk running down the back corresponds to the line of the backbone. If, in proposing visual correspondences between clothes and the body, the image traces the boundaries of the physical apparatus by reinforcing natural outlines through artificial means, there is also a sense in which garments facilitate the interaction between the body and its environment by operating as some-thing of a connecting tissue. The piece of silk extending from the woman's right shoulder to the back of the cat to her right is a subtle indicator of connectibility, its sail-like configuration suggesting the transmission of fluid energy from the breezy, gently dappled sky, through the woman's clothes and body, to her animal companion.

Clothing's ability to initiate a merging of self and other is most explicitly communicated by the analogies set up by the image between the female figure and the animals. At their most blatant, these correspondences may be observed in thc physical positioning of the woman's tail, which constitutes the culmination of a series of parallelisms between the layers of fur and the female figure's silhouette, playfully alluding to the phenomenon of becoming-animal. A related affinity is established by the utilization of similar items of jewellery in the adornment of the woman and of the watchful jaguar. The relationship between the human character and the feline creature situated in the picture's foreground is altogether more puzzling. The animal's body is segmented, as though to suggest it had been assembled out of blocks made of the same stony materials as the neo-classical terrace, jutting out into space in an Alma-Tademaesque fashion. Yet the plasticity and malleable fluidity of the cat's relaxed form is patently at odds with the resilient character of marble. The absence of any realistic allusions to fur may suggest that the animal has been stripped and that its coat has been transformed into the woman's own sumptuous fur. If so, are the seams displayed by its body supposed to signify the animal's surgical reassembling? More to the point, it may be worth considering whether the erotic appeal of the female figure's garments is simply an effect of the sensuous and sensual attributes of the materials of which they are constituted or rather a corollary of the ability of materials to enter so close a relationship with the body as to become a substitute skin or flesh. If silk, by virtue of its delicate semi-transparence, could be said to mimic the literal skin, the animal hide could plausibly represent a proxy for a symbolic skin, woven out of magical affiliations.

Perhaps what the figure of the sleeping cat is implicitly asking us to envisage and take on board is the concept of identity as a hybrid compound, produced through the interfacing of the natural and the artificial, as a metamorphic process playfully encapsulated by dream-like illogicality. As the least mimetic of all the forms presented in *Deva*, the animal shape in the foreground invites the viewer to look again at the total ensemble and evaluate its illusionistic function from a more sceptical perspective than the one afforded by the assessment of other individual characters and objects. We may then become aware of the fact that the correspondences suggested by the painting between human and animal dimensions, fundamentally achieved through clothing and accessories and through the ironic interaction of literal and metaphorical skins, is part of a broader aesthetic plan whose overall effect is a blurring of individuating lines and perceptional schemata. Before proceding to outline the specific features of this effect, it is tempting to speculate that one of the central functions performed by the visual representation of dress in relation to the human body is precisely this: to operate as a microcosmic vehicle for the articulation of a macrocosmic version of reality – hence, to mention just two examples, sartorially bounded bodies may allude to the dream of a territorially circumscribed space, whilst images of bodies engaged in a symbiotic relationship with clothes may connote the vision of an imaginary realm of undifferentiation.

In *Deva*, the world we are presented with, at least in one available reading of the representation, is one wherein pictorial techniques suggest that everything is potentially made of the same substance: this may amount to an endowment of the inanimate with animation or, alternatively, to a uniform draining of vitality from living and inert matter alike. Where clothing is concerned, its notes and melodies may, accordingly, epitomize the verve of a live performance or else the stillness of a tune committed to the prudent silence of parchment. Mirroring this ambivalent perspective, the visual space articulated by the painting is both extremely detailed and latently open-ended, hieratically immense, suggestive of visionary stillness and unreality. *Deva* engineers a disquietingly surreal encounter of concreteness and imponderable bodilessness, by means of which life is immobilized and robbed of any precise location in either space or time, and the barrier between the organic and the inorganic is made to vanish. The female figure condenses these contradictory messages, in that, by coming across as simultaneously languid and energetic, reticent and forward, she encodes a tension-generating exchange bred by symbolic antinomies of erotic import and thus stands for the ultimate object of unslakeable passion: she is not sufficiently individualized and categorizable to be confidently objectified and possessed. Hence the picture bears witness to the ability to make irrational associations pass on to the level of reality as tangible entities, by capitalizing on the lure of illusionism and using familiar tricks of *trompe-l'oeil*. Its analytical and quasi-narrative approach may appear to pander to the tenets of an exactingly imititative art, yet its techniques are invariably geared to the creation not of mimetic exactitude but of solid irrationality. Its cumulative impact may well prove disturbing, for we conventionally expect exactitude of rationalized reality, not reasoned unreality. *Deva* focuses on symbolic instabilities and identity disjunctions that may be culturally negotiated but not globally resolved: by playing with the multiple crosscurrents of meaning that swirl about in all vestimentary systems, this picture reminds us that without ambivalence and ambiguity neither the body nor dress would have anything to fasten on to in order to produce their ephemeral concoctions of 'sense'.

Epilogue

I think it's difficult for us to know what we lose. We're constantly losing things, and often, as we lose them we can't remember what they were. They go, they really do; we lose them totally as we move forward into this increasingly mediated existence. I think that's probably one of the tasks of the contemporary poet: to try to capture that sense of constant loss. (William Gibson, in Mark Harrison [1995], *Visions of Heaven and Hell*, London: Channel Four Television.)

As a means of summing up, albeit provisionally, some of the arguments proposed in the course of this project, it could be suggested that the discourse of dress pertains simultaneously to processes of cultural, social, historical, psychological and ideological compartmentalization and decompartmental-ization, a major leading thread in these processes consisting of the powerful role played by clothing and adornment in the formation of psychosexual personas and constellations. However, although the erotic import of dress is of pivotal significance in both the chronological development of contingent styles and critical decodings of their interweaving languages, the practices of representation of sexual models and orientations enacted by fashion are not determined by a stable referent, to be reflected by garments and decoration in the hall of mirrors of their protean imagery. The absence of fixed signifieds behind the dialogue between sexuality and dress plausibly stems from the ideologically specific and rhetorically embedded character of both parties, as dynamic contributors to the fabrication and dramatization of cultural identities and relations, in both the collective and the individual spheres. These identities and relations, stemming as they do from strategies of symbolic acculturation that endow the subject with an enunciative position only at the price of the extinction of its corporeality, necessarily entail an acceptance of loss. If, in trans-historical psychoanalytical terms, loss is often perceived as a universal precondition for the assumption of adult subjectivity, it would also seem to be the case that the re-mapping of contemporary culture by information-technological means invites a historically specific examination of loss as a process, rather than a state: as Gibson intimates in the opening quotation to this epilogue, loss is an unavoidable concomitant of the pervasiveness of mechanisms of mediation and displacement in the reception and consumption of late-twentieth-century culture.

Contemporary science, particularly where the field of research into Artificial Intelligence is concerned, may supply a fitting metaphor for the shift of emphasis from centred regimes of signification to decentred forms of discursive interaction, such as the one articulated by the overlapping registers of eroticism and fashion. What the scientific model offers is a scenario wherein notions such as depth and surface, centre and periphery, may no longer be envisaged in purely spatial or cartographic terms, since depth and surface, centre and periphery, are seen to inhabit each other in inextricable ways. Computer-based technology has been endeavouring to establish to what extent automata (and, increasingly, virtual simulations of three-dimensional realities) may be capable of autonomous reasoning and learning since at least the advent of cybernetics in the mid-1940s, with its acknowledgement of the flow of information continually passing between the organic and inorganic. Repeatedly, scientists have either had to cope with the frustrating realization that even the most sophisticatedly programmed apparatus turns out to be rather primitive, by comparison with the human brain and the associative powers held by its 'perceptrons', or else confronted the humbling intimation that the apparently watertight logical criteria advocated by cognitive theories prove rather ineffectual when it comes to trying to endow artificial creations with independent mental faculties. In the last two decades, attempts have been made, however, to overcome this impasse, through the construction of automata not on the basis of a centralized mechanism of control but rather according to the principle of layering. The initial robotic model relied on the possibility of reproducing, arguably in line with the aims and objectives of bionics, the structure of the human nervous system. The more recent approach to the learning and reasoning potentialities of the technological body dispenses with the notion of a governing centre and operates, instead, according to the rules of 'subsumption architecture': the robot is assembled through the layering of substantially discrete units, corresponding to different behaviour systems, which may temporarily interact and hence give rise to fresh connections, without these being centrally guided through a neat separation of data and computation.

The artificial system forged on the basis of subsumption architecture may, by virtue of its rejection of central control and reliance on a contingent play of non-hierarchically combined surfaces, bring to mind certain recurring characteristics of postmodern culture and, relatedly, of fashion's penchant for intertextual and antimimetic juxtapositions. If the scientific metaphor is specifically brought to bear on the partnership between sexuality and dress, it could then be argued that the abolition of central control promoted by layered automation provides a parallel to the repudiation of constant underlying concepts, rendered necessary by any concerted attempt to evaluate the ways in which images perform active roles in shaping consciousnesses and relationships. Anchoring the interplay of vestimentary codes and erotic ideals to either a transcendental view of what sexuality is or should be, or a metaphysical distillation of the meaning of dress, would amount to centralizing a bundle of cultural, psychological and biological components, as a means of inferring the developmental outcomes of their interfacing. The adoption of a layering strategy, conversely, constitutes an acknowledgment of contingency, of the possibility of knowledge's emerging, unexpectedly, ironically and perhaps parodically, from a decidedly non-organic coexistence of surfaces. If these surfaces produce meanings, as they crucially and undeniably do, they also, insistently, fashion an enunciative universe predicated on slippage. The cult of knowledge production is as central to the collusion of sexual and sartorial discourses as it is to information-oriented scientific enterprise. Both domains configure knowledge in ways that depart radically from the progress-obsessed mythologies of the Enlightenment and of its heir, Modernity, by severing the idea of generation from the evolutionary imperatives of hierarchically conceived models of humanism, humanity and humaneness, thus underscoring the inevitably coded and mediated status of any prospect of growth.

The scientific analogy proposed above is necessarily experimental, and its pursuit in detail could conceivably justify the production of a distinct study on the interrelations of boundaries, dress and the body and their roles in the fashioning of historical, social and personal frames. Hopefully, this same analogy also bears points of contact with earlier parts of the present project, particularly discussions of the relationship between the natural and the technological bodies, of part-bodies, of fashion's approaches to history, of challenges to the concept of natural reproduction and, last but not least, of the deep function of surfaces.

Studies of representations of the body that, like this one, proceed from the assumption that the body is always something other than its physical structure or appearance will inevitably have to address both the epistemological and the ontological standing of metaphorical realities, which, however simulated, virtual or artificially encoded they may be, cannot be nonchalantly consigned to the province of mere fantasy; in fact, such realities may be all we have today or have, for that matter, ever had. Representations of corporeality compulsively stress the incidence of mediation and metaphoricity in the process of construction of systems of knowledge and being, by dint of the body's versatility as an iconic and symbolic sign and, particularly, openness to figurative appropriation by a plethora of rhetorical, ideological and psychological discourses. The realization that physicality is only one of the body's many attributes prompts the question: if the body is not unproblematically equatable to its carnal properties, what is it, then? One possible answer to this question is that the body is all, and simultaneously, the metaphors into which its physical substance is translated or translatable; that these metaphors are, moreover, unstable and multiaccentual; and that the problematization of what we may call 'reality' instigated by a culturescape of hyperspaces and cyberspaces both makes the body less solid and tangible than ever and spotlights its borderline positioning between the real and the unreal. The symbolically encultured body, like the version of reality put forward by the concept of cyberspace, has no definite mass or extension and is neither incontrovertibly real nor purely fantastic.

The image of the clothed body complicates this ambivalent perspective on both the epistemological and the ontological planes: it forces us to wonder what it may mean to know a clothed body, and whether it is feasible to construct reliable strategies for the decoding of its patterns of adornment; at the same time, it compels an assessment of what the body is or might be, both in relation to and independently of the language of dress. Concomitantly, clothing increases exponentially the body's malleable character by subjecting it to a virtually endless game of combinations and permutations, which, as was argued earlier, dematerializes the corporeal and thus presses us into a consideration of how identities may be forged not out of a sense of continuity and plenitude but rather out of a conscious and critical act of self-dispossession. Although, on a superficial level, the dazzling consumer products supplied by the fashion industry may seem no more than entertaining toys, they are actually instrumental in the formation of subject roles and positions, of self-images and representations predicated on the recognition of the narrative hollowness of symbolic identity. Dress emphasizes that the assumption of subjectivity is necessarily fictional, yet also a necessary fiction. It requires an awareness of the culturally sanctioned, and hence arbitrary and conventional, status of what we may term identity, individuality or selfhood. Yet it also invites a recognition of any fictional identity's own creative ability to generate further fictions. Ultimately, the floating shifter, the purely discursive 'I' constructed by language, has the seductive and arguably ominous power to produce the text(s) of history.

The clothed, or sartorially edited body, like its technologically confected counterparts, is a collection of disparate elements that simultaneously celebrates a temporary attainment of integrity and reactivates a state of disintegration. It continually oscillates between completion and decomposition, the imperative to derive pleasure from its fictionally and rhetorically constructed unity and the playful yearning to revisit the polymorphous time-space prior to the body's capture by the symbolic. The tendency to forge a sense of undividedness, perfection and congruence out of the fragmentary evidence offered by fashion, either in terms of diachronic mutations or in those of synchronic combinations, may be fruitfully challenged by an acceptance of fragmentation as a necessity. This may lead to a realization, unsettling, daunting, yet also tantalizing, of the fact that our access to any past or future is inexorably limited, and that the identities, both past and future, created by dress are, likewise, partial and broken. The preceding chapters have endeavoured to suggest that although the challenge posed by the body-in-pieces may be despotically met by acts of masterful narrativization, the feelings of desire or fear, pleasure or unpleasure, that we experience in the face of fragments serve to question and weaken any such totalizing, essentializing and fundamentally conservative drives, desire and fear alike being directed towards something we cannot have.

Most of us daily confront a reality of fragments, in the act of opening a wardrobe to select an outfit: this act, however trivial, may be seen as a metonym for the undoubtedly much more momentous task we undertake when we attempt to grasp our historical identities. At all times, we are expected to make sense of residues of distorted pasts and shreds of possible futures, displayed before our gaze not by the agents of a rational plan, but by random events of assemblage, discovery, even destruction. Dress thus becomes the vehicle for the expression of concurrently psychological and historical ambiguities, marked by the fluctuation between a rationalistic quest for integrity and a transgressive infatuation with disunity. Destabilizing dissonances constitute a persistent undercurrent in the language of adornment, though only as half-consciously or unconsciously heard whispers, which participate vitally in the orchestration of a discourse, within symbolic thinking, about the permeability of all boundaries.

Bibliography

Adler, K. and Pointon, M. (eds), (1993), *The Body Imaged: The Human Form and Visual Culture Since the Renaissance*, Cambridge: Cambridge University Press.

Armstrong, N., and Tennenhouse, L. (eds) (1989), *The Violence of Representation: Literature and the History of Violence*, London: Routledge.

Arnold, J. (ed.) (1988), *Queen Elizabeth's Wardrobe Unlock'd*, Leeds: W. S. Manley.

Ash, J. and Wilson, E. (eds) (1992), *Chic Thrills: A Fashion Reader*, London: Pandora Press.

Bakhtin, M. (1990), 'Author and Hero in Aesthetic Activity', in *Art and Answerability: Early Philosophical Essays by Mikhail Bakhtin*, trans. Vadim Liapunov and Kenneth Brostrom, Austin: University of Texas Press.

Barkan, L. (1975), *Nature's Work of Art: The Human Body as Image of the World*, New Haven and London: Yale University Press.

Barker, F. (1995), *The Tremulous Private Body*, Michigan: University of Michigan Press.

Barthes, R. (1990), *The Pleasure of the Text*, trans. R. Miller, Oxford: Blackwell.

—— (1990), *A Lover's Discourse*, trans. R. Howard, London: Penguin.

—— (1990), *The Fashion System*, trans. M. Ward and R. Howard, Berkeley and Los Angeles: University of California Press.

Baudrillard, J. (1981), *For a Political Economy of the Sign,* trans. C. Levin, St. Louis, MO: Telas Press

—— (1983), *Simulations*, trans. P. Foss, P. Patton and P. Beitchman, New York: Semiotext[e].

—— (1994), *The Illusion of the End*, trans. C. Turner, Cambridge: Polity Press.

Benthall, J. (1976), *The Body Electric: Patterns of Western Industrial Culture*, London: Thames & Hudson.

Berger, J. (1972), *Ways of Seeing*, London and Harmondsworth: Penguin.

Bond, D. (1981), *The Guinness Guide to 20th Century Fashion*, London: Guinness Superlatives Ltd.

Borges, J. L. (1970), *Labyrinths*, trans. J. E. Irby, Harmondsworth: Penguin.

Bové, Carol Mastrangelo (1984), 'The Politics of Desire in Julia Kristeva', in *Boundary 2: A Journal of Postmodern Literature*, Part 12, pp.217–28.

Bowie, M. (1991), *Lacan*, London: Fontana.

Bradfield, N. (1975), *Costume in Detail – 1730–1930*, London: Harrap.

Brettle, Jane and Rice, Sally (eds), *Public Bodies, Private States – New Viewson Photography, Representation and Gender*, Manchester: Manchester University Press.

Breward, C. (1995), *The Culture of Fashion*, Manchester: Manchester University Press.

Brilliant, R. (1991), *Portraiture*, London: Reaktion Books.

Bryson, N. (1983), *Vision and Painting: The Logic of the Gaze*, London: Macmillan.

Bullock, A. and Stallybrass, O. (eds), (1990), *The Fontana Dictionary of Modern Thought*, London: Fontana.

Burgin, V. (1986), *The End of Art Theory – Criticism and Postmodernity*, London: Macmillan.

Carrithers, M., Collins, S. and Lukes, S. (eds), *The Category of Person*, Cambridge: Cambridge University Press.

Chambers, I. (1986), *Popular Culture: The Metropolitan Experience*, London: Methuen.

Clark, K. (1956), *The Nude: A Study of Ideal Art*, London and Harmondsworth: Penguin.

Collins, J., Radner, H. and Preacher Collins, A. (eds), (1993), *Film Theory Goes to the Movies*, London and New York: Routledge.

Connor, S. (1988), *Samuel Beckett: Repetition, Theory and Text*, Oxford: Blackwell.

Cooper, J. C. (1982), *An Illustrated Encyclopaedia of Traditional Symbols*, London: Thames & Hudson.

Craik, J. (1994), *The Face of Fashion: Cultural Studies in Fashion*, London: Routledge.

Crary, J. (1990), *Techniques of the Observer*, Cambridge, MA: MIT Press.

Davis, F. (1992), *Fashion, Culture, and Identity*, London and Chicago: University of Chicago Press.

Debord, G. (1983), *The Society of the Spectacle*, Detroit, MI: Black & Red.

Deleuze, G. (1994), *Difference and Repetition*, trans. P. Patton, London: Athlone Press.

—— and Guattari, F. (1988), *A Thousand Plateaus – Capitalism and Schizophrenia*, trans. B. Massumi, London: Athlone Press.

De' Marinis, F. (ed.) (1994), *Velvet – History, Techniques, Fashions*, Milan: Rizzoli.

Denvir, B. (1991), *Impressionism – The Painters and the Paintings*, London: Studio Editions.

Derrida, J. (1982), *Positions*, trans. A. Bass, Chicago: Chicago University Press.

Descartes, R. (1968), *Discourse on Method and the Meditations*, trans. F. E. Sutcliffe, Harmondsworth: Penguin.

Devlin, P. (1984), *The Vogue Book of Fashion Photography*, London: Thames & Hudson.

Dijkstra, B. (1986), *Idols of Perversity: Fantasies of Feminine Evil in Fin-de-Siècle Culture*, New York and Oxford: Oxford University Press.

Eagleton, T. (1984), *The Function of Criticism*, London: Verso.

—— (1990), *The Ideology of the Aesthetic*, Oxford: Blackwell.

Eco, U. (1987), *Travels in Hyperreality*, trans. W. Weaver, London: Picador.

Ewing, W. A. (1994), *The Body: Photoworks of the Human Form*, London: Thames & Hudson.

Faursch, D., Singley, P., El Khoury, R. and Efrat, Z. (eds) (1994), *Architecture: In*

Fashion, New York: Princeton Architectural Press.

Featherstone, M., Hepworth, M. and Turner, B. (eds) (1991), *The Body: Social Process and Cultural Theory*, London: Sage.

Feher, M., Naddaff, R. and Tazi, N. (eds) (1989), *Fragments for a History of the Human Body, Part One*, New York: Zone Books.

Felman, S. (1987), *Jacques Lacan and the Adventure of Insight – Psychoanalysis in Contemporary Culture*, Cambridge, MA and London: Harvard University Press.

Ferguson, M. W., Quilligan, M. and Vickers, N. J. (eds) (1986), *Rewriting the Renaissance: The Discourses of Sexual Difference in Early Modern Europe*, Chicago: Chicago University Press.

Fletcher, J. (ed.) (1990), *Abjection, Melancholia and Love*, London: Routledge.

Fontana, D. (1993), *The Secret Language of Symbols*, London: Pavilion.

Foster, H. (ed.) (1988), *Vision and Visuality*, Seattle: Bay Press.

Foucault, M. (1972), *The Archaeology of Knowledge*, trans. Alan Sheridan Smith, London: Tavistock Publications.

—— (1977), *Discipline and Punish*, trans. Alan Sheridan, London: Penguin.

—— (1978), *The History of Sexuality, Vol.I: An Introduction*, trans. R. Hurley, London: Penguin.

—— (1984) *The Foucault Reader*, ed. Paul Rabinow, London: Penguin.

Frascina, F. and Harrison, C. (eds), (1982), *Modern Art and Modernism: A Critical Anthology*, London: Open University Press.

Freud, S. (1983), 'Fetishism', *Sigmund Freud on Sexuality*, Pelican Freud Library Vol. VII, Harmondsworth: Penguin.

Gent, L. and Llewellyn, N. (eds), (1990), *Renaissance Bodies*, London: Reaktion Books.

Glynn, P. (1982), *Skin to Skin: Eroticism in Dress*, London: Allen & Unwin.

Gordon, C. (ed.), (1988), *Power/Knowledge*, Brighton: Harvester Press.

Great Artists Collection, Part 56 (1994), *Boucher*, London: Marshall Cavendish.

Greenblatt, S. (1980), *Renaissance Self-Fashioning*, Chicago: University of Chicago Press.

Gurevich, A. (1988), *Medieval Popular Culture: Problems of Belief and Perception*, trans. J. M. Bak and P. A. Hollingsworth, Cambridge: Cambridge University Press.

Haraway, D. (1985), 'A Manifesto for Cyborgs: Science, Technology and Socialist Feminism in the 1980s', *Socialist Review*, no.80, pp.173–204.

Haynes, D. J. (1995), *Bakhtin and the Visual Arts*, Cambridge: Cambridge University Press.

Hegel, W. F. (1944), *Esthetique*, Vol.III, Part 1, Paris: Aubier.

Heidegger, M. (1962), *Being and Time*, trans. J. Macquarrie and E. Robinson, Oxford: Blackwell.

Helman, C. (1992), *The Body of Frankenstein's Monster: Essays in Myth and Medicine*, London and New York: Norton.

Hollander, A. (1975), *Seeing Through Clothes*, Berkeley: California University Press.

Husserl, E. (1931), *Ideas – General Introduction to Pure Phenomenology*, trans. W. R. Boyce Gibson, London: Allen & Unwin.

—— (1970), *Logical Investigations*, trans. J. N. Findlay, London:

Hutcheon, L. (1989), *The Politics of Postmodernism*, London: Routledge.

Jacobus, M., Fox Keller, E. and Shuttleworth, S. (eds), (1990), *Body/Politics*, London: Routledge.

Jenkins, G. (1990), *The Clothes in Question*, London: The Royal College of Nursing.

Kierkegaard, S. (1974), *Fear and Trembling* and *The Sickness Unto Death,* trans. W. Lowrie, Princeton University Press.

Kristeva, J. (1980), *Desire in Language: A Semiotic Approach to Literature and Art*, trans. T. Gora, A. Jardine and L. Roudiez, New York: Columbia University Press.

—— (1982), *The Powers of Horror*, trans. L. Roudiez, New York: Columbia University Press.

Kroeber, A. L. and Richardson, J. (1940), *Three Centuries of Women's Dress Fashion*, Berkeley and Los Angeles: University of California Press.

Kunzle, D. (1982), *Fashion and Fetishism*, Princeton, NJ: Rowman and Littlefield.

Lacan, J. (1977), *Ecrits: A Selection*, trans. A. Sheridan, London: Tavistock Publications.

—— (1977), *The Four Fundamental Concepts of Psychoanalysis*, ed. Jacques-Alain Miller, trans. A. Sheridan, Harmondsworth: Penguin.

Laver, J. (1937), *Taste and Fashion*, London: Harrap.

—— (1969), *Modesty in Dress*, Boston: Houghton Mifflin.

Lechte, J. (1990), *The Works of Julia Kristeva*, London: Routledge.

Le Corbusier (1924), *The Decorative Art of Today*, trans. J. I. Dunnett, Cambridge, MA: MIT Press.

—— (1931), *Towards a New Architecture*, trans. F. Etchells, London: John Rodker.

Levidow, L. (1995), 'The Cyborg Self: Clean in Mind and Body', abstract of paper given at the conference *Bodily Fictions*, Brunel University College, London, September 1995.

Lewenhaupt, T. and Lewenhaupt, C. (1989), *Crosscurrents: Art–Fashion–Design, 1890–1989*, trans. J. Schiott, New York: Rizzoli.

Lewis, Reina (1994), 'Dis-Graceful Images: Della Grace and Lesbian Sado-Masochism', *Feminist Review*, No.46, p.85.

Loos, A. (1908), 'Ornament and Crime', in U. Conrads (ed.), *Programs and Manifestoes on 20th Century Architecture*, trans. M. Bullock, Cambridge, MA: MIT Press.

—— (1982) *Spoken Into the Void: Collected Essays 1897–1900*, trans. J. Newman and J. Smith, Cambridge, MA: MIT Press.

Lucie-Smith, E. (1991), *Sexuality in Western Art*, London: Thames & Hudson.

Lurie, A. (1982), *The Language of Clothes*, London: Bloomsbury.

Lyotard, J.-F. (1984), *The Postmodern Condition: A Report on Knowledge*, trans. G. Bennington and B. Massumi, Manchester: Manchester University Press.

Marsh, J. (1987), *Pre-Raphaelite Women*, London: Weidenfeld Paperbacks.

Mauss, M. (1985), 'A Category of the Human Mind: The Notion of Person, the Notion of Self', in M. Carrithers, S. Collins and S. Lukes (eds), *The Category of Person*, Cambridge: Cambridge University Press.

Mennel, S. (1989), *Norbert Elias – Civilization and the Human Self-Image*, Oxford: Blackwell.

Merleau-Ponty, M. (1962), *Phenomenology of Perception*, trans. C. Smith, London: RKP.

Mugler, T. (1988), *Thierry Mugler: Photographer*, London: Thames and Hudson.

Nead, L. (1992), *The Female Nude: Art, Obscenity and Sexuality*, London: Routledge.

Nietzsche, F. (1956), *The Birth of Tragedy*, trans. F. Golffing, New York: Doubleday.

Poe, E. A. (1967), *Selected Writings*, ed. David Galloway, New York: Penguin.

Pointon, M. (1990), *Naked Authority – The Body in Western Painting, 1830–1908*, Cambridge: Cambridge University Press.

Ribeiro, A. (1985), *The Art of Dress: Fashion in England and France, 1750–1820*, New Haven and London: Yale University Press.

Rice, A. (1991), *The Witching Hour*, London: Penguin.

Rosaldo, M. and Lamphere, L. (eds), *Woman, Culture and Society*, Stanford, CA: Stanford University Press.

Rudofsky, B. (1972), *The Unfashionable Human Body*, London: Rupert Hart-Davis.

Ryle, G. (1963), *The Concept of Mind*, London: Penguin.

Schopenhauer, A. (1969), *The World as Will and Representation*, trans. E. F. J. Payne, New York: Dover.

Sellers, S. (1989), Interview with Julia Kristeva, *Women's Review*, no.12, pp.19–21.

Silverman, H. J. (ed.) (1990), *Postmodernism – Philosophy and the Arts, Continental Philosophy III*, London and New York: Routledge.

Smitheram, M. (1996), 'Underwear', in A. De La Haye (ed.), *The Cutting Edge*, London: V & A Publications, p.181.

Starobinski, J. (1989), *The Living Eye*, trans. Arthur Goldhammer, Cambridge, MA: Harvard University Press.

Strong, R. (1965), *Hans Eworth: A Tudor Artist and His Circle*, Leicester: Leicester Museum and Art Gallery.

—— (1987), *Gloriana: The Portraits of Queen Elizabeth I*, London: Thames & Hudson.

Summers, D. (1991), 'Real Metaphor: Towards a Redefinition of the "Conceptual" Image', in *Visual Theory: Painting and Interpretation*, New York: Harper Collins.

Thackara, J. (ed.), (1988), *Design After Modernism – Beyond the Object*, London: Thames & Hudson.

Thom, R. (1975), *Structural Ability and Morphogenesis*, trans. D. H. Fowler, Reading, MA: Benjamin Fowler/Cummings.

Todorov, T. (1977), *The Poetics of Prose*, New York: Cornell University Press.

Vigarello, G. (1988), *Concepts of Cleanliness: Changing Attitudes in France Since the Middle Ages*, Cambridge: Cambridge University Press.

Webb, P. (1975), *The Erotic Arts*, London: Secker & Warburg.

White, H. (1978), *Tropics of Discourse: Essays in Cultural Criticism*, Baltimore and London: Johns Hopkins University Press.

Wilson, E. (1985), *Adorned in Dreams*, London: Virago.

—— (1994), 'Bodies in Private and Public', in Jane Brettle and Sally Rice (eds), *Public Bodies, Private States – New Views on Photography, Representation and Gender*, Manchester: Manchester University Press.

Winterson, J. (1990), *Sexing the Cherry*, London: Vintage Press.

Zaczek, I. (1994), *Lovers in Art*, London: Studio Editions.

Index